Interactions 1
Integrated Skills

Linda R. Baker

Pamela Hartmann

Darcy Jack

Elaine Kirn

Paul Most

Jill Korey O'Sullivan

Cheryl Pavlik

Margaret Keenan Segal

Judith Tanka

 **Contemporary**

Photo Credits
Page 1 © Jay Thomas/International Stock; *Page 16* © Michael Newman/Photo Edit; *Page 19* David Young-Wolff/Photo Edit; *Page 33* PhotoLink/PhotoDisc/Nature, Wildlife, Environment; *Page 40* © Nance Trueworthy; *Page 57* © Joel Sohm/The Image Works; *Page 61* © Jason Payne for PictureDesk International, reprinted with permission; *Page 75* © CAP/Corbis CD; *Page 78* © Michael Newman/Photo Edit; *Page 79* © Kevin Cozad/Corbis; *Page 89* © Ethel Wolovovitz/The Image Works; *Page 93 left* © Stone/RKG Photography, *center* © Rudi Von Briel/Photo Edit, *right* © Superstock; *Page 101* © Lionel Delvigne/Stock Boston; *Page 115* © Tony Freeman/Photo Edit; *Page 133* © Jean-Claude Lejeune; *Page 134* © Earl & Nazima Kowall/Corbis; *Page 145* © David Barber/Photo Edit; *Page 150* © Fujifotos/The Image Works; *Page 173* © Barbara Alper/Stock Boston; *Page 183* © Archive Films; *Page 184* © Archive Films; *Page 185* © Photofest; *Page 186* © Photofest; *Page 189 all photos* © The Everett Collection; *Page 190 both photos* © The Everett Collection; *Page 201* © Alexander Lowry/Photo Researchers, Inc.; *Page 221* © Walter Gilardetti; *Page 229* © Superstock; *Page 246* © Tony Freeman/ Photo Edit; *Page 248* © Keenan Ward/CORBIS; *Page 250* © CAP/Corbis CD; *Page 255* © StockTrek/PhotoDisc/ Spacescapes; *Page 261* © AFP/Corbis; *Page 274* © Joe Carini/ The Image Works.

Interactions 1 Integrated Skills Edition

2 3 4 5 6 7 8 9 0 QPD/QPD 0 9 8 7 6 5 4

ISBN 0-07-231394-3
ISBN 0-07-117987-9 (ISE)

Editorial director: *Tina B. Carver*
Development editor: *Annie Sullivan*
Director of marketing: *Thomas P. Dare*
Interior designer: *Michael Warrell, Design Solutions*
Photo researcher: *Amelia Ames Hill Associates/Amy Bethea*
Compositor: *Point West, Inc.*
Typeface: *10.5/12 Times Roman*
Printer: *Quebecor World Dubuque*

www.mhcontemporary.com/interactionsmosaic

The McGraw-Hill Companies

Interactions 1

Integrated Skills

Interactions 1   Integrated Skills

Help your students achieve academic success!

Interactions Integrated Skills is a theme-based, three-level, four-skills ESL/EFL series designed to prepare students for academic content. Derived from the first three levels of the popular *Interactions Mosaic, 4th edition*, the series combines communicative activities with skill-building exercises in listening, speaking, reading, writing, and grammar to boost students' academic success.

Interactions Integrated Skills features:

■ complete scope and sequence in the table of contents

■ consistent chapter structure to aid in lesson planning

■ placement tests and chapter quizzes in the instructor's manuals

■ three videos of authentic news broadcasts to expand the chapter themes

■ audio programs that include both the listening and reading selections

■ additional practice and expansion opportunities on the Website

In This Chapter gives students a preview of the upcoming material.

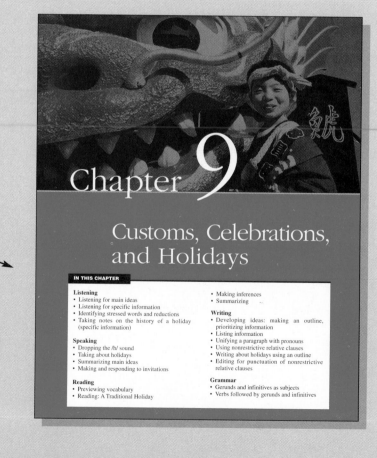

Chapter 9

Customs, Celebrations, and Holidays

IN THIS CHAPTER

Listening
• Listening for main ideas
• Listening for specific information
• Identifying stressed words and reductions
• Taking notes on the history of a holiday (specific information)

Speaking
• Dropping the /h/ sound
• Taking about holidays
• Summarizing main ideas
• Making and responding to invitations

Reading
• Previewing vocabulary
• Reading: A Traditional Holiday

• Making inferences
• Summarizing

Writing
• Developing ideas: making an outline, prioritizing information
• Listing information
• Unifying a paragraph with pronouns
• Using nonrestrictive relative clauses
• Writing about holidays using an outline
• Editing for punctuation of nonrestrictive relative clauses

Grammar
• Gerunds and infinitives as subjects
• Verbs followed by gerunds and infinitives

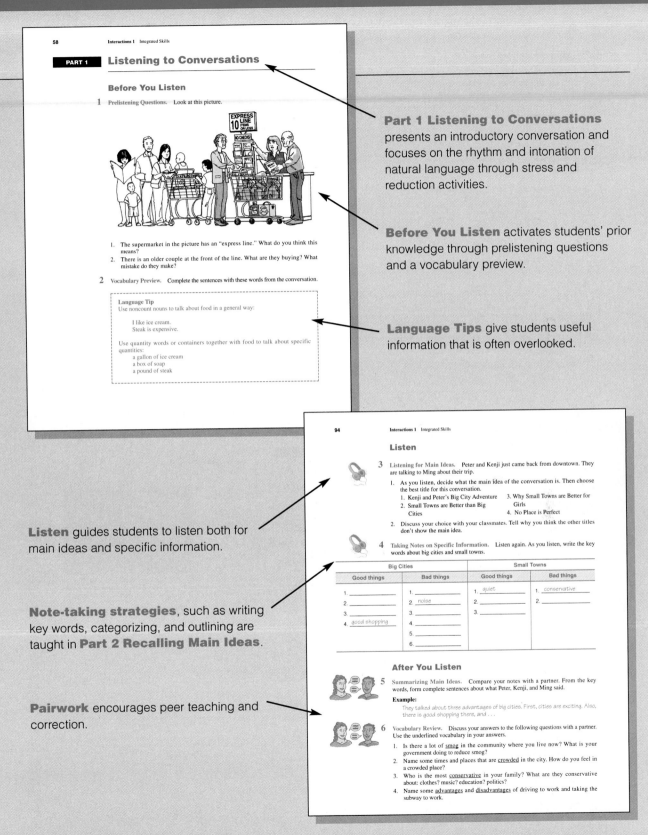

PART 1   **Listening to Conversations**

Before You Listen

1   Prelistening Questions.   Look at this picture.

EXPRESS
LINE
10 ITEMS
OR LESS
NO CHECKS

1. The supermarket in the picture has an "express line." What do you think this means?
2. There is an older couple at the front of the line. What are they buying? What mistake do they make?

2   Vocabulary Preview.   Complete the sentences with these words from the conversation.

> **Language Tip**
> Use noncount nouns to talk about food in a general way:
>
>> I like ice cream.
>> Steak is expensive.
>
> Use quantity words or containers together with food to talk about specific quantities:
>> a gallon of ice cream
>> a box of soap
>> a pound of steak

Part 1 Listening to Conversations presents an introductory conversation and focuses on the rhythm and intonation of natural language through stress and reduction activities.

Before You Listen activates students' prior knowledge through prelistening questions and a vocabulary preview.

Language Tips give students useful information that is often overlooked.

Listen

3   Listening for Main Ideas.   Peter and Kenji just came back from downtown. They are talking to Ming about their trip.

1. As you listen, decide what the main idea of the conversation is. Then choose the best title for this conversation.
    1. Kenji and Peter's Big City Adventure
    2. Small Towns are Better than Big Cities
    3. Why Small Towns are Better for Girls
    4. No Place is Perfect

2. Discuss your choice with your classmates. Tell why you think the other titles don't show the main idea.

4   Taking Notes on Specific Information.   Listen again. As you listen, write the key words about big cities and small towns.

Big Cities		Small Towns	
Good things	Bad things	Good things	Bad things
1. _____	1. _____	1. quiet	1. conservative
2. _____	2. noise	2. _____	2. _____
3. _____	3. _____	3. _____	
4. good shopping	4. _____		
	5. _____		
	6. _____		

After You Listen

5   Summarizing Main Ideas.   Compare your notes with a partner. From the key words, form complete sentences about what Peter, Kenji, and Ming said.

Example:

They talked about three advantages of big cities. First, cities are exciting. Also, there is good shopping there, and . . .

6   Vocabulary Review.   Discuss your answers to the following questions with a partner. Use the underlined vocabulary in your answers.

1. Is there a lot of smog in the community where you live now? What is your government doing to reduce smog?
2. Name some times and places that are crowded in the city. How do you feel in a crowded place?
3. Who is the most conservative in your family? What are they conservative about: clothes? music? education? politics?
4. Name some advantages and disadvantages of driving to work and taking the subway to work.

Listen guides students to listen both for main ideas and specific information.

Note-taking strategies, such as writing key words, categorizing, and outlining are taught in **Part 2 Recalling Main Ideas**.

Pairwork encourages peer teaching and correction.

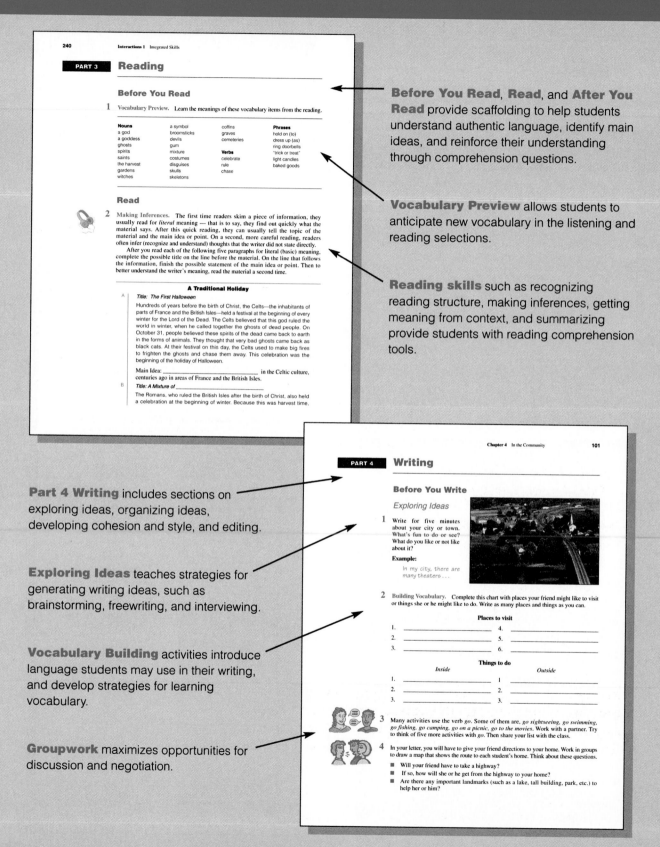

PART 3   Reading

Before You Read

1   Vocabulary Preview.   Learn the meanings of these vocabulary items from the reading.

Nouns			Phrases
a god	a symbol	coffins	hold on (to)
a goddess	broomsticks	graves	dress up (as)
ghosts	devils	cemeteries	ring doorbells
spirits	gum		"trick or treat"
saints	mixture	**Verbs**	light candles
the harvest	costumes	celebrate	baked goods
gardens	disguises	rule	
witches	skulls	chase	
	skeletons		

Read

2   Making Inferences.   The first time readers skim a piece of information, they usually read for *literal* meaning — that is to say, they find out quickly what the material says. After this quick reading, they can usually tell the topic of the material and the main idea or point. On a second, more careful reading, readers often infer (recognize and understand) thoughts that the writer did not state directly.

After you read each of the following five paragraphs for literal (basic) meaning, complete the possible title on the line before the material. On the line that follows the information, finish the possible statement of the main idea or point. Then to better understand the writer's meaning, read the material a second time.

A Traditional Holiday

A   *Title: The First Halloween*

Hundreds of years before the birth of Christ, the Celts—the inhabitants of parts of France and the British Isles—held a festival at the beginning of every winter for the Lord of the Dead. The Celts believed that this god ruled the world in winter, when he called together the ghosts of dead people. On October 31, people believed these spirits of the dead came back to earth in the forms of animals. They thought that very bad ghosts came back as black cats. At their festival on this day, the Celts used to make big fires to frighten the ghosts and chase them away. This celebration was the beginning of the holiday of Halloween.

Main Idea: _____ in the Celtic culture, centuries ago in areas of France and the British Isles.

B   *Title: A Mixture of _____*

The Romans, who ruled the British Isles after the birth of Christ, also held a celebration at the beginning of winter. Because this was harvest time,

Before You Read, Read, and **After You Read** provide scaffolding to help students understand authentic language, identify main ideas, and reinforce their understanding through comprehension questions.

Vocabulary Preview allows students to anticipate new vocabulary in the listening and reading selections.

Reading skills such as recognizing reading structure, making inferences, getting meaning from context, and summarizing provide students with reading comprehension tools.

PART 4   Writing

Before You Write

Exploring Ideas

1   Write for five minutes about your city or town. What's fun to do or see? What do you like or not like about it?

Example:

In my city, there are many theaters . . .

2   Building Vocabulary.   Complete this chart with places your friend might like to visit or things she or he might like to do. Write as many places and things as you can.

Places to visit

1. _____   4. _____
2. _____   5. _____
3. _____   6. _____

Things to do

Inside		*Outside*
1. _____	1	_____
2. _____	2.	_____
3. _____	3.	_____

3   Many activities use the verb *go*. Some of them are, *go sightseeing, go swimming, go fishing, go camping, go on a picnic, go to the movies*. Work with a partner. Try to think of five more activities with *go*. Then share your list with the class.

4   In your letter, you will have to give your friend directions to your home. Work in groups to draw a map that shows the route to each student's home. Think about these questions.

■   Will your friend have to take a highway?
■   If so, how will she or he get from the highway to your home?
■   Are there any important landmarks (such as a lake, tall building, park, etc.) to help her or him?

Part 4 Writing includes sections on exploring ideas, organizing ideas, developing cohesion and style, and editing.

Exploring Ideas teaches strategies for generating writing ideas, such as brainstorming, freewriting, and interviewing.

Vocabulary Building activities introduce language students may use in their writing, and develop strategies for learning vocabulary.

Groupwork maximizes opportunities for discussion and negotiation.

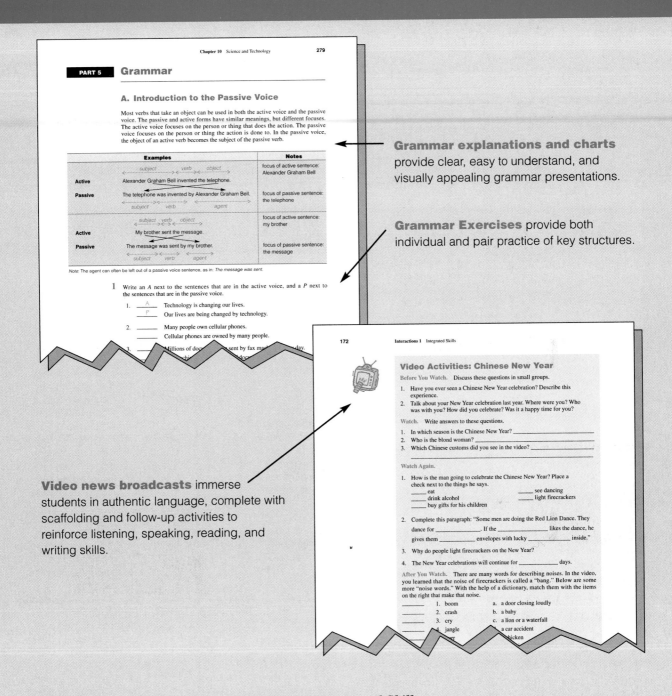

PART 5 **Grammar**

A. Introduction to the Passive Voice

Most verbs that take an object can be used in both the active voice and the passive voice. The passive and active forms have similar meanings, but different focuses. The active voice focuses on the person or thing that does the action. The passive voice focuses on the person or thing the action is done to. In the passive voice, the object of an active verb becomes the subject of the passive verb.

Examples	Notes
subject → *verb* → *object*	focus of active sentence: Alexander Graham Bell
Active Alexander Graham Bell invented the telephone.	
Passive The telephone was invented by Alexander Graham Bell.	focus of passive sentence: the telephone
subject *verb* *agent*	
subject *verb* *object*	focus of active sentence: my brother
Active My brother sent the message.	
Passive The message was sent by my brother.	focus of passive sentence: the message
subject *verb* *agent*	

Note: The agent can often be left out of a passive voice sentence, as in: *The message was sent.*

1 Write an *A* next to the sentences that are in the active voice, and a *P* next to the sentences that are in the passive voice.

1. __A__ Technology is changing our lives.
   __P__ Our lives are being changed by technology.

2. _____ Many people own cellular phones.
   _____ Cellular phones are owned by many people.

3. _____ Millions of doc_____ sent by fax ma_____ day.
   _____ _____ch _____doc

Grammar explanations and charts provide clear, easy to understand, and visually appealing grammar presentations.

Grammar Exercises provide both individual and pair practice of key structures.

Video Activities: Chinese New Year

Before You Watch. Discuss these questions in small groups.

1. Have you ever seen a Chinese New Year celebration? Describe this experience.
2. Talk about your New Year celebration last year. Where were you? Who was with you? How did you celebrate? Was it a happy time for you?

Watch. Write answers to these questions.

1. In which season is the Chinese New Year? _____
2. Who is the blond woman? _____
3. Which Chinese customs did you see in the video? _____
   _____

Watch Again.

1. How is the man going to celebrate the Chinese New Year? Place a check next to the things he says.
   _____ eat   _____ see dancing
   _____ drink alcohol   _____ light firecrackers
   _____ buy gifts for his children

2. Complete this paragraph: "Some men are doing the Red Lion Dance. They dance for _____. If the _____ likes the dance, he gives them _____ envelopes with lucky _____ inside."

3. Why do people light firecrackers on the New Year?

4. The New Year celebrations will continue for _____ days.

After You Watch. There are many words for describing noises. In the video, you learned that the noise of firecrackers is called a "bang." Below are some more "noise words." With the help of a dictionary, match them with the items on the right that make that noise.

_____ 1. boom   a. a door closing loudly
_____ 2. crash   b. a baby
_____ 3. cry   c. a lion or a waterfall
_____ 4. jangle   ___ a car accident
_____ ___rr   ___hicken

Video news broadcasts immerse students in authentic language, complete with scaffolding and follow-up activities to reinforce listening, speaking, reading, and writing skills.

Don't forget to check out the new *Interactions Integrated Skills* Website at www.mhcontemporary.com/interactionsmosaic. It provides additional practice, interactive activities, and links to student and teacher resources.

Interactions 1 Integrated Skills

Chapter	Listening Skills & Tasks	Speaking Skills / Tasks	Reading Type & Topic	Reading Skills / Strategies
1 **School Life Around the World** **Page 1**	■ Listening for main ideas ■ Listening for specific information ■ Identifying stressed words and reductions ■ Taking notes on a speech (main ideas)	■ The -s ending ■ Introducing yourself and others ■ Summarizing main ideas	■ Description: International Students	■ Previewing vocabulary ■ Recognizing reading structure ■ Understanding the main idea ■ Finding definitions in context ■ Finding details
2 **Experiencing Nature** **Page 31**	■ Listening for main ideas ■ Listening for specific information ■ Identifying stressed words and reductions ■ Taking notes on a story (specific information)	■ Can versus can't ■ Talking about abilities ■ Role-playing a story	■ Description: Global Climate Changes	■ Previewing vocabulary ■ Summarizing paragraphs ■ Justifying opinions
3 **Living to Eat or Eating to Live?** **Page 57**	■ Listening for main ideas ■ Listening for specific information ■ Identifying stressed words and reductions ■ Taking notes on advice (specific information)	■ Teens versus tens ■ Interviewing classmates about food and shopping habits ■ Summarizing main ideas ■ Comparing eating habits	■ Description: The Changing Global Diet	■ Previewing vocabulary ■ Recognizing paragraph topics ■ Understanding the main idea ■ Getting meaning by using punctuation clues ■ Recognizing supporting details
4 **In the Community** **Page 87**	■ Listening for main ideas ■ Listening for specific information ■ Identifying stressed words and reductions ■ Taking notes on a conversation (specific information)	■ Describing your neighborhood ■ Summarizing main ideas	■ Description: How Can I Get to the Post Office?	■ Previewing vocabulary ■ Understanding paragraph and whole reading topics ■ Understanding the main idea ■ Finding illustrations of word meanings ■ Recognizing the relationship of detail to the point
5 **Home** **Page 115**	■ Listening for main ideas ■ Listening for specific information ■ Identifying stressed words and reductions ■ Taking notes on apartment information (specific information)	■ The -ed ending ■ Summarizing main ideas ■ Making and answering requests	■ Exposition: A Short History of the Changing Family	■ Previewing vocabulary ■ Understanding time order of paragraphs ■ Understanding the main idea ■ Using punctuation and phrase clues ■ Recognizing time details

Idea Development / Organizing Skills	Writing & Editing Skills	Grammar	Video Topics
■ Interviewing ■ Ordering information ■ Distinguishing fact from opinion ■ Writing topic sentences	■ Connecting ideas with *and, but,* and *so* ■ Writing a personal description ■ Editing for content and form	■ The present tense of *be* and other verbs	■ Exchange Students
■ Ordering information from general to specific	■ Adding details using adjectives and prepositional phrases ■ Using articles ■ Writing a paragraph about art ■ Editing for content, form, and grammar ■ Editing for use of adjectives and articles	■ *There is / there are* ■ Possessive nouns ■ The present continuous tense ■ Modal auxiliaries: *can, may, might, will*	■ Winter Storm
■ Ordering information from general to specific ■ Writing topic sentences	■ Giving examples with *such as* ■ Writing a paragraph about a holiday meal ■ Editing for content, form, cohesion, style, and grammar	■ Count and noncount nouns ■ Quantifiers ■ More modal auxiliaries: requests, offers, and permission	■ Treat Yourself Well Campaign
■ Organizing paragraphs in a letter	■ Using prepositions of place, direction, and distance ■ Writing an informal letter ■ Editing for correct form in an informal letter	■ Future tenses ■ Prepositions of place and time	■ A Homeless Shelter
■ Making a lifeline ■ Limiting information ■ Writing topic sentences	■ Using time words and *because* ■ Punctuating sentences with dependent clauses ■ Writing an autobiographical paragraph ■ Editing for content, form, cohesion, style, and grammar ■ Editing for punctuation with dependent clauses	■ The simple past tense: regular verbs ■ The simple past tense: irregular verbs	■ Asthma and Dust Mites

Interactions 1 Integrated Skills

Chapter	Listening Skills & Tasks	Speaking Skills / Tasks	Reading Type & Topic	Reading Skills / Strategies
6 **Cultures of the World** **Page 145**	■ Listening for main ideas ■ Listening for specific information ■ Identifying stressed words and reductions ■ Taking notes on a lecture (specific information)	■ Discussing cultural values ■ Summarizing main ideas ■ Giving opinions about customs	■ Dialogue: Cross-Cultural Conversation	■ Previewing vocabulary ■ Reading conversation in paragraph form ■ Understanding the point ■ Using context clues ■ Recognizing details of opinions
7 **Entertainment and the Media** **Page 173**	■ Listening for main ideas ■ Listening for specific information ■ Identifying stressed words and reductions ■ Taking notes on a news report (specific information)	■ Expressing opinions, agreeing, and disagreeing ■ Summarizing a news report	■ Exposition: Media Stories	■ Previewing vocabulary ■ Classifying stories ■ Putting events in order ■ Summarizing a plot ■ Explaining reasons for choices
8 **Social Life** **Page 201**	■ Listening for main ideas ■ Listening for specific information ■ Identifying stressed words and reductions ■ Taking notes on a phone conversation (specific information)	■ Intonation with exclamations ■ Discussing dating customs ■ Making a videodating presentation	■ Dialogue: Meeting the Perfect Mate	■ Previewing vocabulary ■ Recognizing the structure of conversations ■ Understanding the main idea ■ Supplying left-out words and references
9 **Customs, Celebrations, and Holidays** **Page 229**	■ Listening for main ideas ■ Listening for specific information ■ Identifying stressed words and reductions ■ Taking notes on the history of a holiday (specific information)	■ Dropping the /h/ sound ■ Talking about holidays ■ Summarizing main ideas ■ Making and responding to invitations	■ Exposition: A Traditional Holiday	■ Previewing vocabulary ■ Making inferences ■ Summarizing
10 **Science and Technology** **Page 255**	■ Listening for main ideas ■ Listening for specific information ■ Identifying stressed words and reductions ■ Taking notes on a speech (main ideas) ■ Outlining notes	■ The American /t/ ■ Discussing technology in the home ■ Summarizing main ideas	■ Exposition: Everyday Uses of Technology	■ Previewing vocabulary ■ Reviewing outline organization ■ Understanding the main idea ■ Using italics and quotation marks

Idea Development/ Organizing Skills	Writing & Editing Skills	Grammar	Video Topics
■ Using a time sequence ■ Limiting information	■ Writing time clauses with *as soon as* and *then* ■ Using quotations ■ Writing an ending to a folktale ■ Using editing symbols	■ The present perfect tense	■ Chinese New Year
■ Categorizing ■ Summarizing ■ Writing a title	■ Using adjectives ■ Using the historical present ■ Writing a summary of your favorite movie ■ Editing for use of two or more adjectives	■ The past continuous tense ■ The simple past versus the past continuous ■ *When* and *while*	■ Quiz Shows
■ Interviewing ■ Writing topic sentences ■ Organizing information in a paragraph ■ Writing concluding sentences	■ Making transitions with *in fact, however, in addition,* and *also* ■ Writing a biographical paragraph ■ Editing for long forms ■ Editing for capitalization	■ Time expressions with the present perfect: *for, since, all, always* ■ Time clauses with *since* ■ The present perfect continuous tense ■ The present perfect continuous versus the present perfect	■ Online Love Story
■ Making an outline ■ Prioritizing information	■ Listing information ■ Unifying a paragraph with pronouns ■ Using nonrestrictive relative clauses ■ Writing about holidays using an outline ■ Editing for punctuation of nonrestrictive relative clauses	■ Gerunds and infinitives as subjects ■ Verbs followed by gerunds and infinitives	■ Puerto Rican Day Parade
■ Supporting opinions ■ Writing e-mail subject lines	■ Unifying writing with synonyms and pronouns ■ Giving opinions and suggestions ■ Writing a persuasive e-mail message ■ Editing spelling and grammar in computer messages	■ The passive voice with the simple present tense ■ The passive voice with the simple past tense	■ Sight for the Blind

Chapter

Appendices

Page 283

Tapescript

Page 291

Chapter 1

School Life Around the World

IN THIS CHAPTER

Listening
- Listening for main ideas
- Listening for specific information
- Identifying stressed words and reductions
- Taking notes on a speech (main ideas)

Speaking
- The -*s* ending
- Introducing yourself and others
- Summarizing main ideas

Reading
- Previewing vocabulary
- Reading: International Students
- Recognizing reading structure

- Understanding the main idea
- Finding definitions in context
- Finding details

Writing
- Developing ideas: interviewing, ordering information, fact vs. opinion, writing topic sentences
- Connecting ideas with *and, but,* and *so*
- Writing a personal description
- Editing for content and form

Grammar
- The present tense of *be* and other verbs

before
previous time

| PART 1 | # Listening to Conversations |

Before You Listen

1 Prelistening Questions.   Look at the picture.

1. What do you think the students are talking about?
2. What does their body language tell you?

109

2 Vocabulary Preview.   Complete the sentences with these expressions from the conversation.

quick

		visit	
take (Chinese)	sounds *seems*	come over	no kidding
you guys* *group*	stop by *drop by*	(just) call me "____"	

take class · study
in
you guys ~ north U.S
you all · ya'll
↓
sauth U.S

* *Note:* "you guys" is a very informal expression used only with people you know very well

1. His name is Kenji. I don't think that's an English name. It ___sounds___ Japanese.

2. My friend is in the hospital. I will ___stop by___ tomorrow and bring her flowers.

3. You have seven brothers and one sister? ___no kidding___!

4. My name is Robert Browning. But please ___call me___ Bob.

5. I don't have a car. When Nancy and I do our homework together, she usually ___come over___ to my house.

6. If your major is Asian Studies, I'm sure you have to ___take Chinese___ and probably some other Asian languages, too.

7. Bye Tom. Bye Reka. See ___you guys___ tomorrow.

Listen

3 **Listening for Main Ideas.** Jack, Peter, and Ming are students at Faber College. They meet in the lobby of their apartment building.

1. Close your book and listen to their conversation. Listen for the answers to these questions.

    1. Who does Jack introduce to Peter? _Ming_

    2. Are Jack and Peter close friends? _No_

    3. Was Ming born in Hong Kong? _No_

    4. What class might Jack take soon? _Chinese_

    5. What do two of the students want to do? _get sth to eat_

    6. Why will the three students probably see each other soon? _they on the same floor._

2. Compare answers with a partner.

Stress

In spoken English, important words are *stressed*. This means that they are spoken *louder, longer,* or *higher* than other words. Stressed words usually give the most important information.

These words are usually stressed: verbs, nouns, adjectives, adverbs, numbers, and negatives like *isn't, don't, can't.*

Examples: My **name** is **Peter.**

I'm in **apartment 212.**

Maybe you could **help** me.

We're on the **same floor.**

4   Listening for Stressed Words.   Listen to the conversation again.

1.   Some of the stressed words are missing. During each pause, repeat the phrase or sentence. Then fill in the blanks with words from the list.

A	B	C	D	E	F
1 born	campus	help	meeting	really	stop
2 building	doing	Hi	met	roommate	term
3 call	eat	hungry	moved	see	thinking
4 came	floor	Jack	name	something	212
5 can't	friend	last	nice *(2 times)*	soon *(2 times)*	220
6 Chinese	good	meet *(2 times)*	over	sorry	

Jack: ____Hi____! How're you ____doing____?

Peter: Hi. You're . . . ____Jack____, right?

Jack: Yeah. And ____sorry____, you're . . . ?

Peter: Peter. Peter Riley.

Jack: Oh, yeah. We ____met____ on ____campus____ last week. Peter, this is my ____friend____, Ming Lee. She's just ____moved____ into the ____building____.

Peter: Hi, Ming Lee.

Ming: ____Nice____ to ____meet____ you. You can just ____call____ me Ming. Lee's my ____last____ ____name____.

Peter: Oh. "Ming." That sounds . . . ?

Ming: Chinese. My parents ____came____ ____over____ from Hong Kong before I was ____born____.

Peter: Really? I was ____thinking____ of taking ____Chinese____ this____term____. Maybe you could ____help____ me.

Ming: Well, my Chinese really isn't very ____good____ . . .

Jack: Listen, Peter. We're ____really____ ____hungry____. Do you want to get ____something____ to ____eat____ with us?

Peter: Sorry, I ____can't____. I have to go ____meet____ my new ____roommate____.

Jack: Oh, OK. Well, ____stop____ by some time. I'm up in ____212____.

Peter: Hey, I'm on the same ____floor____. I'm in ____220____.

Jack: No kidding . . .

Peter: Well, ____nice____ ____to____ you, Ming. I'm sure I'll ____see____ you guys ____soon____.

Ming and Jack: See you later.

2.   Now read the conversation with a partner. Practice stressing words correctly.

Reductions

In spoken English, important words are usually stressed. Other words are not stressed; they are often *reduced*. These words are often reduced: prepositions, articles, pronouns, forms of the verb *to be*, conjunctions.

Reduced Form	Long Form
D'ya . . .	Do you . . .
How're ya doing?	How are you doing?
Niceta meetcha.	Nice to meet you.

5 **Comparing Long and Reduced Forms.** Listen to the following sentences from the conversation. They contain reduced forms. Repeat them after the speaker.

Reduced form*

1. Hi! How're ya doing?
2. Niceta meetcha.
3. D'ya wanna get something to eat with us?
4. I hafta meet my new roommate.
5. I'll seeya guys soon.
6. You k'n jus' call me Ming.

Long form

Hi! How are you doing?

Nice to meet you.

Do you want to get something to eat with us?

I have to meet my new roommate.

I'll see you guys soon.

You can just call me Ming.

_____

* *Note:* The underlined forms are not acceptable spellings in written English.

6 **Listening for Reductions.** Listen to the following sentences. You'll hear the reduced forms of some words.

1. Repeat each sentence during the pause. Then write the long forms in the blanks.

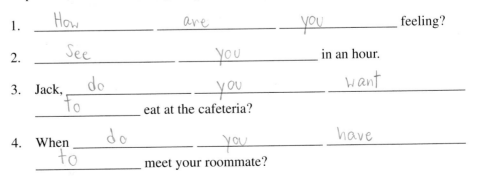

1. ____How____ ____are____ ____you____ feeling?

2. ____See____ ____you____ in an hour.

3. Jack, ____do____ ____you____ ____want____ ____to____ eat at the cafeteria?

4. When ____do____ ____you____ ____have____ ____to____ meet your roommate?

2. With a partner, repeat the sentences for pronunciation practice.

After You Listen

7 **Vocabulary Review.** Discuss the following questions with a partner. Use the underlined vocabulary in your answers.

1. Do you think it is okay to <u>stop by</u> a friend's house without calling first?

2. What class are you going to <u>take</u> after this one?

3. When you were a child, how often did your friends <u>come over</u> to your house?

4. What is your nickname? Does everybody <u>call you</u> "_____", or just some special people?

5. Tell your partner some surprising information about yourself. The other person responds with "<u>No kidding!</u>"

6. Say these names. Can you tell their nationality?

   Example: Xiang — "Xiang sounds Chinese."

Natasha	Isabella
Enrique	Hyun
Mie	Nancy

Pronunciation

> ### The -s Ending
>
> The -s ending is pronounced differently, depending on the end of the word:
>
> - **/iz/** after -ch, -sh, -s, -x, and -z endings
>   **Examples:** teaches, uses, boxes
>
> - **/s/** after voiceless -p, -t, -k, or -f endings
>   **Examples:** drinks, speaks, hits
>
> - **/z/** after voiced consonant endings
>   **Examples:** carries, brings, father's

8 **Distinguishing between -s Endings.**   Listen and write the words. Check the sound you hear. Then practice pronouncing the words.

	/s/	/iz/	/z/
1. plays	☐	☐	☑
2. misses	☐	☑	☐
3. hopes	☑	☐	☐
4. stops	☑	☐	☐
5. drives	☐	☐	☑
6. phones	☐	☐	☑
7. watches	☐	☑	☐
8. summerizes	☐	☑	☐
9. mother's	☐	☐	☑
10. puts	☑	☐	☐

Using Language

Introducing Yourself and Others

Read this part of the conversation between Peter, Jack, and Ming. Notice the words Jack uses to introduce Ming.

> *Jack:* Peter, this is my friend, Ming Lee.
> *Peter:* Hi, Ming Lee.
> *Ming:* Nice to meet you.

The following expressions are often used when English speakers introduce themselves or others.

Functions	Expressions		
	Speaker A	**Speaker B**	**Speaker C**
Introducing others	Sharon, this is my friend, Kim.	Hi, Kim.	Nice to meet you.
	Linda, I'd like you to meet my roommate, Evan.	Good to meet you, Evan.	You, too.
	Mom, I'd like to introduce you to my teacher, Mr. Saunders.	Pleasure to meet you.	Same here. → *mee to same opinion*
Introducing yourself	Hi, I'm Judy. I'm your neighbor in 206.	Nice to meet you.	
	My name is Denise.	Hi, Denise. I'm Ricardo.	

9 **Making Introductions.**   Practice introducing classmates to each other.

1. Sit in a circle if possible.
2. Write your first name on a card and put the card on your desk for everyone to see.
3. Ask a student next to you three or four questions like these.
   - Where are you from?
   - What do you do?
   - Do you work?
   - Do you have a hobby?
4. Now introduce your partner to several other students in the class.

Example:

Jose, this is Noriko. Noriko, this is Jose. Jose is from Mexico. He is here to study engineering.

5. Put away your name cards. Walk around the room and see how many names you remember. If you can't remember someone's name, use expressions like these:

- Excuse me, what's your name again?
- I'm sorry, can you tell me your name again?
- I'm sorry, I don't remember your name.
- You're Noriko, right?

PART 2   Recalling Main Ideas

Before You Listen

1 **Prelistening Questions.**   You will hear a short speech by a school advisor on the first day of an English language program. Before you listen, answer these questions with a partner.

1. What usually happens on the first day in a language program?
2. What information do students probably get?
3. How did you feel on the first day of you English program or course?

2 **Vocabulary Preview.**   You will hear the underlined words in the speech. Before you listen, write the letter of the correct definition beside each sentence.

	Sentences		Definitions
D	1. My <u>advisor</u> always gives me good advice about what classes to take.	a.	timed, planned activities
A	2. David's <u>schedule</u> has two classes in the morning and three classes in the afternoon.	b.	places or areas for special activities
B	3. Many large universities in North America have swimming pools, tennis courts, and other sports <u>facilities</u>.	c.	an exam to find the student's correct place or level
E	4. New workers in my company go to an <u>orientation</u> on their first day of work. This way, they learn all the necessary information about the company rules.	d.	a person who gives opinions on what to do
C	5. I'm not sure if my English is intermediate or advanced, so I have to take a <u>placement test</u>.	e.	informational meeting

Listen

3 Listening for Main Ideas. Listen to the speech. To help you remember, take notes.

Hints for Remembering

- ■ Don't try to write everything.
- ■ Focus only on important information.
- ■ Don't write complete sentences; write key words only.
- ■ Don't write small details.

4 Reviewing Notes. Look at the notes below. They show the main ideas of the speech. Do your notes have the same points? If yes, then you understood the main ideas!

Main Ideas

Speaker: Gina

Schedule Today:

Placement Test

Orientation

Campus Tour

5 Listening for Specific Information. Listen again. Add details to the main ideas in the spaces below. Listen for the answers to these questions.

1. What are the parts of the English test?
2. How long is the test?
3. When is the campus tour?

Main Ideas and Details

Speaker: Gina

Schedule Today:

Placement Test

Orientation

Campus Tour

After You Listen

6 **Summarizing Main Ideas.**   Compare your notes with a partner. Summarize the speech in your own words. As you speak, look at your notes to help you remember.

Example: "In this speech, Gina speaks to new students in an English program. Gina is an advisor. She tells them about…"

7 **Vocabulary Review.**   Discuss your answers to the following questions with a partner. Use the underlined vocabulary in your answers.

1.   What is your daily <u>schedule</u>? Tell the times and activities.
2.   Tell about the <u>placement test</u> you took in your language school. How long was it? How many parts did it have? Which part was the most difficult?
3.   Discuss what type of information is given at:
    - an <u>orientation</u> for first-year students at a college
    - an orientation for a group of tourists visiting your city
4.   What kind of <u>facilities</u> does your school have? Are they free or do you have to pay to use them? Which facilities would you like your school to have?
5.   What is necessary to be a good <u>advisor</u>? Does your school have an academic advisor? Have you ever spoken to her/him?

PART 3 # Reading

Before You Read

1 Discuss the pictures in small groups.

1.   Name the places, things, and people.
2.   Describe the pictures. Where is the place? What kind of place is it? Where are the people from? What do they do?
3.   How is this place like your school? How is it different?

2 Think about the answers to these questions. The reading answers them.

1. What are international students? What are institutions of higher learning?
2. Where do most international students go to school?
3. Why do students want to attend colleges and universities far from home?
4. Why do institutions of higher learning want students from other countries?

3 **Vocabulary Preview.** Learn the meanings of these vocabulary items from the reading.

Nouns		Verbs	Adjectives	Phrases
meaning	governments	mean	international	attend college
a phrase	companies	leave	foreign	by far
culture	workers	attend	abroad	college degrees
nations	knowledge	need	available	real life
a level	skills		expensive	charge tuition
industrialization	internationalism	**Adverb**	private	pay fees
technology	a campus	abroad	legal	away from home
experience	ideas		full	spend money
business	opinions		various	save money
engineering	a state			
subjects	recreation			

Read

4 Read the following material quickly. Then read the explanations and do the exercises after the reading.

main idea

International Students

across , connect

A All around the world, there are international students at institutions of higher learning. The definition of an international student is "a postsecondary student from another country." The meaning of postsecondary is "after high school." Another phrase for international students is "foreign students". The word *foreign* means "of a different country or culture." Even so, some people don't like the word foreign, so they use the phrase "international students." For institution of higher learning, they usually say "university," "college," or "school."

B International students leave their home countries and go to school abroad. One meaning of the word abroad is "in a foreign place." By far, the country with the most students from abroad is the United States. Canada, Great Britain, and some European countries also have a lot of students from other countries. But more and more, students from around the world attend colleges and universities in the developing nations of Latin America, Asia, and Africa. Developing nations don't yet have a high level of industrialization or technology.

C Why do high school and college graduates go to colleges and universities far from their homes? Undergraduates are postsecondary students without college degrees. Often, undergraduates want the experience of life in new cultures. Maybe they want to learn another language well, in school and in real life. Many older students want degrees in business, engineering, or technology. These subjects are not always available in their home countries. Some governments and companies send their best graduate students and workers to other countries for new knowledge and skills. And some students from expensive private schools at home save money through study abroad, especially in developing nations.

D Why do institutions of higher learning want international students? Of course, students from other countries and cultures bring internationalism to the classroom or campus. They bring different languages, customs, ideas, and opinions from many places around the world. Usually, they study hard. Also, educational institutions need money. Tuition is the fee or charge for instruction, and private schools everywhere charge high tuition. One definition of citizens and immigrants is "legal members of a nation or country." International students are not citizens or immigrants, so they pay full tuition and fees to state or government schools. And all students away from home spend money for housing, food, recreation, and other things. For these reasons, many schools and groups of schools want students from other countries.

E For various reasons, many high school and college graduates want or need to study abroad. For other reasons, many nations want or need students from other countries and cultures on their college and university campuses.

After You Read

5   **Recognizing Reading Structure: Readings, Chapters, and Paragraphs.**   Most reading material has structure. The word structure means "organization or form." This book contains twelve chapters. Chapters are the largest divisions of the book. The title of Chapter 1 is "School Life Around the World." Each chapter of this book contains readings. The title of the first reading in Chapter 1 is "International Students." The information of the reading comes in paragraphs. A paragraph is a division or part about one idea or one kind of information. In the reading, there is a capital letter next to each of the five paragraphs. The information in each paragraph of the reading material answers a different question.

Which question does each paragraph answer? Write the letter A, B, C, D, or E on the line. The first one is done as an example.

_~~A~~ C_   1.   Why do international students go to school abroad?

_B_   2.   In what countries do international students attend colleges and universities?

_A_   3.   What are some definitions of words and phrases in international higher education?

_D_   4.   Why do institutions of higher education want foreign students?

_E_   5.   What is the conclusion of this reading material? *the end*

6   **Understanding the Main Idea.**   Often, the information in each paragraph of reading material answers a different question. A one- or two-sentence answer to this question can tell the point or message of the paragraph. It is the main idea. Each paragraph in the reading "International Students" has a point. Here are some possible statements of these main ideas. Write *T* (true) or *F* (false) on the lines.

_T_   1.   International students in institutions of higher learning are foreign students at colleges and universities around the world.

_F_   2.   The United States and European countries have equal numbers of students from abroad. Foreigners don't study in developing countries. *most*

_F_   3.   High school and college graduates go to school in foreign countries for only one reason. They want to leave home.

_T_   4.   Colleges and universities around the world want international students for several reasons, so they advertise and try to get students in other ways. *many*

_F_   5.   Students don't like to go to school abroad. Colleges and universities don't want learners from other countries. *like*

Now change the untrue sentences to true statements of the point of each paragraph. Here is an example of a correction for No. 2: The United States and some European countries have the most students from abroad. Foreigners also study in developing countries.

most , many , like

7 **Finding Definitions in Context.**   You do not need to look up the meanings of all new words and phrases in a dictionary. You can often find their meanings in the context. The context is the other words in the sentence or paragraph. A definition often comes in a sentence after the verbs *be* or *mean*.

Here are some examples of definition sentences. The defined words are in italics. The definitions are in quotation marks.

The definition of a *university* is "an institution of higher learning with one or more undergraduate colleges and graduate schools." The word *college* means "a school of higher learning." And one meaning of the word *school* is "an institution for teaching and learning." What is a *graduate* student? The phrase means "a college student with a bachelor's degree or higher." The word *undergraduate* is for "a college student without a bachelor's degree."

For Nos. 1–4, find definitions of these terms in the preceding explanation. The definitions for Nos. 5–9 are in "International Students" on page 12. (The letters in parentheses are the letters of the paragraphs.)   *colleges and graduate schools*

1. the context *the other words in the sentence or paragraph.*

meaning → 2. a definition *phrase or sentence that says exactly what a word, phrase or idea*

3. a university *an institution of higher learning with one or more undergraduate*

4. a graduate student *a college student with a bachelor's degree*

or foreign students → 5. an international student (A) *postsecondary student from another country*

6. an institution of higher learning (A) *university, college or school.*

7. abroad (B) *in a foreign place*

8. developing nations (B) *don't have a high level of industrialization or technology*

9. citizens and immigrants (D) *legal members of a nation or country*

For more practice, you can find definitions of more words and phrases. Look for these vocabulary items and others: *college, school, undergraduate, foreign, tuition, structure, chapters, paragraph.*

8 **Answering Paragraph Questions with Details.**   The information in each paragraph of a reading can answer a different question. An answer of one or two sentences can tell the point or main idea of the material. Also, most paragraphs give details of the main idea. The definition of *details* is "single or specific pieces of information." Some kinds of details are examples, facts, and reasons.

Here are five different questions about the information in the reading "International Students." Three details correctly answer each question. The other sentence is untrue or unrelated to the main idea. Cross out the untrue or unrelated detail. The first one is done as an example.

1. What are some definitions of words and phrases in international higher education?
    a. The definition of an *international student* is "a postsecondary student from another country."
    b. The meaning of *postsecondary* is "after high school."
    c. ~~The word *school* usually means "a large group of fish."~~
    d. Another phrase for *international students* is foreign students.

2. Where do international students attend colleges and universities? (Give three facts.)
   a. The United States has the most students from other countries.
   b. Developing nations have a high level of industrialization or technology.
   c. Many foreign students attend school in Canada, Great Britain, and some European nations.
   d. More and more students from abroad attend school in Latin America, Asia, and Africa.

3. Why do international students go to school abroad? (Give three reasons.)
   a. They want the experience of life and language in another country and culture.
   b. They need technological information and skills not available in their home countries.
   c. They can't pay full tuition to state or government colleges and universities.
   d. In developing nations, they can save money though lower tuition and living costs.

4. Why do institutions of higher learning want international students? (Give three reasons.)
   a. They don't want to send their students to universities in other countries.
   b. International students bring internationalism to the classroom and campus.
   c. People from other countries are usually very good students.
   d. Foreign students pay high tuition and fees and put money into the economy.

For more practice, you can turn back to the Before You Read section on page 11 and answer the questions. Give definitions in your answer to No. 1. Give facts in your answer to No. 2. Give reasons in your answers to Nos. 3 and 4.

Discussing the Reading

9   In small groups, talk about your answers to the following questions. Then tell the class the most interesting information.

1. On the subject of higher education, what are some important vocabulary items? (Some possible examples are degree, visa, program, enrollment, registration, assignment, and sponsor.) What are some definitions of these words and phrases? Why are the items important to you?

2. Are you an international student, a citizen, or an immigrant? Are you studying at a secondary or a postsecondary school? Are you an undergraduate or a graduate student? Give details for your answers.

3. If you are an international student, do you like attending school abroad? If you are not an international student, do you want to study in another country? Give reasons for your answer.

4. Does your school want or need international students on campus? Give facts and reasons for your answer.

PART 4   # Writing

Before You Write

Exploring Ideas

1 **Interviewing Someone.**   A reporter for a school newspaper is writing an article about new students on campus. He is interviewing some students. Look at some of his questions.

1.   What is your name?
2.   Where are you from?
3.   What classes are you taking?
4.   What do you like about this school?
5.   What do you like to do in your free time?
6.   What are your plans for the future?
7.   Where do you live? . What kind of food do you like?

You are going to interview one of the students in your class for an article for a newsletter about your class. First write some questions. Use some of the above questions and write three other questions. Then choose a partner and interview him or her. Write your partner's answers after the questions.

Organizing Ideas

Ordering Information in a Paragraph

There are different ways to organize or order information in a paragraph. For this paragraph, write facts about the person you interview first. Then write the person's opinions.

Fact vs. Opinion

When you are writing, it is important to understand the difference between fact and opinion. A fact is information that everyone would agree on. It is true and no one would argue with it. An opinion is someone's idea. It may or may not be true. For example, *today's date* is a fact. *Paris is the capital of France* is a fact. *Today is an unlucky day* is an opinion. *Paris is a beautiful city* is also an opinion.

2 The reporter interviewed Maria Vega for her article. After writing her notes, she numbered them in the order she wanted to write the sentences in her paragraph. Look at the reporter's questions and notes. Write *F* for questions about facts about Maria and *O* for questions about Maria's opinions, as in the example.

    F   1. What is your name?

         Maria Vega.

    F   2. Where are you from?

         Puerto de la Cruz, a small village in Guatemala

    F   3. How old are you?

         19

    F   4. Why are you studying in Mexico?

         father is Mexican, aunt lives here in Veracruz

    F   5. What classes are you taking?

         English, art, history

    O   6. Why are you studying English?

         necessary for work

    O   7. What do you like about Veracruz Technical College?

         friendly students, helpful teachers

    O   8. What do you dislike about this college?

         food in the cafeteria

    F   9. What do you do in your free time?

         folk dancing, drawing

    O   10. What are your plans for the future?

         international fashion designer

3   Write *F* or *O* in front of the questions that you asked in Activity 1 on page 16. Then number your questions in the order you want to write the sentences in your paragraph. Show your organization to the person you interviewed. Does she or he agree with it? Does she or he want to add any information?

Writing Topic Sentences

The topic sentence tells the reader the main idea of the paragraph. It should not be too general or too specific. Don't begin paragraphs with "I am going to write about…" or "This paragraph is about…" Which of these sentences would be a good topic sentence. for the paragraph about Maria Vega?

   a. Maria Vega is a girl.
   b. Maria Vega doesn't like the food in the cafeteria.
   c. Maria Vega is one of many new students at Veracruz Technical College.

Sentence a is too general. It doesn't focus on the idea that Maria is a student. Sentence b is too specific. The whole paragraph is not about the food in the cafeteria. Sentence c is the best topic sentence. It focuses on the fact that Maria is a student and points the reader to the writer's purpose in writing about Maria—to talk about new students at the school.

---

4   Write a topic sentence for the paragraph you will write for the newsletter.

Maria Vega is one of many new students
at Veracruz Technical College.

Write

Developing Cohesion and Style

Connecting Ideas

Good writers connect the ideas in their paragraphs. A paragraph with connected ideas has cohesion. Good writers also use clear and simple language. This makes their writing easy to read. A paragraph with clear and simple English has good style.

---

5   Look at the following reporter's article and circle the words *and, but, so,* and *also.* Which words introduce new information? Which word introduces a result? Which word introduces contrasting information?

Maria Vega is one of many new students at Veracruz Technical College. Maria is 19 and is from Puerto de la Cruz, a small village in Guatemala. She is studying here because her father is Mexican, so she wants to learn about his country. She is living in Veracruz with her aunt. Maria likes VTC very much. She likes the friendly students and the helpful teachers. She also thinks her classes are excellent but she doesn't like the food in the cafeteria. In her free time, Maria folk dances and draws. After college, she wants to be a fashion designer.

Using and *to Connect Phrases and Sentences*

When you want to say two things about a subject, use the word *and* to connect the information. Sometimes *and* connects phrases that have the same verb.

Example:

Maria <u>is</u> studying English. Maria <u>is</u> studying art.
Maria Vega is studying <u>English and art</u>.

Sometimes *and* connects sentences that have different verbs. Use a comma before *and* when it connects two sentences.

Example:

Maria Vega <u>is</u> 19. Maria Vega <u>plans</u> to be a fashion designer.
Maria Vega <u>is 19, and plans to be</u> a fashion designer.

6   Write sentences by connecting the phrases with *and*.

1. Ming Su is 26 years old. Ming Su comes from Taiwan.

    Ming Su is 26 years old and comes from Taiwan.

2. Amelia eats breakfast in the cafeteria. Amelia eats lunch in the cafeteria.

    Amelia eats breakfast and lunch in the cafeteria.

3. Reiko is 19 years old. Reiko likes music a lot.

    Reiko is 19 years and likes music a lot.

4. Salma is married. Salma is a student.

    Salma is married and is a student

Susan goes to school and Mark goes also.
                                              too.

5.   Enrique likes soccer. Enrique plays every Saturday.

Enrique likes soccer and plays every Saturday.

6.   The school offers a good program in business. Its recreational facilities are excellent.

The school offers a good program in business and its recreational facilities are excellent.

Using but *and so to Connect Sentences*

You can also connect two sentences with *but* or *so*. Use a comma before these words when they connect two complete sentences.

■   *But* introduces contrasting information.

   Example:

   He thinks his English class is excellent.

   He thinks the food in the cafeteria is terrible.

   He thinks his English class is excellent, *but* he thinks the food in the cafeteria is terrible.

■   *So* introduces a result.

   Example:

   His company sells equipment to American hospitals.

   He needs English for his work.

   His company sells equipment to American hospitals, *so* he needs English for his work.

---

7   Connect the sentences with *so* or *but*.

1.   She has to work all day. She doesn't have time to do all her homework.

She has to work all day, so she doesn't have time to do all her homework

2.   He likes his English class. He doesn't think the American students are very friendly.

He likes his English class, but he doesn't think the American students are very friendly.

3.   Her company is opening an office in the United States. It needs English-speaking workers.

Her company is opening an office in the U.S., so it needs English speaking workers.

4.   She likes school life. She is homesick for her family.

She likes school life, but she is homesick for her family.

5. Pedro wants to work in Japan. He wants to learn Japanese.

Pedro wants to work in Japan, so he wants to learn Japanese.

8 Look at your notes from the interview and write five or six sentences using _and,_ _but,_ and _so_ to connect ideas.

Writing the First Draft

Good writers always write and then revise their work. The first time you write is called the _first draft_. In the first draft, you put your ideas together in the form of a paragraph. When you write the first draft, think about your ideas. Don't worry too much about grammar, spelling, or form.

9 Write a paragraph about the person you interviewed. Use your organization and topic sentence from Activities 3 and 4 on page 18. You can also use some of your sentences with _and, but,_ and _so._ Don't worry about writing everything correctly in this first draft.

Edit and Revise

Editing for Content and Form

You should edit a piece of writing at least two times.

■ The first time you edit, focus on the content of the writing: the writer's ideas, and how they are organized and connected.

■ The second time, focus on the form of the writing: the way the writing looks on the page, and the writer's grammar, spelling, and punctuation.

Editing Practice

10 Edit the following paragraph. Focus only on the writer's ideas and organization. Think about the following questions. Make any corrections you think are necessary.

1. Does the paragraph have a good topic sentence?
2. Are all the sentences about one subject?
3. Is the order of sentences correct?
4. Can any sentences be combined?
5. Which connecting words can you use?

A New Class Member

This is about Wichai Tongkhio. ~~is~~ a new member of the English composition class at Amarin Community College. There many classes at ACC. he generally likes life in Bangkok He likes the school, He doesn't like his dormitory. He is 18 years old. He is from a village in the north. He studying business administration, English and accounting. In his free time, he play basketball, He goes to movies. He plans to visit the United States next summer, so he needs to learn English.

11   Now edit the paragraph above again. This time, focus on the form. Check the writer's use of third-person singular verbs in the present tense; they should end with -s. Check the writer's use of negative verb forms. Check capitalization and punctuation Finally, check the writer's sentence and paragraph form. Use the following rules to help you. Make any corrections you think are necessary. Then rewrite the paragraph using correct form.

Rules for Sentence and Paragraph Form

1.   Write the title in the center of the first line.

2.   Capitalize all important words in the title.

3.   Don't capitalize small words like *a, the, to, with,* and *at* in titles, except at the beginning of a title.

4.   Skip a line between the title and the paragraph.

5.   Indent (leave a space) at the beginning of every paragraph.

6.   Begin every line except the first at the left margin. (Sometimes a line for the left margin is on the paper. If it isn't, leave a space of one inch.)

7.   Leave a one-inch margin on the right.

8.   Use a period (.) at the end of every sentence. (For rules on punctuation, see Appendix 4, pages 289-290.)

9.   Leave a small space after the period.

10.   Begin every sentence with a capital letter.

11.   Also capitalize names of people and places.

12.   If the last word of a line doesn't fit, use a hyphen (-) to break it. You can break a word only between syllables (**e•quip•ment**).

13.   Periods and commas (,) must follow words. They can't begin a new line.

14.   Every sentence in the paragraph follows the sentence before it. Start on a new line only when you begin a new paragraph.

15.   In formal writing, most paragraphs have four to ten sentences. A paragraph usually has more than one or two sentences.

Editing Your Writing

12   **Editing Using a Checklist.**   Edit your first draft using items 1, 2, and 3 in the following checklist. Then edit it for grammar and form using items 4 and 5.

Editing Checklist

1. Content
   a.   Is the information about your partner interesting?
   b.   Is it complete?
   c.   Is it correct?

2. Organization
   a.   Are all the sentences about one topic?
   b.   Is the order of the sentences easy to follow?

3. Cohesion and Style
   a.   Are your sentences clear and simple?
   b.   Are they easy to understand?
   c.   Can you connect any sentences?

4. Grammar
   a.   Is the grammar correct?
   b.   Are your verbs correct? Remember that third-person singular verbs end with -s in the present tense. Also check that your negative verb forms are correct.
   c.   Are singular and plural nouns correct?
   d.   Is the word order in your sentence correct?

5. Form
   a.   Is your punctuation correct?
   b.   Is your spelling correct?
   c.   Are your paragraph and sentence forms correct?

 **13**   **Peer Editing.**   Show your article to the person you interviewed. Does she or he think the information in it is correct? Does she want to add anything to the paragraph? Does he think you should correct any of the grammar, spelling, punctuation, or sentence or paragraph form? If you are not sure that your classmate's suggestions are correct, check with your teacher.

Writing the Second Draft

14   Rewrite your article using correct form. Check the grammar and form one final time. Then give your article to your teacher for comments and corrections. When your teacher returns your paper, ask him or her about any comments or corrections you don't understand. The next time you write, look back at your teacher's comments. Follow your teacher's instructions, and try not to make the same mistakes again.

PART 5

Grammar

A. Present Tense of *Be*: Affirmative and Negative Statements, Contractions

The verb *be* has different forms after different subjects.

	Examples	Notes
Affirmative	I **am** from Japan. The students **are** late. You **are** twins! The teacher **is** over there.	Use *am* with the pronoun *I*. Use *are* with plural nouns and these pronouns: *we, you, they, these,* or *those.* Use *is* with singular nouns and these singular pronouns: *he, she, it, this,* or *that.*
Negative	I **am not** late. She **is not** in this class.	Use *not* after the verb *be* in negative sentences.

Contractions are short forms. They are used in conversation and informal writing. Full forms are used in more formal writing.

	Full Forms	Contractions	
Affirmative	**I am** Mexican. **He is/she is/it is** over there. **We are/you are/they are** at home.	**I'm** Mexican. **He's/she's/it's** over there. **We're/you're/they're** at home.	
Negative	**I am not** interested. **He/she/it is not** here. **We/you/they are not** late.	**I'm not** interested. **He's/she's/it's not** here. **We're/you're/they're not** late.	(no contraction) **He/she/it isn't** here. **We/you/they aren't** late.

1   Complete the sentences with the correct forms of the verb *be*. Use contractions when possible.

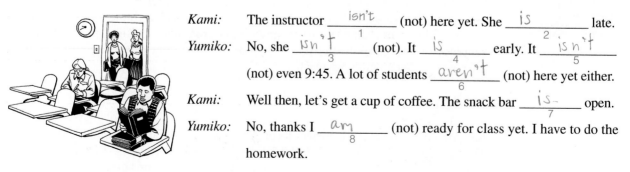

Kami: The instructor ___isn't___ (not) here yet. She ___is___ late.
                                  1   2
Yumiko: No, she ___isn't___ (not). It ___is___ early. It ___isn't___
                          3   4   5
(not) even 9:45. A lot of students ___aren't___ (not) here yet either.
                                              6
Kami: Well then, let's get a cup of coffee. The snack bar ___is___ open.
                                                                           7
Yumiko: No, thanks I ___am___ (not) ready for class yet. I have to do the
                                  8
homework.

Kami: The homework ___is___ difficult! The exercises ___are___
9   10

complicated and confusing. Fifteen minutes ___isn't___ (not) enough
11

time is singular

time to do it.

Yumiko: Ssshhh! You ___are___ making me nervous.
12

Kami: I ___'m___ sorry. But it really ___is___ too late to do the
13   14

homework now.

Yumiko: You ___are___ probably right.
15

B. *Be: Yes / No* Questions and Short Answers

Affirmative Questions	Affirmative Answers	Negative Answers	
Am I early?	Yes, you are.	No, you're not.	No, you aren't.
Is she/he/it Japanese?	Yes, she/he/it is.	No, she's/he's/it's not.	No, she/he/it isn't.
Are you/we late?	Yes, you/we are.	No, you're/we're not.	No, you/we aren't.
Are they late?	Yes, they are.	No, they're not.	No, they aren't.
Negative Questions			
Aren't you early?	Yes, I am.	No, I'm not.	
Isn't that woman a professor?	Yes, she is.	No, she's not.	No, she isn't.
Aren't we late?	Yes, we are.	No, we're not.	No, we aren't.
Aren't they late?	Yes, they are.	No, they're not.	No, they aren't.

Notes: In a yes/no question, the verb comes before the subject.

Negative questions are used to express the speaker's belief or expectation.

Contractions are not used in affirmative short answers. They are used in negative short answers.

2   Write missing questions for the answers below. Different questions are possible.

Example: A: Is Marco a good student?

           B: Oh, yes. He's the best student in the class.

1. A: Is he is in the Chinese Department?

    B: No, he isn't. He's in the English Department.

2. A: Is she from Texas?

    B: No, she isn't. She's from New York.

3. A: Are we early?

    B: Yes, we are.

4. A: Are they doing dance?

    B: Yes, they are.

5. A: Are you student?

    B: No, I'm not.

C. The Simple Present Tense: Affirmative and Negative Statements

The simple present tense is used to describe everyday activities and habits, to make general statements of fact, and to express opinions. With some verbs, the simple present shows an existing condition. The first three notes in the chart below apply to each type of affirmative and negative statement.

	Examples	**Notes**
Everyday activities and habits	Andres and Ricardo often **study** math together.	An object sometimes follows the verb.
Statements of fact	Lu **speaks** three languages. Dave **runs** quickly.	With third-person singular subjects, the verb ends in -s.
Opinions	I **don't like** the instructor. He **doesn't teach** math very well.	In negative statements, *do* or *does* comes before *not*. The contractions are *don't* and *doesn't*. The main verb always appears in the simple form.
Existing conditions	I **hear** music. He **doesn't understand** your question.	Other verbs that describe an existing condition include *like, need, want, seem, know,* and *believe.*

Notes:

1. Most verbs add -s to the simple form to make the third person singular: *She works at the library.*
2. For verbs ending in -y after a consonant, change the y to i and add -es: *carry/carries; try/tries.*
3. For verbs ending in -s, -z, -sh, -ch, -x, or -o (after a consonant), add -es: *teach/teaches; pass/passes; go/goes.*
4. Two verbs are irregular: *be/is; have/has.*

3   Use the words provided to make present tense statements about the people in the pictures. When an *A* appears in parentheses after the words, make an affirmative statement. When an *N* appears in parentheses, make a negative statement.

Examples: Mr. Sommers

32 years old (A)   Mr. Sommers is 30 years old.

have a beard (A)   Mr. Sommers has a beard.

Mr. Sommers

1. be a teaching assistant (A)
2. be a professor (N)
3. help Mr. Michaels (A)
4. teach three days a week (A)
5. give lectures (N)
6. work with students in small groups (A)
7. wear a suit and a tie (N)
8. like to wear jeans every day (A)
9. carry a briefcase (N)
10. have a board in his classroom (N)

D. The Simple Present Tense: *Yes / No* Questions and Short Answers

In simple present yes/no questions, a form of the verb *do* comes before the subject with verbs other than *be*. Use *does* with *he, she,* and *it.* Use *do* with *I, you, we,* and *they.* In these questions, the main verb always appears in the simple form. The appropriate form of *do* appears in short answers.

Affirmative Questions	Affirmative Answers	Negative Answers
Do I look like my mother? **Does he/she/it** do work? **Do we/you/they** need change?	Yes, you do. Yes, he/she/it does. Yes, we/you/they do.	No, you don't. No, he/she/it doesn't. No, we/you/they don't.
Negative Questions *use when you guess or not sure*		
Don't I need a ticket? **Doesn't she/he** need change? **Doesn't it** bite? **Don't we/you/they** leave soon?	Yes, you do. Yes, she/he does. Yes, it does. Yes, we/you/they do.	No, you don't. No, she/he doesn't. No, it doesn't. No, we/you/they don't.

4 Student A asks yes / no questions using the words below. Student B answers the questions with short answers. Student A adds some questions of his or her own.

> **Example:** A: *Does* ~~Do~~ this school have a cafeteria?
> B: Yes, it does. (or: No, it doesn't. It only has a snack bar.)
> A: Is the food good?
> B: No, it isn't. It's terrible.

1. this school have a cafeteria
2. students study there
3. it open late
4. any students work there
5. it *has* ~~have~~ coffee
6. the prices high

5 Change roles. Now student B asks yes/no questions using the words below. Student A gives short answers. Student B adds some questions of his or her own.

1. your English class difficult
2. you like your English class
3. the instructor give many exams
4. you often late to class
5. the teacher check your homework
6. you study enough

E. The Simple Present Tense: Information Questions and Answers

An information question begins with a question word and cannot be answered by *yes* or *no*. When a form of *do* separates a question word from the subject, the main verb must appear in its simple form.

Question Words	Questions	Possible Answers	Notes
Who	**Who** are your teachers? **Who** is your adviser? **Who** helps you?	Mr. Sommers and Ms. Lee. Mr. Michaels. Ben and Tom.	*Who* refers to people. *Who* can be the subject of a question. *Who* is usually followed by a singular verb.
Whom	**Who** **Whom** } do you ask?	My tutor.	*Who* (or *Whom*) is also used as an object. *Whom* is used only in formal questions. *Who* is used in informal speech.
What	**What** interests you? **What** is in the bag? **What** does she teach?	Books and movies. My lunch. History.	*What* refers to things. *What* can be the subject of a question *What* can also used as an object.
Where	**Where** is the snack bar? **Where** do we go now?	In the student center. To English class.	*Where* is used to ask questions about places.
When	**When** are our papers due? **When** does class begin?	On Wednesday. In five minutes.	*When* is used to ask questions about time.
Why	**Why** is the building closed? **Why** does he come so late?	Because it's a holiday. He has a job after school.	*Why* is used to ask questions about reasons.
How	**How** is your math class? **How** are you? **How** do you get to school?	Very hard. Pretty good. By bus and subway.	*How* can refer to a degree (of something). *How* can refer to a state or condition (for example, health). *How* can refer to a way or a method of doing something.

Note: Contractions for question words + *be* used in informal speech are: *who + is = who's*; *what + is = what's*; *where + is = where's*; *when + is = when's*; *why + is = why's*; *how + is = how's*.

6   Make information questions for each of the answers given below. Use the simple present tense and the question words *who, what, where, when, why,* or *how*.

Example: How are you?
          I'm very well, thanks.

1. ___Who is she_____?
   She's my English teacher.

2. <u>How do you get to school</u> ?
I walk to school.

3. <u>What does he teach</u> ?
He teaches math.

4. <u>When do we go shopping</u> ?
On Friday.

5. <u>Why don't you buy that a pair of shoes</u> ?
Because it's too expensive.

6. <u>Where is my vegetables</u> ?
In the refrigerator.

7. <u>What is your favorite color</u> ?
It's blue.

8. <u>Who is pay your tuition</u> ?
My father.

9. <u>Where is your classroom</u> ?
On the first floor.

10. <u>How is the weather in your country</u> ?
Horrible!

7 Work in pairs. Take turns asking and answering information questions using the words below. Add some questions of your own.

Examples: How / your classes this term?
A: How are your classes this term?
B: They're boring.
Why / you like them?
A: Why don't you like them?
B: Because the courses are too easy.

1. Who / your English teacher?
2. How / you like him/her?
3. When / your English class?
4. Where / your English class meet?
5. What / you bring to class?
6. What / the first thing you do in the morning?
7. How / you get to school?
8. Who / you usually come to school with?
9. When / your first class begin?
10. When / you usually go home?

Video Activities: Exchange Students

Before You Watch.   Discuss these questions in small groups.

1.   Did you have exchange students in your school?
2.   What are the advantages and disadvantages of studying in an overseas high school?
3.   How do students celebrate graduation from high school?

Watch.   Write answers to these questions.

1.   Where does Eda come from?
2.   How old do you think she is?
3.   Where does she live?
4.   What event is Eda going to?
5.   At the end of their year in the U.S., how do the visiting students feel about going back to their home countries?

Watch Again.   Read the following statements. Are they true or false? Write *T* for true, *F* for false.

_____   1.   Brian thinks Turkish people are very different from American people.

_____   2.   Eda is not homesick because she talks to her parents frequently.

_____   3.   About 12 foreign students are studying in San Diego.

_____   4.   The students are going to return to their countries in five months.

_____   5.   The students are planning to meet again in the future.

After You Watch.   Work with a partner. Student 1 is a high-school senior who is spending a year as an exchange student in the United States. Student 2 is a relative back home. Write a phone conversation asking and answering questions about Student 1's daily life. Use the simple present tense with frequency adverbs. Then role-play your conversation for your classmates.

Here are some topics to discuss; add any other topics you want.

- Student 1's host family (describe the people)
- Student 1's home, room, and school
- The kind of food Student 1 eats regularly
- The typical weather in Student 1's U.S. home

Chapter 2

Experiencing Nature

IN THIS CHAPTER

Listening
- Listening for main ideas
- Listening for specific information
- Identifying stressed words and reductions
- Taking notes on a story (specific information)

Speaking
- *Can* versus *can't*
- Talking about abilities
- Role-playing a story

Reading
- Previewing vocabulary
- Reading: Global Climate Changes
- Summarizing paragraphs
- Justifying opinions
- Using the organization of an information article

Writing
- Developing ideas: ordering information from general to specific
- Adding details using adjectives and prepositional phrases
- Using articles
- Writing a paragraph about art
- Editing for content, form, and grammar
- Editing for use of adjectives and articles

Grammar
- *There is / there are*
- Possessive nouns
- The present continuous tense
- Modal auxiliaries: *can, may, might, will*

| PART 1 | # Listening to Conversations |

Before You Listen

1 **Prelistening Questions.** Before you listen, talk about weather and vacation activities with a partner.

1. Are you familiar with four seasons? Describe the weather in each season.
2. What activities do people enjoy doing in each season?
3. Describe your perfect outdoor vacation. Where would you go? What would you do there?

2 **Vocabulary Preview.** Complete the sentences with these expressions from the conversation. Then go back and write the meanings of the expressions in the chart.

Expressions	Meanings
It's raining cats and dogs.	It's raining hard a lot of rain
sick of verb + -ing	sick of studying → I'm tired, I'm boring
to get a tan	brown my skin
crazy about → *driving me crazy* / *making me crazy*	I'm crazy about vacation → you like very much
freezing	cold
degrees	measure of temperature
weather forecast → *make a guess*	predicting the weather
chance of → *possible*	chance of rain

chance of ~rain *follow n* [something] → chance of [n]

chance to win [opportunity] → chance to [v]

follow verb

1. A: What happened to you? You're all wet!
    B: _It's raining cats and dogs_ outside, and I forgot my umbrella.
2. Ming is _crazy about_ skiing. It's her favorite sport.
3. In the summer, I love to lie in the sun and _to get a tan_.
4. The weather report in the newspaper says there's a ninety percent _chance of_ snow tomorrow. We probably won't be able to go to school.
5. The oven temperature is only 200 _degrees_ F.* It's not hot enough to cook a pizza.
6. When are we going to get to Las Vegas? We've been on the road for six hours. I am _sick of_ driving.
7. A: Did you watch the news at 6 p.m.?
    B: Yeah.
    A: Did you hear the _weather forecast_ for tomorrow?
    B: Yes. It's going to be sunny and warm. A perfect day for the beach!
8. A: Why don't you turn on the heater? It's _freezing_ in this room!
    B: It's broken. We'll have to sleep in our coats tonight.

_____

* 200 degrees Fahrenheit is about 93 degrees Celsius.

Listen

3 **Listening for Main Ideas.**   Jack, Peter, and Ming are talking about weather and vacations.

1. Close your book and listen to the conversation. Listen for the answers to these questions.
    1. Why is Peter complaining? He doesn't like the weather.
    2. What's the weather like? It's raining cats and dogs
    3. What month is it? October
    4. Where do Jack and Peter want to go? Why? They like sunny
    5. What activities can they do there? lie in the sun , get a tan
    6. Where does Ming prefer to go? What activities can she do there? skiing, snowboard mountain
    7. What's the weather forecast for tomorrow?
        cloudy, cold and 90% chance of rain
2. Compare answers with a partner.

beach. Hawaii Florida

Stress

4   **Listening for Stressed Words.**   Listen to the conversation again.

1.   Some of the stressed words are missing. During each pause, repeat the phrase or sentence. Then fill in the blanks with words from the list.

A	B	C	D	E
again	crazy	hate	sick of	umbrella
anyplace	December	last	ski	warm
beach	degrees	library	swimming	weather
break	don't	mountains	sun	year
chance	dry	October	sunny	
cloudy	fell	planning	tan	
come	freezing	same	that's	

Peter: Hey, look outside. It's raining cats and dogs — __again__! I __hate__ this weather. When does winter __break__ start?

Jack: Winter break? It's only __October__.

Peter: I know, but I'm __sick__ __of__ studying. I want to go someplace __warm__ and lie on the __beach__ for a week. Someplace where it's __sunny__ and __dry__. Florida or Hawaii, maybe?

Jack: Yeah. We can go __swimming__ and snorkeling and get a great __tan__. Now __that's__ my idea of a perfect vacation.

Ming: Not mine. I can't swim very well, and I __don't__ like lying in the __sun__. I prefer the __mountain__, especially in winter. I'm __crazy__ about skiing and snowboarding. In fact, I'm __planning__ to go to Bear Mountain with some friends in __December__. Do you want to __come__?

Jack: No thanks. I went there __last__ __year__. I was __freezing__ the whole time. Anyway, I don't know how to __ski__ very well. I __fail__ about a hundred times.

Ming: How about you, Peter?

Peter: Sorry, I agree with Jack. I don't want to go __anywhere__ where it's below 70 __degrees__.

Jack: By the way, what's the __weather__ forecast for tomorrow?

Ming: The __same__ as today. __Clody__, cold, and a 90 percent __chance__ of rain.

Jack: Oh, no! How am I going to go to the __library__?

Ming: Take an __umbrella__!

_____

Cross-Cultural Note

In North America, the school year begins in September, and there is a long vacation in December called "winter break." In most cases, school starts again after the New Year.

_____

2.   Now read the conversation with a partner. Practice stressing words correctly.

Reductions

5   **Comparing Long and Reduced Forms.**   Listen to the following sentences. They contain reduced forms. Repeat them after the speaker.

Reduced form*	**Long form**
1. It's raining cats 'n' dogs *in*	It's raining cats and dogs.
2. I wanna go someplace warm.	I want to go someplace warm.
3. We kin swim.	We can swim.
4. I'm gonna go ta Bear Mountain.	I'm going to go to Bear Mountain.
5. How bouchu?	How about you?
6. I dowanna go.	I don't want to go.

_____

* *Note:* The underlined forms are not acceptable spellings in written English.

6   **Listening for Reductions.**   Listen to the following conversation. You'll hear the reduced forms of some words.

1.   Repeat each sentence during the pause. Then write the long forms in the blanks.

Jack: Hi Ming. Hi Peter.

Ming and
Peter: Hey Jack.

Ming: What's happening?

Jack: I'm going to the campus recreation center. __Do__ __you__ __want__ __to__ come?

Ming: What are you __going__ __to__ do there?

Jack: Well, it's a nice day. We __can__ swim __and__ lie in the sun.

Ming: Thanks, but I __don't__ __want__ __to__ go. I'm too tired.

Jack: How __about__ __you__, Peter?

Peter: I can't. I've __got__ __to__ stay home __and__ study. Maybe tomorrow.

2.   With a partner, repeat the sentences for pronunciation practice.

After You Listen

7   Vocabulary Review.   Discuss the following questions with a partner. Use the underlined vocabulary in your answers.

1.   Are you <u>sick of studying</u> English? Do you need a vacation?

2.   Which sports are you <u>crazy about</u>?

3.   In your hometown, what is the coldest temperature, and what is the hottest temperature? (Use the word <u>degrees</u> in your answer.)

4.   Do you enjoy lying in the sun to <u>get a tan</u>?

5.   Are you afraid to drive if it's <u>raining cats and dogs</u>?

6.   What is the <u>chance of rain</u> tomorrow in the area where you live?

7.   Do you check the <u>weather forecast</u> before you go out each morning?

8.   Which is worse for you: to be <u>freezing</u> or to be too hot?

Pronunciation

Can vs. Can't

Notice the difference between the verb forms *can* and *can't* in the following sentences.

I can **meet** you tomorrow.

I **can't meet** you tomorrow.

Can is unstressed, so the vowel is reduced. Stress only the main verb: kin **meet**.

Can't is stressed, so the vowel is not reduced. Stress both *can't* and the main verb: **can't meet**.

8   Distinguishing between *Can* and *Can't*.   Listen and repeat each statement. Circle *Yes* if the statement is affirmative and *No* if the statement is negative.

1.	Yes	(No)	6.	(Yes)	No
2.	(Yes)	No	7.	Yes	(No)
3.	(Yes)	No	8.	(Yes)	No
4.	Yes	(No)	9.	Yes	(No)
5.	Yes	(No)	10.	(Yes)	No

Using Language

Talking about Abilities

You can use *can* and *can't* to talk about abilities.

For example:

Ming can ski, but she can't swim.

Here are some other expressions for talking about abilities:

- I'm (not) able to . . .
- I (don't) know how to . . .   +   verb
- I wish I could . . .

- I'm (not) good at . . .   +   verb + *ing*
- I'm (not) really good at . . .

9   **Talking About Abilities.**   Complete this chart. Then tell a partner about your abilities. Use all of the expressions from the explanation box.

Things I am good at	Things I am not good at
1. I'm good at cooking a typical Thai food	1. I'm not good at speaking English
2. I'm good at doing exercise	2. I'm not good at dancing
3. I'm good at cleaning my home	3. I'm not good at drawing picture
4. I'm good at going shopping	4. I'm not good at driving

PART 2

Recalling Main Ideas

Before You Listen

1 Prelistening Questions.   Before you listen, talk about camping with a partner.

1. Have you ever gone camping? Tell about this experience. Where did you go? When? With whom?
2. Why do many people enjoy camping?
3. What unpleasant or dangerous things can happen when people are camping?

2 Vocabulary Preview.   Before you listen, write the letter of the correct definition beside each word from the conversation.

Words	Definitions
_____ 1. incredible	a. afraid
_____ 2. muddy	b. walking out in nature
_____ 3. hiking	c. hurried to do something
_____ 4. clear	d. unbelievable; very surprising
_____ 5. hit the trail	e. covered with wet earth
_____ 6. couldn't wait	f. not cloudy
_____ 7. scared	g. start a hike

Listen

3 Listening for Main Ideas.   A man and a woman are checking into a motel. They tell the manager a very unusual story. As you listen, answer these questions.

1. What starts all of the trouble?
2. What happens to the couple's clothes?

4 Taking Notes on Specific Information. Listen to their story again.

1. During the pauses, fill in the missing key information in the spaces provided. Remember:

   ■ Don't try to write everything. Write the important information only.
   ■ Don't write complete sentences; write key words only.

   1. Decided to go _____.

   2. Weather was _____.

3. After half an hour, started to _____.

4. Hiked back to _____ to change _____.

5. Couldn't find _____.

6. Went back _____.

7. Saw_____ wearing_____.

8. Felt _____.

9. Problem now: _____.

2. Listen to the story again. This time there are no pauses.

After You Listen

5 **Summarizing Main Ideas.** In groups of three, use your notes to role-play the story in Activity 3.

6 **Vocabulary Review.** Write the letter of the correct response beside each sentence. Then read the dialogues with a partner.

Sentences

_____ 1. Why did you start eating without me?

_____ 2. Where are you going on Saturday afternoon?

_____ 3. I want to hit the trail by 8 A.M.

_____ 4. Are you worried about your English exam this afternoon?

_____ 5. What's the weather like?

_____ 6. Who walked on the floor with muddy feet?

_____ 7. That was an incredible story.

Responses

a. Then we'd better get up at 7.

b. I was so hungry, I couldn't wait.

c. Clear but cold. Take a sweater when you go out.

d. Yeah, I'm very scared.

e. I don't believe it. Do you?

f. The dog!

g. We're going hiking by the lake.

Talk It Over

Truth or Lie Game

1. Tell the class about a dangerous, unusual, or exciting experience that you have had in nature. Your teacher will give you a card. If the card says "Truth", you must tell a true story. If the card says "Lie", tell an imaginary story, but you should make it sound real.

2. After each story, the class will take a vote: how many people think the story was true? How many think it was a lie? See which student in your class is the best storyteller — or the best liar!

Role-play

1. Discuss the following questions.
    1. What do the words on the T-shirt mean?
    2. Do you think laws against *littering* (throwing paper and garbage on the ground or street) improve parks and streets?
2. Role-play the following situation in groups of three (George, Lou, and Rick).

George and Lou are brothers. They have just spent a wonderful weekend camping. Now they're getting ready to leave, but they are leaving their campsite dirty and full of trash. Rick is a park ranger. He stops the brothers to explain their responsibilities and to ask them to clean up.

The following expressions may help you express your ideas:

Explaining Rules

You need to . . .	It's against the rules to . . .
You shouldn't . . .	You're not allowed to . . .

Cross-Cultural Note

North America has many large, beautiful national parks. It is illegal to leave garbage in a park. It is also illegal to take plants or animals out of a park. Parks and camping areas always have rangers. Their job is to protect the parks and help park visitors.

PART 3   # Reading

Before You Read

1   **Vocabulary Preview.**   Learn the meanings of these vocabulary items from the reading.

Handwritten notes (left margin):
delsert : hot
delssert : sweet
admire → respect
Degree
major ⟵
extreme
freezing
typical
average
common
extreme
boiling

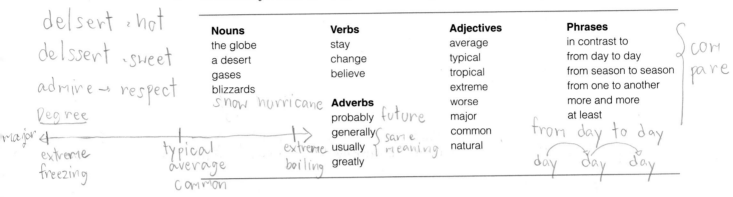

Nouns	Verbs	Adjectives	Phrases
the globe	stay	average	in contrast to
a desert	change	typical	from day to day
gases	believe	tropical	from season to season
blizzards		extreme	from one to another
	Adverbs	worse	more and more
	probably	major	at least
	generally	common	
	usually	natural	
	greatly		

Handwritten notes: snow hurricane — future — same meaning — from day to day — day day day — compare

Read

2   A reading selection of several paragraphs is probably about one general subject. The title of a reading often gives its subject. Each paragraph of the reading is usually about a more specific (narrower) topic within the general (wide) subject. For example, here are four paragraph titles that go with the reading selection "Global Climate Changes."

Handwritten notes (left margin):
I Title = general idea
A. Sub-title = main idea
   of paragraph
   or section
1. Detail
2 Detail
3. Detail
B. Sub-title = main idea
1. Detail
2.. Detail
3. Detail

- General Changes in the Nature of Weather
- The Powerful Effect of People on Nature
- Climate in Regions of the Globe
- Global Warming and the "El Niño" Effect

Notice that the titles are phrases, not full sentences. The important words begin with capital letters. Quickly read each paragraph of the reading. Then choose the best title from the list and write it on the line below the paragraph. Also, underline the topic sentence in each paragraph. Remember — a topic sentence tells the general subject of the paragraph. It is a short statement of the main idea.

Global Climate Changes

The word weather means "the atmospheric conditions at a specific place and time." The weather can vary from day to day. In contrast to weather, climate is "the general or average atmospheric conditions of a region." <u>In different areas of the globe, the climate generally stays the same from year to year.</u> For example, the climate in the desert is usually very dry. It may be cold in winter and hot in summer, but there is very little rain or humidity. In contrast, in tropical rain forests there is very high humidity. In most other areas of the world, the weather is cool or cold and wet or dry in the winter season. It is warm or hot and dry or humid in the summer months.

Climate in Regions of the Globe

According to some meteorologists (weather researchers), the earth's climate is changing slowly. In most places on the planet, the weather varies from season to season or even from day to day. In contrast, the typical climate is similar every year. Even so, there may be global climate changes from one long time period to another. What are these changes? Some scientists believe the weather is becoming more extreme. There are longer periods of very cold and very hot temperatures. There are more and more powerful hurricanes and tornados (storms with strong fast winds) and blizzards (heavy snowstorms). Floods (large amounts of water on dry land) and long droughts (times without enough rain) are causing greater and greater physical damage to the human communities on earth. These extreme forces of nature will get even worse in the future, say some people. And every change in climate in one part of the globe will bring more extreme changes in other areas.

Global Warming and the "El Niño" Effect

I. GW & El Niño
A. GW
1. Def: slow increase in temp
2 cause: increase of gases in the atmosphere
B. El Niño
1. Def: seasonal weather disorder
2 Effection in Tropic
a. Atmosphere
b. Rain
c. Wind
D. Hurricane
3. Effect Other Places [North]
a. Draught
b. Blizzard
c. Snow
d. Low temperature

Global warming and El Niño are having major effects on the earth's atmosphere, the weather, and the changing world climate. At least that's the opinion of many researchers and scientists. What is global warming? It is a slow increase in the average yearly temperature of the planet. The cause is an increase of gases in the atmosphere. What is El Niño? The Spanish phrase means "The Little Boy" or "The Christ Child." It names a weather condition most common in the month of December. This "seasonal weather disorder" is a change in the atmosphere of the tropical areas of the Pacific Ocean. It increases the amount of rain in the Americas and can bring strong winds and hurricanes. In contrast, El Niño may cause drought in the southern and western Pacific (Asia). Blizzards, snow, and long periods of low temperatures may follow in the northern regions of the globe.

The Powerful Effect of People on Nature

Not all meteorologists believe there is much natural global warming. According to these scientists, the El Niño effect is not getting stronger. So why is the temperature of the earth going up? Why are tropical storms like hurricanes causing more and greater flood and wind damage? Probably, human beings are the main cause of the extreme effects of weather and climate changes. Cars and factories are putting more and more gases like carbon dioxide (CO_2) into the earth's atmosphere. Coal and oil add carbon dioxide to the air too. Trees and plants take in carbon dioxide, but humans are cutting down the rain forests and putting up buildings where green plants grow. The world has a lot of people now, and it will have a lot more people in the future.

____

After You Read

3 Summarizing Paragraphs. A summary is a short statement of the most important information in a reading. How can you learn to summarize better? In your own words, begin with the most general point about the topic. Then give the important details or examples of that point. Here is a summary of the first paragraph of "Global Climate Changes."

All over the world, the typical climate is generally similar every year. It is dry in desert areas and wet in tropical regions. In most places, it is colder in winter and warm or hot in summer.

Work in groups of four. Choose a different paragraph from the reading and read it carefully. Begin with the title or topic. Identify the main idea and the important details. Then tell or read your summary to your group.

Discussing the Reading

4   In small groups, talk about your answers to these questions. Then tell the class the most interesting information.

1. Describe the typical climate in your area of the world. Does the weather change in the various seasons? If so, how?
2. Do you think the earth's climate is changing? If so, how and why is it changing? If not, why not?
3. What are your opinions on the future of the atmosphere and nature?

Talk It Over

People have many different beliefs about nature and the weather. Some ideas come from scientific facts. Others come from people's experiences or culture. In your opinion, which of these statements are true? Explain them to the group, and give the reasons for your opinions.

- In nature, there is no good or bad. There is no right or wrong. There is only the power of cause and effect.
- Why does it rain? It's useless to ask. It just does.
- Meteorologists and other researchers can study the weather, but they can't know or tell about future weather.
- A lot of people complain about the weather. Do they have the power to change it? Of course not.
- Nature doesn't listen to criticism or complaints. Do human beings have to listen to them? No, they can be like nature.
- If you ask for rain, don't be surprised if you get thunder and lightning.
- Why do people get depressed about the rain? Without rain, there would be no rainbows.
- Two people can never see exactly the same rainbow. But they can take a picture of it.
- Do you want sunshine today? Carry a big umbrella and wear a heavy raincoat. Then it won't rain.
- Is your arthritis pain increasing? This means wet weather is coming.

PART 4   # Writing

Before You Write

Exploring Ideas

1 In small groups, use these questions to discuss the painting.

1. What is the title of the painting? What is a shark?
2. Which man is Watson? Why do you think he is naked?
3. What is happening in the picture? How does the picture make you feel?
4. What can you see in the background? Where do you think this is happening?
5. When do you think this scene happened?
6. Do you think this really happened? Why or why not?

Watson and the Shark, John Singleton Copley, U.S., 1738–1815. Oil on canvas; 72 x 90¼ in. (182.9 x 229.2 cm). Gift of Mrs. George von Lengerke Meyer. Courtesy, Museum of Fine Arts, Boston. Reproduced with permissions. © 2000 Museum of Fine Arts, Boston. All rights reserved.

More about Watson and the Shark

The scene in *Watson and the Shark* really happened. Mr. Brook Watson was swimming in the Havana harbor in Cuba when the shark attacked. The shark bit his leg, but Mr. Watson did not die. He was a politician, and he wanted to get publicity, so he asked the American painter John Singleton Copley (1738–1815) to paint the scene. Watson later became Lord Mayor of London.

Organizing Ideas

Ordering Information in a Paragraph

Descriptions often begin with general information — information that describes the whole picture. Then a writer writes specific information — information that describes smaller parts of the picture.

The first sentence in a paragraph is often the topic sentence. In a paragraph about a work of art, it tells the name of the painting and the name of the artist. (Notice that we underline or *italicize* names of works of art.)

2   Read the following paragraph, which describes the painting below. Which sentences give general information? Which sentences give specific information? Underline the topic sentence in the paragraph. Circle the adjectives.

George Seurat, French, 1859–1891, *A Sunday on La Grande Jatte*, 1848; oil on canvas, 1884–1886, 207.5 x 308 cm, Helen Birch Bartlett Memorial Collection, 1926.224. Photograph © 1994, The Art Institute of Chicago. All Rights Reserved.

A Sunday on La Grande Jatte is a picture of a park on a warm and sunny day. It seems very peaceful. In the park there are many large trees. On the left you can see a lake with some small sailboats. There are people in the park. They might be European. Some people are walking, and some are lying or sitting on the grass. Many of the people are looking at the lake. The people in the park are wearing old-fashioned clothes. The women are wearing long dresses, and some of them are carrying umbrellas. In the middle of the painting there is a small child. She is walking with her mother.

3   Now look back at the painting of *Watson and the Shark*. Which of the following sentences is a good topic sentence for a paragraph about the painting?

1. *Watson and the Shark* is a good painting.
2. In this painting there are some men in a boat.
3. The men in this painting are afraid.
4. *Watson and the Shark*, by John Singleton Copley, shows a dramatic rescue.

4   List six general points of the painting that you should mention in your description. Then number the points in the order that you will describe them.

1. the rowboat เรือพายขนาดเล็ก   4. the shark
2. the sea   5. rescue
3. the men   6. _____

Write

Developing Cohesion and Style

Adding Details: Adjectives

An adjective is a word that describes a noun. Colors are adjectives. Words such as *tall, thin, curly, hungry, round, happy,* and *sick* are adjectives too. Adjectives make descriptions more interesting. They can be in two different positions:

1. After the verbs *be, seem,* and *look*.

   Examples:
   The men are *young*.
   The men look *horrified*.

Note: If you want to use more than one adjective you can connect them with *and*:
The shark is huge *and* frightening.

2. Before a noun.

   Example:
   The *young* men are in a boat.

5   Look at the picture *Watson and the Shark* again. With a partner, make a list of adjectives to describe the following. Use your imagination to describe the colors.

- the boat   small, overloaded
- the men in the boat   scared, excited
- the weather   bad weather
- the shark   is a big and dangerous
- the man in the water   scary
- the water   dark and cold freezing

choppy [adj.] used especially about the ocean, having a lot of small waves an uneven movement

6 Add the adjectives from your list to the following sentences.

1. The boat is in the water. _The small, overcrowded boat is in the water._
2. There is a shark in the water. _There is a big and dangerous in the water_
3. The men are wearing clothes. _The men are wearing old-fashioned clothes._
4. The man in the water seems _scary_
5. The weather looks _clody_ and _choppy_

Adding Details: Prepositional Phrases

Prepositions are words such as *on, in, towards, during, with*. They give information about location, direction, and time. Prepositions occur in prepositional phrases such as:

preposition	+	noun
on		the table
near		the door

Prepositions of location will be the most useful for you paragraph. Some common prepositions of location are:

on	in	at	near	beside	above
next to	in front of	behind	in the middle of	under	

Notice that prepositional phrases can be at the beginning of a sentence or at the end.

Examples:

In the park there are many large trees.
There are people *in the park*.

To make your writing more interesting, put prepositional phrases in different places — not always at the beginning of a sentence.

---

7 Look at the paragraph about the Seurat painting again. Underline all the phrases that show position or location. Most of these phrases begin with prepositions.

8 Look at the painting of *Watson and the Shark* again. Write four sentences about it using prepositions of location.

1. _There are several men in a small boat._
2. _There is a big shark in the dark water._
3. _In the boat there are several men are scared the shark._
4. _In front of the rowboat there is a harpoon._
5. _____

harpoon [n] = a long thin weapon with a sharp pointed end and a rope attached to it that is thrown or fired when hunting large animal in the ocean

Using Articles: a/an *and* the

A, *an*, and *the* are articles. They appear before nouns. *A* and *an* are indefinite articles. They describe general nouns. *The* is a definite article. It describes specific nouns.

	Examples	Notes
Indefinite Articles	*A:* I can drive **a** car, but I can't fly **an** airplane. *B:* Really? I can do both.	The speakers are talking about cars and airplanes in general — any cars or airplanes.
Definite Articles	*C:* Are you finished writing **the** reports yet? *D:* Not yet. Do you want to use **the** computer? *C:* That's all right. I can wait.	The speakers are talking about specific reports and a specific computer — the reports that *D* is writing and the computer that *D* is using.

Usually *a* or *an* comes before a noun when the noun appears for the first time. After that, *the* appears before the noun.

Examples	Notes
This is a painting of **an** island near Paris. **The** painting is very famous.	It is *one* painting of *one* island. It is *the* <u>specific</u> painting described in the first sentence.

9   Complete this paragraph about *The Tree of Life* with *a*, *an*, or *the*.

There is _____ large tree in the middle. Two children are standing under
       1

_____ tree, and two children are climbing in _____ tree. _____ children
   2   3   4

are waving. On the left is _____ man and _____ woman in _____ boat.
                              5   6   7

_____ man is fishing. _____ woman is holding _____ child. _____ large bird
   8   9   10   11

is flying over _____ boat. To the right is _____ smaller tree. Two people
                 12   13

are sitting under _____ tree at _____ table. On _____ table is _____ plant.
                    14   15   16   17

Writing the First Draft

10   Write a paragraph about the painting *Watson and the Shark*. Use your notes from Activity 4 on page 46 and Activity 8 on page 47. Remember to use the present continuous to tell what is happening. Use *there is* and *there are* to name the things in the painting. Don't worry about mistakes in form and grammar.

Edit and Revise

Editing Practice

11 Edit the following paragraph for content and organization. Does it contain all of the important elements of the painting *The Starry Night*? Does the order of the description make sense? Check it also for the quality of the description. Does it make good use of adjectives? Does it describe the painting accurately?

The Starry Night is the painting by Vincent van Gogh, a Dutch artist. There are some other houses and buildings around a church. In the front of the painting are some tall, curving trees, and in the back are some rolling mountains. Our eyes follow their shapes up, around, down, and back again, like a ride on a roller coaster. In the center is a church. The stars, trees, and mountains look like they are moving. It is the beautiful scene of a sky full of bright stars.

Vincent van Gogh. *The Starry Night* (1889). Oil on canvas, 29 x 36¼". The Museum of Modern Art, New York. Acquired through the Lillie P. Bliss Bequest. Photograph © 1995 The Museum of Modern Art, New York.

12   Now edit the paragraph for form. Check it for correct use of *a*, *an*, and *the*. Make any changes you think are necessary. (*Hint:* There are five incorrect uses of *a/an* and *the*.)

Editing Your Writing

13   **Editing Using a Checklist.**   Edit your paragraph for content and organization using items 1 and 2 in the following checklist. Then go back and edit your paragraph for cohesion, style, and form using items 4 and 5 in the editing checklist.

Editing Checklist

1. Content
   a. Are there interesting adjectives in the paragraph?
   b. Do the adjectives describe the picture well?
2. Organization
   a. Does the paragraph move from general to specific?
   b. Do you need to change the order of the sentences?
3. Cohesion and Style
   a. Can you connect any sentences?
   b. Are there appropriate descriptive adjectives?
   c. Are the prepositional phrases appropriate?
4. Grammar
   a. Are the verb forms correct? Is there an *-s* on all third-person singular verbs?
   b. Is the use of *a, an* and *the* correct?
5. Form
   Does the paragraph follow the rules for correct form? If you aren't sure, look back at the rules for sentence and paragraph form on page 22.

14   **Peer Editing.**   Show your paragraph to another student. He or she will check your work and tell you if anything is unclear.

Writing the Second Draft

15   Write the second draft of your description of *Watson and the Shark* using correct form. Check the form and grammar one more time. Then give it to your teacher for comments and corrections. When your teacher returns your paragraph, compare it with your paragraph from Chapter 1. Do you see any improvements? What problems do you still have?

<table>
<tr><td>**PART 5**</td><td># Grammar</td></tr>
</table>

A. *There is / There are*

Statements and questions can be formed with *there is / there are*. *There* is used to show that something exists or is in a place. *There is* is used when the noun that follows it is singular; *there are* is used when the noun that follows is plural.

	Examples	**Notes**
Affirmative Statements	**There is** a bee on the flower. **There are** meadows on the way.	The contraction for *there is* is *there's*. There is no contraction for *there are*.
Negative Statements	**There is no** water in my canteen. **There are no** rocks on the trail.	There are two contractions for *there is no*: *there isn't* AND *there's not*. The contraction for *there are no* is *there aren't*.

Affirmative Questions	**Affirmative Answers**	**Negative Answers**	
Is there a river near the trail? **Are there** any sleeping bags?	Yes, there is. Yes, there are.	No, there isn't. No, there aren't.	No, there's not. No, there's not.
Negative Questions			
Isn't there a map of the park? **Aren't there** hills on the hike?	Yes, there is. Yes, there are.	No, there isn't. No, there aren't.	No, there's not.

1   Fill in the blanks with *there is, there are, there isn't, there aren't, is there* or *are there*.

Harold: Maude, _____there's_____ nothing to do in the city. Let's go camping!
                                    1

Maude: Camping? But _____there aren't_____ any people our age in the mountains.
                                          2

Harold: Sure _____there are_____. And _____there is_____ camping equipment in the
                              3   4

garage. Let's see . . . I think _____there is_____ a tent and _____there are_____ two
                                              5   6

sleeping bags.

Maude: But _____is there_____ a camp stove?
                          7

Harold: Yes, _____there is_____. But _____there are_____ no backpacks, and _____there aren't_____
                        8   9   10

any hiking boots.

Maude: That's alright. I don't want to hike anyway. <u>Are   there</u>
                                                                      11

bathrooms and showers at the campground?

Harold: Of course <u>there   are</u>.
                            12

Maude: <u>Is   there</u> a hotel nearby? Just in case it rains...
              13

Harold: I think <u>there   is</u>. Come on! Let's go hiking!
                        14

<u>there   is</u> nothing to lose.
       15

2 Describe the picture below. Use sentences beginning with *there is/there are.*

Examples: There is a deer standing in the meadow.
              There are two people by the river.

B. Possessive Nouns

	Examples		**Notes**
Singular Nouns	Carlos Hiroshi tomorrow the boy the lady	Carlos's or Carlos' (car) Hiroshi's (boots) tomorrow's (weather) the boy's (pencil) the lady's (ring)	If a singular noun ends in -*s*, add '*s* or ' for the possessive form. If a singular noun does not end in -*s*, add '*s*.
Plural Nouns	the boys the ladies the men the children people	the boys' (bicycles) the ladies' (coats) the men's (team) the children's (toys) the people's (choice)	If a plural noun ends in -*s*, add '. If a plural noun does not end in -*s*, add '*s*.

Mr. Jones'
Mr. James's
ใช้ได้ ทั้ง 2 แบบ

ถ้าลงท้าย ด้วย S ใส่ ' อย่าง เดียว

3 Complete the sentences below. Use the possessive forms of the nouns in parentheses.

1. (Mrs. Jones) That's __Mr. Jones's__ canteen by the tent.
2. (today) __today's__ weather is going to be hot and sunny.
3. (Sarah parents) __Sarah's parents__ house is on a farm in the country.
4. (women) The __women's__ showers are over there.
5. (boyfriend) I don't have a backpack, but you can use my __boyfriend's__.
6. (brothers) His __brothers'__ names are John and Jeff.
7. (campers) The __campers'__ tents are falling down in the storm.
8. (wife) My __wife's__ brother is a forest ranger.
9. (birds) The __birds'__ nest is high up in the tree.
10. (fishermen) The __fishermen's__ boat is in the harbor.

C. The Present Continuous Tense

The present continuous tense is formed with the present tense of the verb *be* + the *ing* form of a verb. This tense is used to talk about an action happening at the moment of speaking, or an action currently in progress.

Statements		
	Examples	**Notes**
Affirmative	**She's carrying** a heavy bag. **They're relaxing** by the lake. **We're learning** Italian this semester. **She's majoring** in biology.	In these examples, the action is happening at the moment of speaking. In these examples, the action is currently in progress.
Negative	Hiroshi **isn't wearing** boots. They **aren't** going on the hike. She **isn't** keeping a journal.	Form the negative by placing *not* between the form of *be* and the verb in the *-ing* form.

Yes / No Questions			
	Examples	**Possible Answers**	
		Affirmative	**Negative**
Affirmative	**Is** Carlos **carrying** her backpack? **Are** they **picking** flowers?	Yes, he is. Yes, they are.	No, he isn't. No, they aren't
Negative	**Isn't** he **walking** on the trail? **Aren't** you **getting** tired?	Yes, he is. Yes, I am.	No, he isn't. No, I'm not.

Information Questions		
	Examples	**Possible Answers**
Affirmative	**When are** we **leaving**? **Why are** you **sneezing**?	We're leaving at noon. I'm getting a cold.
Negative	**Who isn't carrying** a canteen? **Why aren't** they **wearing** shoes?	Anita and Paul aren't. Their feet are hurting them.

4 Look at the pictures with a partner. Student A asks present continuous questions with the cue words provided. Student B answers the questions.

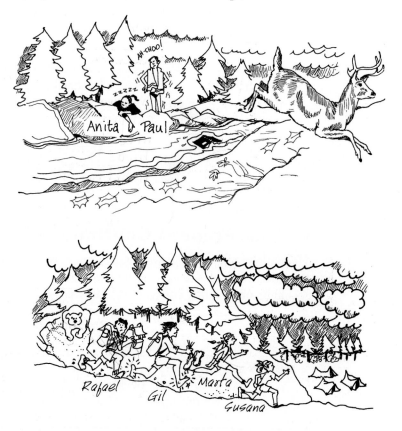

Example: Who / run / with no backpack?

A: Who is running with no backpack?
B: Susana is running with no backpack.

1. the sky / get cloudy?
2. Who / sleep?
3. What / the bear / do?
4. What / Paul / wear?

5. the hikers / have trouble?
6. What / the deer / do?
7. What / happen / to the tents?
8. What / Gil / do?

Change roles. Now Student B asks present continuous questions with the new cue words, and Student A answers.

9. the weather / change?
10. What / the hikers / do?
11. Who / carry / an extra backpack?
12. What / Paul / do?

13. anyone / swim?
14. What / happen / Anita's book?
15. Why / Gil / carry / the boots?
16. What / Anita / do?

D. Modal Auxiliaries: *Can, May, Might,* and *Will*

Can, may, might, and *will* are all modal auxiliaries. These are special verb forms. Modals do not change forms; they do not take *-s* or *-ed*. Modals are followed immediately by the simple form of a verb.

Statements

	Examples	Notes
Affirmative	I **can** swim. The rain **may** stop soon. The tents **might** fall down. We **will** call you tonight. She**'ll** go to the store.	In statements, modals come before the simple form of a verb. Don't use *to* before the verb. *Will* is the only one of these modals that can appear as a contraction.
Negative	I **cannot** find my watch. We **may not** need the compass. I **might not** come back. He **will not** go with us.	*May not* and *might not* cannot appear as a contraction. The contraction for *cannot* is *can't;* the contraction for *will not* is *won't.*

Modals	Meaning	Examples
can	ability	I **can** speak English. (I am able to speak English.) He **can't** swim. (He isn't able to swim.) **Can** you dance? (Are you able to dance?)
may **might**	future possibility	It **may** rain. (Maybe it will rain; maybe it won't.) I **might not** go. (Maybe I won't go; maybe I will.)
will	intentions predictions	I**'ll** see you tomorrow. (I intend to see you tomorrow.) The movie **won't** be crowded. (I predict the movie won't be crowded.) **Will** you buy a tent? (Do you intend to buy a tent?)

5 Circle the correct words in each set of parentheses.

There are some clouds, but it (willn't rain / (won't rain)) today.
1

At least I don't think it ((will rain) / will rains). It (can be / (will be))   *Predict*
2   3

a beautiful day. I (might to catch / (might catch)) some fish. They
4

(can might be / (might be)) big fish. Uh-oh. There's water coming
5

into the boat. There ((might be) / will to be) a leak. I (not / (can't))
6   7

((see) / to see) the bottom of the boat under all the water. Help!
8

Help! What's that noise? It ('ll / (might)) (is / (be)) a waterfall. Oh, no!
9   10

It is a waterfall! Well, I (mayn't / (may not)) (will save / (save)) the boat,
11   12

but I (can / ('ll)) be able to save my life. I (can / (can't)) ((swim) / to swim)!
13   14   15

Video Activities: Winter Storm

Before You Watch.

1. The following places are mentioned in the video. Find them on a map of the United States before you watch: Washington, D.C; New York; Ohio; New England; North Carolina.

2. Work in small groups. Make a list of words to describe winter weather in a cold climate.

    Examples: snow   icy   freezing

Watch.

1. This video mainly shows a storm in the _____ part of the U.S.

    a. southern   b. western   c. northern   d. eastern

2. Which of the following words describe the weather conditions you saw in the video?

    snow   fair   storm   rain   icy
    freezing   wind   warm   humid

Watch Again.   Match the places on the left with the weather conditions on the right.

Place	Weather Conditions
_____ 1. Washington D.C.	a. 12 inches of snow are expected
_____ 2. New York City	b. drivers of salt trucks and snow plows didn't go to work
_____ 3. New England	c. 5 inches of snow are expected
_____ 4. North Carolina	d. 6 inches of snow fell
_____ 5. Long Island	e. schools, businesses, and government offices closed
	f. slush

After You Watch.   Walk around the classroom and talk to your classmates. Write the name of a person who…

1. _____ has never seen real snow.
2. _____ loves winter.
3. _____ was in a hurricane.
4. _____ enjoys thunderstorms.
5. _____ has built a snowman.
6. _____ was born in the winter.
7. _____ likes to walk in the rain.
8. _____ knows how to ice skate.
9. _____ has stayed home from school when the weather was bad.
10. _____ checks the weather forecast in the morning.

Chapter 3

Living to Eat or Eating to Live?

IN THIS CHAPTER

Listening
- Listening for main ideas
- Listening for specific information
- Identifying stressed words and reductions
- Taking notes on advice (specific information)

Speaking
- *Teens* versus *tens*
- Interviewing classmates about food & shopping habits
- Summarizing main ideas
- Comparing eating habits

Reading
- Previewing vocabulary
- Reading: The Changing Global Diet
- Recognizing paragraph topics
- Understanding the main idea
- Getting meaning by using punctuation clues
- Recognizing supporting details

Writing
- Developing ideas: ordering information from general to specific, writing topic sentences
- Giving examples with *such as*
- Writing a paragraph about a holiday meal
- Editing for content, form, cohesion, style, and grammar
- Editing for commas with appositives

Grammar
- Count and noncount nouns
- Quantifiers
- Modal auxiliaries: requests, offers, permission

PART 1

Listening to Conversations

Before You Listen

1 Prelistening Questions.   Look at this picture.

1. The supermarket in the picture has an "express line." What do you think this means?
2. There is an older couple at the front of the line. What are they buying? What mistake do they make?

2 Vocabulary Preview.   Complete the sentences with these words from the conversation.

Language Tip
Use noncount nouns to talk about food in a general way:

> I like ice cream.
> Steak is expensive.

Use quantity words or containers together with food to talk about specific quantities:
> a gallon of ice cream
> a box of soap
> a pound of steak

---

		fruit & vegetable	
groceries	pound[1]	produce (noun)	aisle
gallon[2]	in line	to take checks *accept check*	

[1] 2.2 pounds equal one kilogram.
[2] A gallon is equal to about 4 liters.

1. Strawberries are cheap now. They cost $1.29 a ___*pound*___ .

2. We have a big family. We buy a ___*gallon*___ of milk every week.

3. You can pay with cash or a credit card, but this market doesn't ___*take checks*___ .

4. I hate frozen or canned vegetables and fruit. I only eat fresh ___*produce*___ .

5. I just spent $90.00 on ___*groceries*___ . Last week I spent $85.00. Food is really expensive here!

6. A: Excuse me, where is the bread?

    B: It's on ___*aisle*___ four.

7. The market was very crowded. I had to wait ___*in line*___ for fifteen minutes to pay.

Listen

3   **Listening for Main Ideas.**   Mr. and Mrs. Nutley are doing their weekly grocery shopping.

1. Close your book and listen to the conversation. Listen for the answers to these questions.

    1. What are Mr. and Mrs. Nutley discussing? *groceries shopping*

    2. Why is Mr. Nutley buying so much food? *he is hungry*

    3. How much did the strawberries cost? *$1.19 a pound*

    4. What did Mr. Nutley forget? *soap*

    5. Why did Mrs. Nutley say "*More* ice cream?" *The have a gallon at home.*

    6. Why can't the Nutleys use the express line? *The have too much stuff.*

2. Compare answers with a partner.

Stress

4   **Listening for Stressed Words.**   Listen to the conversation again.

1.   Some of the stressed words are missing. During each pause, repeat the phrase or sentence. Then fill in the blanks with words from the list.

aisle	cookies	have	not	sorry	too
always (2 times)	expensive	I'll	$1.19	steak	wait
aren't	express	isn't	produce	strawberries	what's
army	few	like	really	take	why
back	forgot	line	sale	that	
box	gallon	many	see (2 times)	$3.99	
checks	grocery	more	soap (2 times)		

Mr. N: Well, dear, I got a _____few_____ things that _____aren't_____ on the _____grocery_____ list.

Mrs. N: I can _____see_____ _____that_____! You're _____not_____ shopping for an _____army_____, you know.

Mr. N: You know I _____always_____ do this when I'm hungry.

Mrs. N: Well, let's _____see_____ what you _____have_____ here.

Mr. N: Some nice, fresh _____strawberries_____ for only _____$1.19_____ a pound.

Mrs. N: Well, that's fine. They _____always_____ have nice _____produce_____ here. But _____why_____ do you have all these _____cookies_____?

Mr. N: I don't know; don't you _____like_____ them?

Mrs. N: Oh, I suppose. I hope you have a _____box_____ of _____soap_____ here.

Mr. N: Oops, I _____forgot_____. Where's the _____ in this market?

Mrs. N: _____Aisle_____ 3.

Mr. N: _____I'll_____ go get it.

Mrs. N: _____Wait_____ — This _____steak_____ you got looks _____really_____ _____expensive_____!

Mr. N: Well, it _____isn't_____. It's on _____sale_____ for just _____$3.99_____ a pound.

Mrs. N: And ___What's___ this? ___More___ ice cream? We already have a ___gallon___ at home. Go put it ___back___. Meanwhile, I'll get in ___line___.

Cashier: I'm ___sorry___, ma'am; this is the ___express___ line. You have ___too___ ___many___ groceries, and we don't ___take___ ___checks___ here.

2.   Now read the conversation with a partner. Practice stressing words correctly.

Reductions

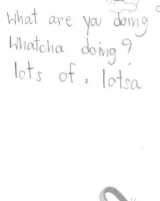

what are you doing?
whatcha doing?
lots of = lotsa

5   **Comparing Long and Reduced Forms.**   Listen to the following sentences from the conversation. They contain reduced forms. Repeat them after the speaker.

Reduced form*	**Long form**
1. Let's see <u>whatcha</u> have here.	Let's see what you have here.
2. Why <u>d'ya</u> have all these cookies?	Why do you have all these cookies?
3. I <u>dunno</u>.	I don't know.
4. <u>Doncha</u> like <u>'em</u>?	Don't you like them?

phrase (handwritten above "what you")

_____
* *Note:* The underlined forms are not acceptable spellings in written English.

6   **Listening for Reductions.**   Listen to the following sentences. You'll hear the reduced forms of some words.

1.   Repeat each sentence during the pause. Then write the long forms in the blanks.

Customer: Waiter?

Waiter: Yes, sir. Do you know _____ _____ want?

Customer: _____ _____ have the spaghetti with mushroom sauce tonight?

Waiter: Yes, we do.

Customer: Well, are the mushrooms fresh or canned?

Waiter: We get _____ _____ fresh mushrooms from

the produce market every day.

Customer: Great, I'll have that.

Waiter: What kind of wine _____ _____ want with that?

Customer: I _____ _____. Why _____

_____ recommend something?

Waiter: Our California wines are excellent.

2.   With a partner, repeat the sentences for pronunciation practice.

After You Listen

7   **Vocabulary Review.**   Discuss the following questions with a partner. Use the underlined vocabulary in your answers.

1.   Who shops for groceries in your family? How often?

2.   What kinds of produce do you buy every week?

3.   How much does a gallon of gasoline cost right now in your country? Recently has this price gone up, gone down, or stayed the same?

4.   Which of the following places usually take checks: restaurants, supermarkets, department stores, car dealers, or movie theaters?

5.   When you fly in an airplane, do you prefer to sit by the window or by the aisle?

6.   How many pounds do you weigh, approximately?

7.   Do you get angry when you have to stand in line?

Pronunciation

Teens or Tens?

Notice the differences in stress between the following pairs of words. In the numbers 13 to 19, stress the first syllable **and** -*teen*. For 20, 30, 40, etc., to 90, stress the first syllable only. Listen.

thirteen	thirty	fourteen	forty	fifteen	fifty
sixteen	sixty	seventeen	seventy	eighteen	eighty
nineteen	ninety				

8   **Distinguishing between Teens and Tens.**   Listen to the sentences and circle the number you hear.

1.   13   (30)
2.   (14)   40
3.   (15)   50
4.   16   (60)

5.   17   (70)
6.   (18)   80
7.   19   (90)

9   **Listening for Teens and Tens.**   Listen to these sentences. Write the number you hear on the blank line in each picture.

Talk It Over

Interview. You are going to use count and noncount nouns as you interview people about food and shopping habits.

1. Work in groups of four. Write the names of your group members in the spaces at the top of the chart.

2. Write your teacher's name in the space marked "Teacher." Take turns asking your teacher questions with "How much?" or "How many?" using the words on the left side of the chart.
   - Use present tense.
   - Pay attention to count and noncount nouns.
   - Add time expressions as needed. For example, "How much coffee do you drink *every week*?"

3. Then ask your group members the questions and write their answers on the chart. The other members of your group will ask you the questions, too. Follow the example for Stacy.

   Example:
   How much coffee do you drink *every day*?   2 cups a day
   How many candy bars do you buy a month?   2 bars

Questions	Stacy	Teacher	Name	Name	Name
coffee / drink	2 cups a day				
beer / drink	3 glasses a week				
candy / buy / week	2 bars				
food / eat / breakfast	only a little				
money / spend / groceries / each week	about 20 dollars				
gasoline / buy / month	about 15 gallons				
bananas / eat / week	3 or 4				
times / eat / restaurants / month	8 or 9				

PART 2   # Recalling Main Ideas

Before You Listen

1   **Prelistening Questions.**   In the United States people learn that they should eat food from the four major food groups: grains (wheat, corn, etc.), fruits and vegetables, dairy (milk), and protein (meat, fish, etc.) Before you listen, answer these questions with a partner.

1.   Talk about the picture. Is this man a healthy eater?
2.   Do you eat like this man? For example, do you like junk food? What is your favorite type?
3.   Do you ever eat canned or frozen food?
4.   Have you ever lost weight? How did you do it?

2   **Vocabulary Preview.**   You will hear the underlined words in the speech. Before you listen, write the letter of the correct definition beside each sentence.

		Sentences	Definitions
D	1.	Angela weighs 160 pounds. The doctor says she is <u>overweight</u>.	a. (to) get fatter
F	2.	After Christmas I'm going to <u>go on a diet</u> because I ate too much during the holidays.	b. avoid; not eat
A	3.	If I don't exercise, I <u>gain weight</u>.	c. a diet where you lose weight very fast because you only eat one type of food
B	4.	If you want to lose weight, you should <u>stay away from</u> fattening foods like ice cream.	d. too fat
H	5.	A piece of bread has about 75 <u>calories.</u>	e. medicine that helps people lose weight
G	6.	Fresh food is healthier than <u>prepackaged</u> food.	f. to start a program for losing weight
E	7.	<u>Diet pills</u> are very dangerous.	g. canned or frozen food
C	8.	Marta lost ten pounds in a week on a <u>crash diet</u>, but she gained it all back.	h. unit for measuring the energy value of food

Listen

3   **Listening for the Main Idea.**   Listen to the following advice about losing weight. As you listen, answer this question.

What is the best way to lose weight?

4   **Taking Notes on Specific Information.**   Listen again. This time, take notes on the *dos* and *don'ts*.

Do	Don't
Lose weight slowly 2 pounds a week one kilo	Take diet pills
eat right stay away from fast food, canned food	go on crash diet
exercise regularly 1 hour 3 times a week	eat canned food
be patience	eat quickly

After You Listen

5   **Summarizing Main Ideas.**

1.   Compare notes with a partner. Together, summarize the advice you heard in complete sentences. Tell your partner if you have tried these ideas for losing weight.

Example:

You should lose weight slowly.

You shouldn't eat fast food.

2.   With your class, make a list on the board of additional *dos* and *don'ts* about losing weight and dieting. Tell the class which ones you have tried and how well they worked.

6   **Vocabulary Review.**   Discuss your answers to the following questions with a partner. Use the underlined vocabulary in your answers.

1. In the United States, many people <u>go on a diet</u> starting on January 2. That's because they ate too much on Christmas and New Year's Day. When do you eat too much? Do you go on a diet afterwards?

2. Many people are overweight, but do you know anybody who is underweight? What can this person do <u>to gain weight</u>?

3. Are there any <u>prepackaged</u> foods that you buy regularly?

4. Some people try to lose weight by counting <u>calories</u>. Have you ever done that?

5. Have you ever tried <u>diet pills</u> or a <u>crash diet</u>? Did they work?

6. If you want to lose weight, which foods should you *stay away from*?

Talk It Over

Comparing Eating Habits.   "Eating habits" means your eating customs. It includes when, where, and what you eat. Use the chart below to talk about differences between your eating habits at home with the way you eat when you travel somewhere.

When I'm at home	When I travel
1. what you eat for breakfast, lunch, and dinner *Example:* I eat rice for breakfast.	I eat cereal for breakfast.
2. the time and size of meals and snacks	
3. the price of food	
4. restaurants	
5. table manners	

PART 3   # Reading

Before You Read

1 Discuss the pictures in small groups.

1. Where are the people in each scene and what are they doing?
2. How are the foods in each picture similar? How are they different?

2   Think about the answers to these questions. The reading "The Changing Global Diet" answers them.

1.   What might the word *diet* mean?
2.   How is "fast food" becoming the same around the globe?
3.   Why might people like or dislike quick and convenient eating places?
4.   How are fast foods and convenience foods becoming more nutritious?
5.   How are global eating customs and food choices changing?

3   **Vocabulary Preview.**   Learn the meanings of these vocabulary items from the reading.

Nouns	Verbs	Adjectives	Phrases
choices	include	basic	lose weight
habits	grow	certain	go on a diet
nourishment	prepare	expensive	food stands
nutrition	serve	universal	fast-food chains
menus	contain	famous	have the same look
style	snack	convenient	home-cooked meals
taste	produce	cheap/cheaper	convenience foods
customers		familiar	salad bars
value	**Adverbs**	nutritional	junk food
vitamins	typically	fresh	nutrition bars
minerals	quickly	canned	for instance
dairy	generally	frozen	
elements	widely	packaged	
ingredients	perfectly	healthful	
markets		nourishing	

Read

4   Read the following material quickly. Then read the explanations and do the exercises after the reading.

The Changing Global Diet

A   Most words in the English language have more than one simple, or basic, meaning. One example is the word *diet*. The most general definition of the noun is "a person's or a group's usual food choices and habits." In a more specific definition, *diet* means "an eating plan with only certain kinds or amounts of food." For instance, a diet is often a plan to lose weight. And as a verb, *diet* means "go on a diet."

B   All over the world, the global diet includes *fast food*—prepared items from inexpensive restaurants, snack bars, or food stands. Some examples of typically American fast food are *hamburgers, hot dogs, sandwiches, fried chicken,* and so on. Some types of international fast foods might be German *sausage* and *schnitzel,* Italian *pizza* and *pasta,* Mexican *tacos* and *burritos,* Middle Eastern *shish kebab* and *falafel,* Japanese *sushi* and *tempura,* Chinese *eggrolls* and *noodles,* and the like. The variety of fast foods available on the planet is growing. Even so, this kind or style of nourishment is becoming *universal*, or worldwide. Fast-food places usually prepare and serve the items quickly. Many are part of *fast-food chains* (eating places with the same name and company owner). For instance, the biggest and most famous American fast-food chain serves hamburgers in every continent on the planet except Antarctica. In over 120 different countries, its 25,000 eating places have the same look. They have a similar atmosphere. The menu items may not be exactly alike from one culture to another, but the style and taste of the foods don't differ much.

C   For several reasons, many people choose fast food. First, it is quick and convenient. Second, it is cheaper than special home-cooked meals or formal restaurant dinners. And third, it is identical in every eating place with the same company name. The atmosphere and style of most fast-food places is casual, comfortable, and familiar. So why do other eaters dislike or stay away from this fast, easy kind of nourishment? The main reason is its low nutritional value. Fast food doesn't contain large amounts of *fiber, vitamins, minerals*, and the like—elements necessary for good nutrition and health. In contrast, most types of fast food have a lot of fat, cholesterol, sugar, or salt in them. Possibly, these substances can cause or increase health disorders, like heart disease, strokes, and some kinds of cancer.

D   Some people believe food should be perfectly fresh and "natural." According to natural food eaters, fast food is not good for human beings. They don't believe *convenience foods*—canned, frozen, or packaged in other ways—are very nutritious either. On the other hand, these quick and easy kinds of worldwide nourishment are generally getting better and more healthful. For instance, many fast-food restaurants now have salad bars and put vegetable items on their menus. In some places, customers can get fish or *veggieburgers* instead of hamburgers and grilled chicken instead of fried. Also, some newer kinds of packaged and prepared foods contain less fat, cholesterol, sugar, or salt than before. Of course, people everywhere like to snack on *junk food* (candy, cookies, potato chips, ice cream, and other things without much nutritional value). For health and sales reasons, some snack food companies are producing packaged items with less fat, sugar, or salt. And *nutrition bars*—snacks with a lot of protein, vitamins, and other nourishing food elements—are becoming more widely available.

E   Of course, human beings around the world don't always eat in fast-food places. They don't buy only canned, frozen, or packaged convenience items from stores or machines. A few families are producing food on their own, but most people buy it from markets in their communities. Some choose only *natural food*, items without chemical substances. Many families prepare good meals at home. Other people are restaurant customers. Universally, more meals include the basic necessary food elements—protein, carbohydrates, and fats. A greater number of dishes contains the necessary vitamins and minerals. Almost everywhere, some kind of meat, fish, dairy product, or another protein food is part of a good breakfast, lunch, or dinner. There are also grains, breads, vegetables, fruit, and the like. The variety of food choices is large now and is probably going to increase. The number of food preparation methods is growing too. Cooking customs, eating habits, and food preferences all over the world are becoming more healthful. In these and other ways, the global diet is changing.

After You Read

5 **Recognizing Paragraph Topics.** A well-structured paragraph has a clear topic. Within the subject of the reading, it is about a different topic from all the other paragraphs. The material in each paragraph answers a question about that topic.

What is the topic of each paragraph from the reading "The Changing Global Diet"? Write the paragraph letter on each line.

____E____ 1. ways the global diet is changing

____C____ 2. why people choose or stay away from fast food

____D____ 3. how convenience foods are becoming more nutritious

____B____ 4. how fast food is the same around the globe

____A____ 5. some definitions of the word *diet*

For each of the five topics, make a different question about the material in the reading. Remember—for questions, you'll have to change the word order or add words to the topic phrases. Examples:

1. In what ways is the global diet changing?
2. Why do people choose or stay away from fast food?

6 **Understanding the Main Idea.** Usually, a main-idea statement is a good answer to a question about the topic of each paragraph of reading material. This one- or two-sentence answer also tells the point or message of the paragraph.

In order A–E, here are some possible main-idea statements about the topics of the paragraphs in the reading "The Changing Global Diet." Write *T* (true) or *F* (false) on each line. Change the false sentences to true statements of the main idea. Then use them as answers to the five questions in Exercise 2.

____F____ 1. The word *diet* has two basic definitions—"usual food choices" and "an eating plan."

____F____ 2. Fast food has very little variety around the world. It is always hamburgers, hot dogs, and fried chicken. But the style of the nourishment and the atmosphere of the eating places varies a lot in different countries.

____T____ 3. Some eaters enjoy the convenience, price, and familiar comfort of fast food. Other people dislike its low nutritional value.

____F____ 4. Fast foods and convenience foods are getting less and less healthful. The restaurant items are always fried, and there are no vegetables. The packaged items are going to contain more fat, sugar, salt, and so on.

____F____ 5. The global diet is changing mostly in bad ways. Few people buy fresh, natural foods at markets. No families cook at home. Not many meals contain the necessary food elements. And there is a smaller variety of food choices and preparation methods.

7   **Getting Meaning by Using Punctuation Clues.**   Often, the context of reading material contains clues to the meanings of vocabulary items. New or unusual words or phrases may be in italics. Short definitions, similar words, explanations of the items, or examples of their meanings might come between certain kinds of punctuation marks, like quotation marks (" ") or parentheses ( ). They can also appear after a comma (,) or a dash (—).

In the reading selection "The Changing Global Diet," some of the new or less common vocabulary items are in italics. Short explanations of their meanings may appear between or after various kinds of punctuation marks. For each of these definitions, find the words and phrases. (The letters in parentheses are the letters of the paragraphs.) Write them on the lines, as in the example.

1.   a person's or group's usual food choices or habits: (A) ___*diet*___

2.   an eating plan with only certain kinds or amounts of food: (A) ___*diet*___

3.   prepared items from inexpensive restaurants, snack bars, or food stands: (B) ___*fast food*___

4.   another word for worldwide: (B) ___*universal*___

5.   eating places with the same name and company owner: (B) ___*fast - food chains*___

6.   elements necessary for good nutrition and health: (C) ___*fiber, vitamins, minerals.*___

7.   prepared canned, frozen, or packaged items: (D) ___*convenience food*___

8.   candy, cookies, potato chips, ice cream, and other things without much nutritional value: (D) ___*junk food*___

9.   snacks with a lot of protein, vitamins, and other nourishing food elements: (D) ___*nutrition bars*___

10.   food items without chemical substances: (E) ___*natural food*___

For more practice, find other vocabulary items in italics, such as *hamburgers, hot dogs, sandwiches, fried chicken, sausage, schnitzel, pizza, pasta, tacos, burritos, shish kebab, falafel, sushi, tempura, eggrolls, veggieburgers, candy, cookies, potato chips, ice cream, protein, carbohydrates, fats, fiber, vitamins, minerals*, and the like. For each item and others, you can explain the meaning in a sentence like this.

Hamburgers are a kind of typical American fast food.

Sausage is a type of German fast food.

Protein is an example of a necessary food element.

(A/An) _____   is/are   a kind   of _____ .
                                    a type
                                    an example

8 **Recognizing Supporting Details.**   Usually, each paragraph of a reading includes not only a main idea but also details about it. These details support the main idea of the paragraph with specific facts, examples, reasons, or the like. The supporting details are answers to a question about the main idea. A paragraph may also contain other information or ideas, but these are not part of the main idea.

Here are five different questions about the information in the reading "The Changing Global Diet." Which details answer each question? Cross out the unrelated sentence.

1. What are some examples of possible meanings of the word *diet*?
    a. ideas or information to think about
    b. a person's or a group's usual food choices or habits
    c. an eating plan with only certain kinds or amounts of food
    d. a way to lose weight

2. For what reasons is fast food becoming the same or similar in various cultures around the globe?
    a. It includes typical American kinds of food like hamburgers, hot dogs, and fried chicken.
    b. Quick and convenient items from Germany, Italy, Mexico, China, and other countries are available too.
    c. Formal restaurant meals can be expensive or cheap, fast or slow, nutritious or low in fiber.
    d. The eating places have a similar look and atmosphere, and they may be part of a chain.

3. Some people like to eat fast food, but others don't. What are the reasons for their preferences?
    a. Fast food is usually quick, convenient, and inexpensive.
    b. Fast-food restaurants, snack bars, and other eating places are informal, comfortable, and familiar.
    c. Fast food may not contain the necessary elements or substances for good nutrition and health.
    d. People can't get vegetables and fruit or kinds of nourishment from stores or machines.

4. In what ways are fast foods and convenience foods becoming better and more healthful?
    a. Some people buy and eat only natural foods without chemicals of any kind.
    b. Many fast-food eating places have salad bars and include vegetables on their menus.
    c. Instead of hamburgers high in fat and cholesterol, customers can get fish or veggieburgers or grilled chicken.
    d. Some newer kinds of packaged foods contain less fat, sugar, or salt than before.

5. The global diet is changing in some good ways. What are some examples of these changes for the better?

   a. A few families are producing their own food, and many more are buying natural or nutritious food from markets.

   b. Health disorders like heart disease, strokes, and cancer are no longer related to food and eating.

   c. Many people are preparing, cooking, and eating healthful meals in their own homes.

   d. The available variety of healthful nourishment choices—protein foods, grains, vegetables, and fruits—is large and growing.

For more practice, turn back to the Before You Read section on page 69 and answer the questions.

Discussing the Reading

9   In small groups, talk about your answers to the following questions. Then tell the class the most interesting information and ideas.

1. What are your opinions of fast food and fast-food eating places? Give reasons for your answer.

2. What kinds of food do you usually buy from machines, stores, or markets? How do you prepare or cook it? When and where do you eat it? Give examples of your food customs and habits.

3. In general, do you think the global diet is changing? In the same ways or in different ways? In good or bad ways? What are the reasons for your opinions?

PART 4   # Writing

Before You Write

Exploring Ideas

1   **Describing Holiday Foods.**   Write in your journal about typical everyday meals that you eat. Write as much as possible in about five minutes. Don't worry about form or grammar.

2   Thanksgiving is an important American holiday. On this day, Americans give thanks for everything that they have. They eat a big meal with many special foods. Some of these foods are in the list below.

turkey   stuffing   sweet potatoes   pumpkin pie   cranberry sauce

Think of the food you eat on a holiday. Sometimes there is no English word for a special dish. Write the word in your first language and explain it.

Your holiday: *New Year*

Foods that you eat: *sticky rice , grilled chicken*

3   Write some sentences that compare the special food you eat on holidays with the food you eat every day.

Example: People usually prepare and eat a lot of food on Thanksgiving. The Thanksgiving meal is more delicious than our everyday meals.

_____

_____

_____

_____

_____

_____

Foods from Japan

Organizing Ideas

Ordering Information in a Paragraph

People often begin a paragraph with general ideas and then write more specific ones. The last sentence of a paragraph often describes a personal reaction, opinion, or feeling. For example, here are some notes about Thanksgiving:

1. Thanksgiving is a family celebration to remember the first harvest of American colonists.
2. People eat traditional foods from the first Thanksgiving feast.
3. Some typical Thanksgiving foods are turkey, stuffing, sweet potatoes, homemade bread, and pies.
4. People eat more than usual on Thanksgiving, but they feel full and happy.

4   Organize these sentences into the correct order. Number them from 1 for the first to 7 for the last.

_____7_____ 1. Everyone eats more than usual, and at the end of the day we are as stuffed (full) as the turkey.

_____4_____ 2. In my family, everyone brings a special dish for the Thanksgiving meal.

_____5_____ 3. My aunt bakes a turkey and fills it with stuffing, a mixture of bread and spices.

_____1_____ 4. Thanksgiving is a family celebration.

_____3_____ 5. They prepare many traditional foods such as turkey, sweet potatoes, and cranberry sauce.

_____2_____ 6. On this day Americans remember the first Thanksgiving feast of the early American colonists.

_____6_____ 7. My relatives also make bread, vegetables, salad, and at least four pies.

5   Make similar notes for your paragraph. Answer these questions in your notes. You may want to look back at Activities 2 and 3 on page 75.

1. What's the name of the holiday? What does it celebrate?
2. Why do people eat special dishes on this holiday?
3. What does your family eat on the holiday?
4. How do you feel about the holiday?

Writing Topic Sentences

The topic sentence:

- gives the main idea of the paragraph
- is always a complete sentence and has a subject and a verb
- is often the first sentence in a paragraph but is sometimes the second or even the last sentence

---

6 Which of these main ideas about Thanksgiving are complete sentences? Write a *C* in front of the complete sentences.

_____C_____ 1. The Thanksgiving meal is a special celebration.

_____ 2. Thanksgiving, an important celebration.

_____ 3. Families eat typical American dishes on Thanksgiving.

_____ 4. A Thanksgiving feast for a family celebration.

_____ 5. Thanksgiving is an important American holiday.

7 Look at the sentences about the Thanksgiving meal in Activity 4. Which sentence is the topic sentence? Underline it.

8 Look at the notes you wrote for your paragraph. First, decide if you want to add or change anything. Then write a topic sentence for your paragraph. Remember, it may be the first or second sentence in your paragraph. Exchange your notes and your topic sentence with a partner and answer these questions:

1. Is the topic sentence a complete sentence?
2. Does it give the main idea that was in your partner's notes?

Write

Developing Cohesion and Style

Giving Examples with such as

When you write, you can introduce examples with the phrase *such as*.

Example:
- On Thanksgiving Day we eat many traditional foods. The foods are turkey, sweet potatoes, and cranberries.
- On Thanksgiving Day we eat many traditional foods *such as* turkey, sweet potatoes, and cranberries.

9   Look at the following list of dishes from around the world. In small groups, discuss what the different dishes are. Then write the name of each dish under the correct heading as in the example.

Example:

A: Who knows what ravioli is?

B: It's a kind of Italian food.

C: Right. It's a kind of small, square pasta. It's filled with cheese or meat.

- ■ dim sum
- ■ tacos
- ■ samosas
- ■ ravioli

- ■ enchiladas
- ■ spring rolls
- ■ curry
- ■ cannoli

- ■ tamales
- ■ mulligatawny soup
- ■ minestrone soup
- ■ moo shu pork

Italian	Chinese	Mexican	Indian
ravioli	_____	_____	_____
_____	_____	_____	_____
_____	_____	_____	_____
_____	_____	_____	_____

10   Now write sentences with *such as*. The first sentence is done for you.

1. Italian restaurants serve many wonderful dishes such as ravioli, cannoli, and minestrone soup.   .

2. In Chinese restaurants you can try delicious dishes _____ _____ _____

3. _____ _____ _____

4. _____ _____ _____

Writing the First Draft

11 Write your paragraph. Include the name of the holiday in your title, such as in the title "A Thanksgiving Meal." Use the topic sentence and your notes. Try to use *such as* in your paragraph.

Edit and Revise

Editing Practice

12 Edit this paragraph twice. First, find a place to add *such as* before examples. The second time check to see if the count and noncount nouns are correct. Make any other changes you think are necessary.

Special Christmas Foods

Christmas is an important holiday for many people in the United States. It is the celebration of the birth of Christ. People in North America prepare many special Christmas food from all over the world. Many Christmas specialties fruitcake and eggnog come from Great Britain. North Americans make fruitcakes with fruits, nuts, and

liquors. Eggnog is a drink of eggs, milks, and sometimes rum. American also eat a lot of Christmas cookies. I love all the special Christmas food.

Editing Your Writing

13   **Editing Using a Checklist.**   Edit your paragraph using the following checklist.

Editing Checklist

1. Content
   a. Is the paragraph interesting?
   b. Is the information clear?
2. Organization
   a. Does the topic sentence give the main idea of the paragraph? Is it a complete sentence?
   b. Are all the sentences about the holiday?
   c. Are the sentences in logical order?
3. Cohesion and Style
   a. Can you connect any sentences with *and, so*, or *but*?
   b. Does *such as* introduce examples?
4. Grammar
   a. Are the present-tense verbs correct?
   b. Are the count and noncount nouns correct?
5. Form
   a. Is the paragraph form (indentation, capitalization, and punctuation) correct?
   b. Is the spelling of words with *-s* endings correct?

14   **Peer Editing.**   Show your paper to another student. Does he or she understand your paragraph? Does he or she think you need to make any other corrections?

Writing the Second Draft

15   Write the second draft of your paragraph using correct form. Then give it to your teacher for comments.

When your teacher returns your paragraph, look at her or his comments. If you don't understand something, ask about it. Then make a list of things you do well and the things you need to work on.

What I do well: **What I need to work on:**

1. _____   _____

    _____   _____

2. _____   _____

    _____   _____

3. _____   _____

    _____   _____

PART 5 **Grammar**

A. Count and Noncount Nouns

There are two basic types of nouns — count nouns and noncount nouns. Count nouns are things you can count, such as books and pens. Noncount nouns are things you can't count, such as paper and ink.

	Examples		Notes
	Singular	**Plural**	
Count Nouns	a **meal** an **egg** one **waiter** a **chair** one **restaurant**	three **meals** some **eggs** **waiters** some **chairs** **restaurants**	Count nouns have both singular and plural forms. Singular count nouns can have *a/an* before them; most plural count take an *-s/-es* ending.
Noncount Nouns	**butter** some **juice** **electricity** **salt** some **jewelry** **traffic** **freedom** **anger** some **luck**		Noncount nouns are always singular and have no plural form; they do not take *-s* or *-es* endings. Most noncount nouns refer to a whole that is made up of smaller or different parts. Some noncount nouns describe abstract things, such as ideas, feelings, and concepts.

B. *Some* and *Any*

Some and *any* refer to an unspecified number or amount. *Some* and *any* may appear before both count and noncount nouns.

	Examples	Notes
some	Please buy **some** napkins. There's **some** milk in that cup. Would you like **some** spaghetti?	*Some* expresses an indefinite amount. *Some* is used in affirmative statements and questions.
any	There aren't **any** plates on the table. I don't use **any** salt. Do you have **any** pots in your kitchen?	*Any* is used in negative statements and in affirmative and negative questions.

Note: Not any before noncount and plural count nouns means *no*. For example: *There aren't any hot dogs. = There are no hot dogs.*

1   Fill in each blank in the following sentences with *some* or *any*. In some cases, either answer may be correct.

1. Mary always eats ___some___ fruit for breakfast.
2. I'm going to the supermarket. Do we need ___some___ *or any* bread?
3. I need to buy ___some___ food; I don't have ___any___ fruit or vegetables.
4. I want ___some___ coffee, but there isn't ___any___ decaffeinated coffee left.
5. Are there ___any___ supermarkets near your apartment?
6. Taro doesn't have ___any___ experience as a cook.
7. I'd like ___some___ onions and ___some___ mushrooms on my pizza.
8. I don't want ___any___ ice cream, but I'd like to try ___some___ frozen yogurt.
9. There doesn't seem to be ___any___ waiters in the restaurant.
10. I'm full. I can't eat ___any___ more food.

C. *A lot of/many/much*

A lot of, many, and *much* are used to express a large quantity of something. *A lot of* may appear before both noncount and plural count nouns. *Many* appears only before plural count nouns. *Much* appears only before noncount nouns.

	Examples	**Notes**
a lot of	She doesn't eat **a lot of** hamburgers. Isn't there **a lot of** salt in this soup? Are there **a lot of** apples at home?	*A lot of* is used in affirmative and negative statements and questions.
many	**Many** fast-food restaurants serve hamburgers I don't like **many** kinds of vegetables. Do **many** people have a poor diet?	*Many* is used in affirmative and negative statements and questions.
much	They don't eat **much** red meat. We don't drink **much** tea or coffee. Does chicken have **much** cholesterol? Don't they eat **much** fish?	*Much* is used mainly in negative statements and affirmative and negative questions. *Much* usually isn't used in affirmative statements.

2   Write one question and one answer about each picture, using *a lot of, many,* or *much.*

1. Is there much ice cream in the bowl ___?
    Yes, there is a lot of ice cream in the bowl ___.

2. Are there many cookies on the plate ___?
    No, there aren't many ___.

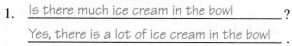

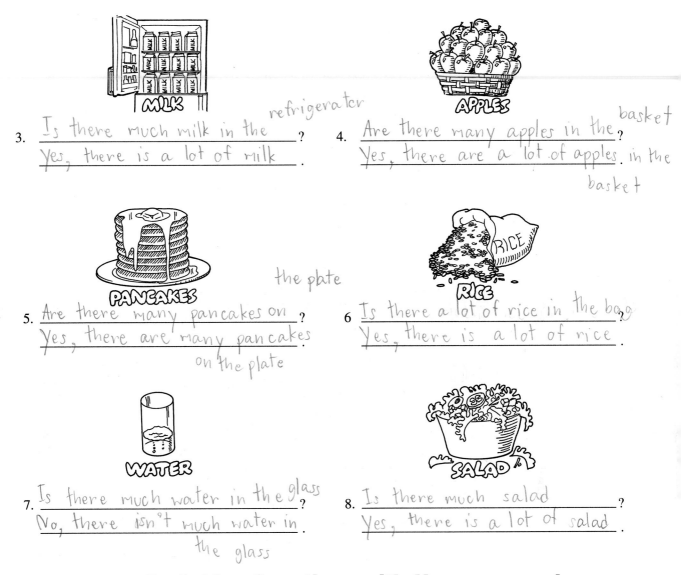

3. Is there much milk in the refrigerator ?
   Yes, there is a lot of milk .

4. Are there many apples in the basket ?
   Yes, there are a lot of apples in the basket .

5. Are there many pancakes on the plate ?
   Yes, there are many pancakes on the plate .

6. Is there a lot of rice in the bag ?
   Yes, there is a lot of rice .

7. Is there much water in the glass ?
   No, there isn't much water in the glass .

8. Is there much salad ?
   Yes, there is a lot of salad .

D. Asking Questions with *How many* and *How much*

How many is used in questions before plural count nouns. *How much* is used in questions before noncount nouns.

	Examples	**Answers**
how many	**How many** eggs do you want? **How many** cakes are you making?	Two. Only one.
how much	**How much** coffee does he drink? **How much** rice do we need?	Three cups. Ten pounds.

Note: If a unit of measurement is used with a noncount noun, *how many* should be used. For example: *How much coffee does he drink?* can also be expressed as *How many cups of coffee does he drink?*

3 Take turns asking and answering questions about the pictures on pages 82–83. Use *how many* or *how much* in your questions.

Example: A: How much ice cream is in the bowl?
  B: There's a lot of ice cream. How many cookies are on the plate?
  C: Two. (*or* There aren't many.)

E. Modal Auxiliaries: Requests, Offers, and Permission

The modals *may, can, could, will,* or *would* can be used with the simple form of a verb to make requests, offers, and to request permission. In questions, the modal appears before the subject.

Making Requests		
Examples	**Possible Answers**	**Notes**
Could you please **bring** a fork?	Of course.	In these cases, we are asking someone else to do something.
Would you **suggest** a dessert?	I'd be glad to.	*Could* and *would* are used in both informal and formal situations.
Will you **pass** the salt, please?	Certainly	
Can we **have** a menu, please?	Sure.	*Can* and *will* are informal.

Note: Please makes any request more polite.

Making Offers		
Examples	**Possible Answers**	**Notes**
May I **help** you?	Yes. Can I get a menu?	In these cases, we are offering to do something for someone. *May* is considered formal. *Can* is less formal.
Can I **get** you something to drink?	I'd like an iced tea, please.	

when you ask people to
do sth for you →use
Would
will

Polite
May
Would / Could
Can / Will

impolite

Requesting Permission		
Examples	**Possible Answers**	**Notes**
May we **join** you? **Could** I **borrow** some money? **Can** I **use** a credit card?	No, you may not. Yes, you can. No, you can't.	In these cases, we want something or want to do something and are asking for someone's help or permission. *May* is considered formal. *Could* is used in formal and informal requests. *Can* is the least formal.

Note: *May* is not used in questions in which the subject is *you*.

4   Imagine yourself in the following situations. Decide on appropriate requests, offers, or requests for permission for each situation.

A. You are having dinner at your good friend's house.

1. You want to help your friend bring the food to the table.
    Can I help you bring the food to the table?

2. You want a second helping of rice.

3. You want the last piece of bread.

4. You want your friend to give you the recipe.

5. You want to start clearing the table.

B. You are having tea with a classmate in a cafe. Your teacher walks in.

1. You want your teacher to join you. Would you like to join with us?

2. You want the waiter to bring another cup.

3. You want to pour the tea for your teacher.

4. You want your friend to pass you the sugar.

5. You want the waiter to bring the check.

Video Activities: Treat Yourself Well Campaign

Before You Watch.   Discuss these questions in small groups.

1.   What is the difference between healthy and unhealthy food?

2.   Do you think low-fat or nonfat food can be delicious?

3.   Do you like American fast food?

Watch.   Write answers to these questions.

1.   What kind of food do the Wood brothers like to eat?

2.   Describe some of the dishes that the tasters are eating.

Watch Again.   Complete the following statements.

1.   The Wood brothers don't eat light dishes because _____.
    a.   they're more expensive than fast food
    b.   they don't taste as good as "fat" food
    c.   they don't care if they get fat

2.   Healthy food contains _____.
    a.   butter
    b.   cream
    c.   vegetables
    d.   lots of salt

3.   The pizza does <u>not</u> contain _____.
    a.   nonfat cheese
    b.   vegetables
    c.   nonfat dressing
    d.   low-fat sausage

After You Watch.   Bring a menu to class from a restaurant you like. Work in small groups. Your teacher will divide the menus among the groups, and you should read them together. Decide which restaurant has the healthiest food. Tell the class about it. When all the groups have told about their restaurants, the class should vote for the best restaurant. Maybe you can go there together for lunch or dinner!

Chapter 4

In the Community

IN THIS CHAPTER

Listening
- Listening for main ideas
- Listening for specific information
- Identifying stressed words and reductions
- Taking notes on a conversation (specific information)

Speaking
- Describing your neighborhood
- Summarizing main ideas

Reading
- Previewing vocabulary
- Reading: How Can I Get to the Post Office?
- Understanding paragraph and whole reading topics

- Understanding the main idea
- Finding illustrations of word meanings
- Recognizing the relationship of detail to the point

Writing
- Developing ideas: organizing paragraphs in a letter
- Using prepositions of place, direction, & distance
- Writing an informal letter
- Editing for correct form in an informal letter

Grammar
- Future tenses
- Prepositions of place and time

PART 1

Listening to Conversations

vivid : clear

Before You Listen

1 **Prelistening Questions.**   Before you listen, talk about your community with a partner.

1.   In the community where you live now, where do you go to do the following:
    - to get some cash
    - to clean your dirty clothes
    - to develop some film
    - to pay a traffic ticket
    - to buy some medicine
2.   Can you walk to these places from your home? If not, how do you travel there?
3.   Look at the picture. What is happening?

2   **Vocabulary Preview.**   Complete the sentences with these expressions from the conversation. Then go back and write the meaning of the expressions in the chart.

Expressions	Definitions
Give (me) a ride	can you drive me
Run errands *a little job outside house* *take a short trip*	I need to do a little job [common]
Drop off (something/somebody)	leave off ... ... car
Dry cleaners	place that wash clothes
Do laundry	wash clothes
Convenient	feel comfortable , easy
Cash (a) check	to have money , get money
Have got to	have to , need to
Jaywalking	walk a middle on street

have got to more urgent than have to

1. I'm very busy this afternoon. I have to go to the bank, mail a package, and _____run_____ some other ___errands___.

2. Most teenagers don't know how to __do laundry__; their mother or father usually washes their clothes for them.

3. It's very _convenient_ to have a bus stop in front of my house.

4. My car doesn't work and I need to be at my job in 30 minutes. Can you _give me a ride_?

5. I'm sorry, I can't talk to you right now. My class starts in 5 minutes. I _have got to_ go.

6. I can't wash my beautiful new jacket in a washing machine. I need to take it to the _dry_ _cleaners_.

7. Before you can _cash a check_, you need to sign your name on the back. Then, you have to show your ID.

8. David _drops off_ his daughter at school every morning, _routine_ and picks her up every afternoon.

9. A police officer stopped me when I crossed in the middle of the street. I didn't know that _jay walking_ is illegal in the United States. Next time I'll cross at the corner.

Listen

3   **Listening for Main Ideas.**   Peter and Kenji both plan to go downtown.

1. Close your book as you listen to the conversation. Listen for the answers to these questions.
    1. What does Kenji ask Peter to do? _he has to_ Give him a ride, run some errands
    2. Where will Peter drop Kenji off? _Downtown_ At the corner King Blvlavard and second photo
    3. Kenji needs to run four errands. What are they? bank, dry cleaner, court, shop
    4. What does Peter need to do downtown? He need to go to court house
    5. Why does Kenji miss Japan? He got a ticket for jay walking because He can jay walking in Japan
2. Compare answers with a partner.

Stress

4   **Listening for Stressed Words.**   Listen to the conversation again.

1. Some of the stressed words are missing. During each pause, repeat the phrase or sentence. Then fill in the blanks with words from the list.

A	B	C	D
bank	cross	film	need
cheaper	do	give	photo
check	door	go	ride
cleaner's	downtown	going	rules
clothes	drive	got	street
convenient	drop	jaywalking	traffic
corner	drugstore	laundry	use
courthouse	errands	miss	

Kenji: Peter, are you going ____Downtown____ today?

Peter: Uh-huh. Why?

Kenji: Can you ____give____ me a ____ride____? I have to run some ____errands____.

Peter: Where do you need to ____go____?

Kenji: Uh, a lot of places. First, I've got to go to the ____bank____. Could you ____drop____ me off at the ____corner____ of King Boulevard and Second Avenue?

Peter: King and Second? Oh, sure. I know where that is. But why are you ____going____ to the bank? Why don't you ____use____ the ATM on campus?

Kenji: 'Cause I ____need____ to cash a ____check____ my dad sent me. And the ____cleaner's____ is next ____door____ to the bank. I have to pick up some ____clothes____ there anyway.

Peter: There's a ____laundry____ room right here on the first floor. You can ____do____ your laundry there much ____cheaper____.

Kenji: I'm not picking up laundry. It's dry cleaning. By the way, is there a ____photo____ shop near there? I need to drop off some ____film____ to develop.

Peter: A photo shop? Oh, yeah. There's probably one in the ____drug store____, across the ____street____ from the bank.

Kenji: Oh, that's ____convenient____. So what are *you* going to do downtown?

Peter: I'm going to the ____courthouse____. I've got to pay a _____traffic_____ ticket.

Kenji: No kidding! I'm going there, too. I also _____got_____ a ticket.

Peter: But, Kenji, you don't _____drive_____!

Kenji: I know. I got a ticket for _____jaywalking_____!

Peter: Really?!

Kenji: Yeah. *Man*, sometimes I _____miss_____ living in Japan. I could _____cross_____ the street and not worry about stupid _____rules_____ like jaywalking!

2. Now read the conversation with a partner. Practice stressing words correctly.

Reductions

5 **Comparing Long and Reduced Forms.** Listen to the following sentences from the conversation. They contain reduced forms. Repeat them after the speaker.

did and do
sound same way

Reduced form*	**Long form**
1. <u>Kinya gimme</u> a ride?	Can you give me a ride?
2. Where <u>d'ya</u> need ta go?	Where do you need to go?
3. I <u>hafta</u> run some errands.	I have to run some errands
4. I've <u>gotta</u> (godda) pay a traffic ticket.	I have got to pay a traffic ticket.
5. <u>Couldja</u> drop me off?	Could you drop me off?
6. A <u>lotta</u> places.	A lot of places.
7. What <u>arya gonna</u> do downtown?	What are you going to do downtown?

_____
* *Note:* The underlined forms are not acceptable spellings in written English.

6 **Listening for Reductions.** Listen to the following conversation. You'll hear the reduced forms of some words.

1. Repeat each sentence during the pause. Then write the long forms in the blanks.

    A: ___Do___ ___you___ know where the Central Library is?
    B: Sure. You ___have___ ___to___ take Bus #9.
    A: ___Could___ ___you___ walk with me to the bus stop?
    B: I'm sorry. I don't have time _____ I've ___got___ ___to___ do a ___lot___ ___of___ things.
    A: Oh. Then _____ _____ just _____ _____ directions to the bus stop?
    B: ___Are___ ___you___ kidding? It's right there across the street.

2. With a partner, repeat the sentences for pronunciation practice.

7 **Reductions Game.** Pretend that you are at home and a hurricane is about to strike your area. There are police cars with loudspeakers in the streets telling people that they have five minutes to evacuate (leave) their homes.

Reductions

because	'cause	has to	hasta
going to	gonna	have to	havta
got to	gotta	want to	wanna

---

1. Sit in a circle. The first student says what he or she has to do. Use the reduced forms above and the words in the Word Bank.
2. The next student repeats the first student's sentence. Then, he or she gives his or her own sentence.
3. The third student repeats the first two sentences and adds his or her own.
4. The student who can remember all of the sentences is the winner.

Example:

Student 1: I hafta rescue my cat.

Student 2: She hasta rescue her cat. And I hafta find my medicine.

Student 3: She hasta rescue her cat. He hasta find his medicine. And I hafta call my brother.

Word Bank

turn off	medicine	family photos	the gas
take	TV	jewelry	my cat / dog
find	brother / sister	money	clothes
call	rescue	save	look for

After You Listen

8 **Vocabulary Review.**   Discuss the following questions with a partner. Use the underlined vocabulary in your answers.

1. Last week, did you <u>drop</u> anything <u>off</u> before school or after school?
2. How do you get to school? Do you drive, take a bus, or does someone <u>drop you off</u>?
3. Who <u>does the laundry</u> in your family? When you travel, do you do your own laundry or do you take it to a cleaner?
4. Name some <u>errands</u> that you have to run this week. What type of transportation will you use to run errands?
5. Is it a good idea to <u>give</u> a stranger <u>a ride</u>? Why?
6. Is the place where you live now <u>convenient</u>? For example, is there good transportation nearby? Can you walk to a market easily?
7. What are some things you <u>have got to</u> do before you go to bed tonight?
8. Explain the difference between "<u>cashing a check</u>" and "depositing a check."

PART 2	# Recalling Main Ideas

Before You Listen

Village

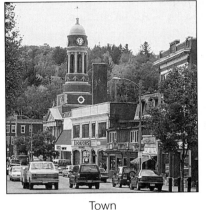

Town

City

1 **Prelistening Questions.** You will hear a conversation about large and small communities. Before you listen, discuss these questions with a partner.

1. Which photo looks most like your community?

2. Size is one difference between a village, a town, and a city. What other differences can you think of? What are the good things and bad things about living in each type of community?

Cross-Cultural Note

Many large cities in North America have a busy downtown in the center and a quiet suburb outside the city. Many people prefer to work downtown, but to live in the suburbs. These people commute (travel) from home to work and back.

2 **Vocabulary Preview.** You will hear the underlined words below in the speech. Before you listen, write the letter of the correct definition beside each sentence.

	Sentences	Definitions
_D_ 1.	Do you know why the color of the sky is brown? It's the <u>smog</u> from all the cars and factories.	a. good thing, positive point
_E_ 2.	I don't like to take the bus at 5:00 in the afternoon. It's always <u>crowded</u> with so many people coming home from work.	b. old-fashioned, traditional
_B_ 3.	Linda's grandmother is very <u>conservative</u> in her thinking; she doesn't like Linda to wear short dresses or to go out with boys before she is 18 years old.	c. bad thing, negative point
_A_ 4.	Winter in Canada is very cold, but there is also an <u>advantage</u>: there are great places to ski.	d. dirty air
_C_ 5.	Patrick wants to work in the United States His big <u>disadvantage</u> is that he doesn't speak English.	e. full (of people)

Listen

3   **Listening for Main Ideas.**   Peter and Kenji just came back from downtown. They are talking to Ming about their trip.

1. As you listen, decide what the main idea of the conversation is. Then choose the best title for this conversation.
   1. Kenji and Peter's Big City Adventure
   2. Small Towns are Better than Big Cities
   3. Why Small Towns are Better for Girls
   4. No Place is Perfect

2. Discuss your choice with your classmates. Tell why you think the other titles don't show the main idea.

4   **Taking Notes on Specific Information.**   Listen again. As you listen, write the key words about big cities and small towns.

Big Cities		Small Towns	
Good things advantages	**Bad things** disadvantages	**Good things**	**Bad things**
1. exciting	1. traffic	1. quiet, peace	1. conservative
2. make more money	2. noise	2. friendly	2. boring
3. can find anything	3. smog	3. thing cheaper	
4. good shopping	4. crowded		
	5. dangerous		
	6. long line		

After You Listen

5   **Summarizing Main Ideas.**   Compare your notes with a partner. From the key words, form complete sentences about what Peter, Kenji, and Ming said.

Example:

They talked about three advantages of big cities. First, cities are exciting. Also, there is good shopping there, and . . .

6   **Vocabulary Review.**   Discuss your answers to the following questions with a partner. Use the underlined vocabulary in your answers.

1. Is there a lot of <u>smog</u> in the community where you live now? What is your government doing to reduce smog?

2. Name some times and places that are <u>crowded</u> in the city. How do you feel in a crowded place?

3. Who is the most <u>conservative</u> in your family? What are they conservative about: clothes? music? education? politics?

4. Name some <u>advantages</u> and <u>disadvantages</u> of driving to work and taking the subway to work.

PART 3	# Reading

Before You Read

1 Discuss the picture in small groups.

1. Who are the two young travelers? What are they doing? What is their problem?

2. What are the other people in the picture doing?

3. Does this situation ever happen to you? Do you use a map or ask for directions — or both? Do people sometimes ask you for directions? What do you answer?

2 Think about the answers to these questions. The reading selection answers them.

1. How do people in different places give directions?

2. Sometimes you might ask, "How can I get to the post office?" What if a person doesn't know the answer? What might he or she do?

3. How can body language help you in getting around the community?

3 **Vocabulary Preview.**   Learn the meanings of these vocabulary items from the reading.

Nouns	Verbs	Adjectives	Phrases
advantages	find out	confused	ask for directions
tourists	measure	flat	the American Midwest
travelers	motion	impolite	a sense of direction
the countryside	gesture		get lost
the flatlands	lead	**Adverbs**	have a good time
gestures	guess	straight	body language
motions		seldom	facial expressions
movements		rarely	

Read

4   Read the following material quickly. Then read the explanations and do the exercises after the reading.

How Can I Get to the Post Office?

A | I have a special rule for travel: Never carry a map. I prefer to ask for directions. Sometimes I get lost, but I usually have a good time. And there are some other advantages: I can practice a new language, meet new people, learn new customs, and the like. I can find out about different "styles" of directions every time I ask, "How can I get to the post office?" Here are some illustrations of those differences.

B | Tourists are often confused in Japan. That's because most streets there don't have names; outside big cities, people most often use landmarks in their directions. For example, the Japanese might tell travelers something like this: "Go straight down to the corner. Turn left at the big hotel with the sushi bar and go past the fruit market. The post office is across from the bus stop—next to the fast-food fried chicken place."

C | In the United States, people might give directions in different ways according to their region or community. As an example, in the countryside of the American Midwest, there are not usually many landmarks. There are no mountains, so the land is very flat; in many places there are no towns or buildings for miles. Instead of landmarks, residents of the flatlands will tell you directions and distances. In the states of Kansas or Iowa, for instance, people will say, "Go straight north for two miles. Turn right, and then go another mile in a northeast direction."

D | On the other hand, people in Los Angeles, California, have no idea of directions or distance on the map. Residents of this Pacific coast area are almost always in their cars, so they measure distance in time. "How far away is the post office?" you ask. "Oh," they might answer, "I guess it's about five minutes from here." You say, "Yes, but how many miles away is it—or how many kilometers or blocks?" They rarely know—or can seldom say.

E | Sometimes, people in the European country of Greece do not even try to give directions; that's because tourists seldom understand the Greek language. Instead, a Greek may motion or gesture or say, "Follow me." Then that person will lead you through the streets of a city to the post office.

F | What if a person doesn't know the answer to your question about the location of a place? A New Yorker might say, "Sorry, I have no idea" and walk away quickly. But in Yucatan, Mexico, not many residents answer, "I don't know." People in Yucatan may believe that a quick "I don't know" is impolite; they might stay and talk to you—and usually they'll try to give an answer, sometimes a wrong one. A tourist without a good sense of direction can get very, very lost in this southern region!

G | One thing will help you everywhere—in Japan, the United States, Greece, Mexico, or any other place. You might not understand a person's words, but you can probably understand the body language—the facial expressions, gestures, motions, movements, etc. He or she will usually turn and then point. Go in that direction and you'll find the post office—maybe!

After You Read

5   **Recognizing Paragraph and Whole Reading Topics.**   Reading material with simple, basic structure might begin with an introductory paragraph and end with a short conclusion. The several paragraphs between the first and the last might give the same *kind* of information — for instance, illustrations of the main point of the whole reading. (An illustration serves as an example or proof of an idea or statement.) Each of the paragraphs will give *different* illustrations of the message.

Of course, the subject of a *whole* reading should be more general than the specific topics of the individual paragraphs. It should be clearly related to the narrower topics.

In the reading "How Can I Get to the Post Office?" there is a capital letter next to each of the seven paragraphs. Write the specific topic of each paragraph next to its letter. A and B are done as examples.

A.   The Introduction to the Reading
B.   Directions in Japan
C.   Directions in the U.S.
D.   People in L.A. and California measure distance in time
E.   Directions in Europe and Greece.
F.   When people don't know
G.   Conclusion

Which phrase best tells the subject of the whole reading "How Can I Get to the Post Office?" Circle its letter. Give the reasons for your answer.

a.   the importance of body language for tourists and travelers

b.   how people give street directions in various places in the world

c.   different kinds of maps for travel and weather

6   **Understanding the Main Idea.**   How can readers get and tell the point of reading material in a simple way? One basic method is to ask one question about the information in each paragraph — and then a general question about the point of the whole reading. A one- or two-sentence answer to each question gives the main idea.

For each of paragraph topics from the reading "How Can I Get to the Post Office?", complete a different question about the information. (Write the necessary words on the lines.) Also, finish the question about the main idea of the whole reading. Two items are done as examples.

A.   What is the point of _____ the introduction to the reading material?
B.   How do people often give _____ directions in Japan?
C.   How do people often give _____ directions in the region of the American Midwest?

D. _How do people give_ directions in the city of Los Angeles, California?

E. _How do people give_ directions in European country of Greece?

F. _How do people often give_ directions in some areas of Mexico like Yucatan?

G. _What is_ the conclusion to the reading material?

In what ways _do people give_ directions in various cultures around the world?

7 In order, here are some false sentences about the information in paragraphs A–G of the reading. The possible statement of the point of the *whole* reading is not right, either. Change the eight wrong sentences to true statements of the point. Then use them as correct answers to the eight questions in Exercise 6.

1. If you ~~don't~~ (do) carry a map on your travels, you won't have to ask for directions.
2. In Japan, people ~~most often~~ don't use street names in their directions.
3. In the ~~mountainous~~ (flat) land of the American Midwest, people will tell you directions with ~~landmarks~~. distance
4. In Los Angeles, California, the most common way to give directions is in ~~kilometers~~. time
5. Even if visitors to Greece don't understand the language, the people will usually give directions with ~~a lot of words in long sentences~~. motion or gesture or say "follow me"
6. In some parts of ~~Mexico~~ New York, people may be impolite, so they always say "I don't know" in answer to questions about directions.
7. All over the world, words in sentences are ~~easier~~ more difficult to understand than body language.
8. In various cultures around the world, people give directions to travelers and tourists in exactly the ~~same way~~. many different ways.

8 **Finding Illustrations of Word Meanings.** Sometimes illustrations of the meaning of vocabulary items are in another sentence or sentence part. The words *for example, for instance, as an illustration, like,* and *such as* can be clues to meaning through illustrations.

Example: People in Los Angeles talk about <u>distance in time</u>. They'll say such things as "It's about five minutes from here." (An illustration of distance in time is the phrase "about five minutes from here.")

On the lines, write illustrations of the words from the reading material. (The letters in parentheses are the letters of the paragraphs.) Some items are partly done as examples.

1. landmarks: (B) _the corner_ , _the big hotel with the sushi bar_ , _____ , _____ , _____ , and so on.

2. directions: (C) _straight north_ , _two miles_ , _turn right and then go another mile_, _in a north east_ , _____ , and so on.

3.   distances: (∅) ___mile___ , ___minutes___ ,
___kilometers___ , ___blocks___ , and the like.

4.   body language: (G) ___facial expressions___ ,
___gestures___ ___motions___ , ___movements___ , and so on.

For more practice, find other illustrations of vocabulary items, such as names of countries, names of nationalities, names of American states, names of regions, kinds of places, phrases in street directions, and the like.

9   **Recognizing the Relationship of Detail to the Point.**   Punctuation marks might show the relationship between the point of reading material and some of the supporting detail. For instance, a colon (:) can introduce a list of things — usually illustrations or examples of an idea.

Commas (,) can separate the different items of the list or series.

Example: In Japan, people typically use *landmarks* in their directions: they talk about hotels, markets, bus stops, and so on. (What are some examples of landmarks for directions? *Hotels, markets,* and *bus stops.*)

A semicolon (;) can separate two closely related sentence parts. The second sentence part can explain or add useful information to the point of the first.

Example: In the American Midwest, there are no mountains and few hills; the land is very flat. (The word *flat* can mean "without mountains or hills.")

Quotation marks separate direct quotes (people's exact words) from the rest of the sentence.

Example: A Greek will say, "Follow me." (What does a Greek often say instead of giving directions? "Follow me.")

Here are some questions about the supporting details of the reading. Look at the punctuation and the related sentence parts. Then find the answers to these questions in the material. With words from the paragraphs and your own words, write the answers on the lines.

1.   The writer of the reading material has a special rule for travel. What is it?

_____

2.   What are some advantages of travel without maps?
___Practice a new language, meet new people and lern new customs.___

3.   Why are foreign tourists often confused in Japan?

_____

_____

4. What are some illustrations of Japanese directions?

   _Go_____

   _____

5. What directions might residents of the American Midwest give people? (Tell some examples.)

   _____

   _____

6. Why don't people in Los Angeles give directions in miles, kilometers, or blocks?

   _They don't have idea of directions or distance in the map.___

7. Why do Greeks seldom give foreigners directions in words and sentences?

   _____

   _____

8. If a resident of New York City doesn't know the location of a place, how might he or she answer a question about directions?

   _"Sorry I have no idea" and walk away quickly.___

   _____

9. Why won't a polite resident of Yucatan answer a lost tourist, "I don't know"?

   _____

   _____

10. How does a person give directions with body language?

   _Facial expressions, gestures, motions, movements.___

For more practice, turn back to the Before You Read section on page 95 and answer the questions in your own words.

Discussing the Reading

10 In small groups, talk about your answers to the following questions. Then tell the class the most interesting information and ideas.

1. Do you ever get lost — in your own town, city, region, or in new places? If so, do you ask for directions? Why or why not? If so, in what way?

2. How do most people give directions in your city or in the countryside? Do you give directions the same way? Why or why not?

3. In your opinion, why do people in different places give directions in different ways?

4. Do you have a good sense of direction? Can you find new places quickly and easily? Explain your answer with examples.

PART 4	# Writing

Before You Write

Exploring Ideas

1 Write for five minutes about your city or town. What's fun to do or see? What do you like or not like about it?

Example:

In my city, there are many theaters . . .

2 **Building Vocabulary.** Complete this chart with places your friend might like to visit or things she or he might like to do. Write as many places and things as you can.

Places to visit

1. _____   4. _____
2. _____   5. _____
3. _____   6. _____

Things to do

Inside   *Outside*

1. _____   1 _____
2. _____   2. _____
3. _____   3. _____

3 Many activities use the verb *go*. Some of them are, *go sightseeing, go swimming, go fishing, go camping, go on a picnic, go to the movies.* Work with a partner. Try to think of five more activities with *go*. Then share your list with the class.

4 In your letter, you will have to give your friend directions to your home. Work in groups to draw a map that shows the route to each student's home. Think about these questions.

- ■ Will your friend have to take a highway?
- ■ If so, how will she or he get from the highway to your home?
- ■ Are there any important landmarks (such as a lake, tall building, park, etc.) to help her or him?

Organizing Ideas

Organizing Paragraphs in a Letter

Your letter will have three paragraphs. Each paragraph has a different purpose.

■ The first paragraph will say hello, discuss the visit, and describe some of the activities you and your friend might do.

■ The second paragraph will give directions to your home.

■ The last paragraph will have only one or two sentences. The purpose of this paragraph is to say good-bye and end the letter.

---

5 Look at the following sentences. Decide if they belong in paragraph 1, 2, or 3. Write 1, 2, or 3 on the line before each sentence.

___1___ a. We can also go to a baseball game.

___2___ b. There's a gas station on the corner.

___1___ c. There's a concert at the City Auditorium.

___2___ d. Make a left turn on Maple Avenue.

___3___ e. Please write and tell me what time you will arrive.

___2___ f. It won't be hard to find my house.

___1___ g. It won't be easy to get theater tickets.

___2___ h. I'm glad to hear that you are doing well.

___3___ i. See you in two weeks.

1   2   3
h   f   e
a   d   i
c   b.
g

Write

Developing Cohesion and Style

Using Prepositions

Prepositions often show:

1. **Place**

> **Examples:** The shoe store is *in* the mall.
> The concert is *at* the music hall.
> The school is *behind* the post office.
>
> There's a store *on* { the right.
> the left.
> the corner.
> Main Street.

Using Prepositions *(continued)*

2. **Direction**

   Examples: Take Highway 6 *to* Exit 14.
   Turn right *onto* Apple Avenue.
   Drive *down* Main Street.

3. **Distance**

   Example: Go straight *for* two blocks.

6   Underline the prepositions of place, direction, and distance in the following paragraph. Then exchange papers with another student and compare them.

Take Route 44 south to Exit 12. Turn right at the first light. You will be on Maple Avenue. Go straight down Maple Avenue for two miles. At the corner of Bryant and Maple you will see an elementary school. Turn right at the first street after the school. The name of the street is Roosevelt Drive. Go straight for five blocks. Then make a left turn onto Broadmoor. My apartment building isn't difficult to find. It's on the left, Number 122. You can park your car behind the building.

7   Complete the paragraph with the prepositions below. There may be more than one possible answer.

at   on   in   to   for   off

I live ____in____ the old part of the city. Take the number 5 bus. Get off ___at_, on___ Franklin Street. You will see a large church down the street. Walk ___to___ the church and turn right. Walk two blocks and turn left at _____—_____ Smith's Drugstore. You will be ___on___ Ames Avenue. Go straight ___on___ Ames for two blocks. Then turn left ___at___ the corner of Ames and Findlay. My house is the third one ___on___ the left.

Writing the First Draft

HW.

8   Write the letter to your friend. In the first paragraph, describe what you are going to do during her or his visit. In the second paragraph, give directions to your home. In the third paragraph, say good-bye and tell your friend how excited you are about the visit.

Edit and Revise

Editing Practice

Date   July 12, 20XX

Dear Bill,   Salutation

I am excited about your visit. There's a lot to do here, and I'm sure we'll have a great time. On Saturday afternoon we can go to a basketball game. I think I can get tickets. In the evening we're going to go to Randy's house for dinner. After dinner we might go to a rock concert. I'm going to try to get tickets. If you want, on Sunday we can play tennis in the morning and visit the planetarium in the afternoon.   } Body

It's easy to find my house. Just take the Connecticut Turnpike east to Exit 5. Turn left at the first light. Then you will be on Bradford Boulevard. Go straight on Bradford for three miles. Then turn left on Apple. You will see a large supermarket on your left. Go to the second light. Make a right turn on Woodgate Road. My building is on the right, three houses from the corner. It's number 417.

See you in two weeks.

Closing { Sincerely,
Steve

Using Correct Form in an Informal Letter

Date   The date usually appears in the upper right-hand corner. The order of the date is month, day, year. Capitalize the name of the month and put a comma after the day and before the year. Do not use a comma in the year.

Example: April 4, 20XX

Salutation   Most letters begin with *Dear*. Use the name that you usually call the person. In an informal letter a comma goes after the name.

Examples: Dear Professor Hudson,   Dear Mr. and Mrs. White,
                  Dear Dr. Fitzgerald,   Dear Melinda,

Body   Indent each paragraph. In letters, paragraphs may have only one or two sentences. Although it is important to write each paragraph on a different topic, the paragraphs in a letter do not always begin with a topic sentence.

Closing   The closing of a letter begins either at the left or in the center of the page. There are many different closings. The closing that you choose depends on your relationship with the person you are writing to.

Examples: Regards,
                  Best wishes,   }   for informal letters
                  Fondly,
                  Love,   }   for letters to close friends or relatives

9 Edit this letter using the editing checklist on page 22, Chapter 1. Then rewrite the letter using correct letter form.

June 15, 20XX

Dear Mary, I'm very glad that you visit me next week. We will ~~do~~ have a good time. It's easy to find my house. Make left turn at the corner of Broadway and Fifth Street. Drive down Fifth two blocks. Make a right turn on Henry Street. There are a park on the corner. My house is on the left side. It are number 150. the weather is warm so we might going hiking and swimming. Please to bring your photo album. I want see the pictures of your family.

Addressing An Envelope

Return Address Write your address in the top left-hand corner of the envelope.

Address Write the address clearly. You may want to print it. Make sure the address is complete. If there is an apartment number, be sure to include it. It is also important to use the zip code or the postal code.

Carol Martin
128 Lake Drive, Apt. 8
Muskegon, Michigan 49441
U.S.A.   } Return Address
                  Zip Code

                                                                    Stamp

                      Mr. and Mrs. Daniel Kaufman
                      432 St. George Street
          Address {   Toronto, Ontario
                      CANADA M562V8

                              Postal Code

10   Address an envelope for the letter on page 105. Write your name and address as the return address. Then correct this address and write it on the envelope below.

Mary pirewali, 256 rose avenue, san jose 519478 california united states.

```
                                                        ┌──────┐
                                                        │ Stamp │
                                                        └──────┘
```

Editing Your Writing

11   **Editing Using a Checklist.**   Edit your letter using the following checklist.

Editing Checklist

1. Content
    a.   Are the activities interesting?
    b.   Are the directions clear?
2. Organization
    Is each paragraph about a different topic?
3. Cohesion and Style
    Are the prepositions correct?
4. Grammar
    Are the verb forms correct?
5. Form
    a.   Are the date and salutation correct?
    b.   Do the paragraphs begin with an indentation?
    c.   Is the closing in the right place?

12   **Peer Editing.**   Exchange letters with another student. Discuss the letters. Are there any other changes you should make?

Writing the Second Draft

13   Write the second draft of your letter using correct form. Then give the letter to your teacher for comments. When your teacher returns your letter, ask him or her about any comments you don't understand. Is there any improvement in your writing?

PART 5

Grammar

A. The Future with *be going to*

The structure *be* + *going to* + the simple form of a verb is used to express predictions as well as plans and intentions. It is common in conversation and often sounds like *gonna* in quick, informal speech. Do not use *gonna* in writing.

	Statements	
Purpose	**Examples**	
	Affirmative	**Negative**
Predictions	The sky looks grey. **It's going to rain**. The policeman **is going to give** you a ticket if you park there.	Tomoko **isn't going to arrive** on time for the movie. The cafe **isn't going to be** crowded this early.
Plans and intentions	We**'re going to eat** at a new restaurant tonight. I**'m going to walk** to school more often.	They **aren't going to go** to the post office today. He **isn't going to run** for mayor again.

	Yes/No Questions		
	Examples	**Possible Answers**	
		Affirmative	**Negative**
Affirmative	**Is** the doctor **going to be** in today? **Are** we **going to meet** downtown?	Yes, she is. Yes, we are.	No, she isn't. No, we aren't
Negative	**Isn't** Raymond **going to come** to the park? **Isn't** it **going to rain** on Saturday?	Yes, he is. Yes, it is.	No, he isn't. No, it isn't.

	Information Questions	
	Examples	**Possible Answers**
Affirmative	Where **is** she **going to go**? When **are** we **going to meet**?	The supermarket. At five o'clock.
Negative	Why **aren't** you **going to come**? Who **isn't going to be** there?	I have to work. Ellen.

1 The following pictures show people thinking about a change they have decided to make or an action they have decided to take. Write a sentence with *be going to* to express the intention of the person or people in each picture.

1.

The man is going to join a gym.

2.

She is going to ride a bicycle.

3.

He is going to recycle.

4.

He is going to have a hair cut.

5.

They are going to travel around the world.

6.

She is going to visit her sister.

B. The Future with *will*

Like *be going to*, *will* expresses intentions. However, *be going to* implies that some planning has gone into an intention, while *will* often implies a spontaneous, unplanned intention. Also, unlike *be going to*, *will* is used to express offers, promises, and requests. Only the simple form of the main verb is used with *will*.

Statements		
Purpose	**Examples**	
	Affirmative	**Negative**
Intentions	He**'ll buy** a computer this semester.	She **won't shop** in that store anymore.
Offers and promises	I**'ll come** to the park with you.	I **won't be** late.
Predictions	It **will** be sunny today.	It **won't** rain.
Requests	**Will** you **drive** me to the store?	**Won't** you **come** with me?

Yes/No Questions			
	Examples	**Possible Answers**	
		Affirmative	**Negative**
Affirmative	**Will** you **make** an appointment with the doctor?	Yes, I will. Yes, we are.	No, I won't. No, we aren't
Negative	**Won't** they **meet** us at the restaurant?	Yes, they will.	No, they won't.

Information Questions		
	Examples	**Possible Answers**
Affirmative	What **will** you **do** on Saturday?	I'll go shopping.
Negative	Why **won't** you **come** with us?	I don't feel well.

2 Circle the correct answer in each set of parentheses. In some cases, both answers may be correct.

Chiara: Hi, Angela.

Angela: Chiara!

Chiara: Those shopping bags must be heavy. I ('ll / 'm going to) carry a few for you.
                                                    1

Angela: Thanks. What are you doing in town?

Chiara: I ('ll / 'm going to) see if there are any good movies playing at the theater.
                        2

Angela: I'm free tonight. I ('ll / 'm going to) go with you if you'd like.
3

Chiara: That would be great.

Angela: I just have to get these groceries home. (Will you / Are you going to) meet
4

me at the movie theatre?

Chiara: Sure. But I don't see your car. How (will you / are you going to) get home?
5

Angela: I ('ll / 'm going to) take the bus.
6

Chiara: Don't be silly. I ('ll / 'm going to) drive you. My car is right here.
7

Angela: That would be great. Oh no, this bag is ripping. The groceries (will / are
8

going to) fall out. I ('ll / am going to) be right back.
9

Chiara: Where are you going?

Angela: I ('ll / 'm going to) get another bag.
10

Chiara: I ('ll / 'm going to) wait for you here.
11

Angela: I ('ll / 'm going to) be back in a minute!
12

3   In a group, brainstorm a list of ways in which you can help your community. Then, choose a way that you personally want to help your community. Make a statement of your intention, then outline the steps you will take to follow through on your intention.

Example: I'm going to help at the local soup kitchen.

First, I'll find the number of the soup kitchen in the phone book or from the community center. Then I'll call up the kitchen and find out how to volunteer. I think I'll either sign up to cook food or to serve it. That'll depend on what they need more.

C. The Future Using the Present Continuous and the Simple Present

In specific situations, the present continuous and the simple present can be used to express future time.

The Future Using the Present Continuous	
Examples	**Notes**
We **are moving** to Main Street next week. The town council **isn't meeting** this week.	The present continuous can be used to express future time when the idea of the sentence concerns a planned event or a definite intention.
Where **are** we **meeting** tonight? **Aren't** you **going** downtown this weekend?	Unlike *going to*, the future continuous is used when plans have not only been decided on, but have actually been arranged. Normally a time expression or the context makes it clear that the action or situation is in the future.

The Future Using the Simple Present	
Examples	**Notes**
The movie **begins** at 8:00. I **leave** town on Friday. His train **arrives** at 3:00. The museum **opens** at 9:00 tomorrow.	The simple present can be used to express future time in sentences that concern events that are on a definite schedule. Normally a time expression or the context makes it clear that the action or situation is in the future.

4   Fill in the blanks with either the simple present or the present continuous form of the verbs in parentheses.

1. The bus (arrive) _____arrives_____ at 9:00.
2. She can't come to the park with us this afternoon. She (work) _is working_.
3. (go)_Are_ you _going_ to the concert tonight?
4. She (leave) _is leaving_ in a few minutes. Do you want to go with her?
5. The train (leave) _leaves_ London at 3:00 and (arrive) _arrives_ in Cambridge at 4:00.
6. The museum (open) _opens_ at 9:00.
7. What time (meet)_are_ you _meeting_ your mother tomorrow?
8. What (do)_are_ you _doing_ this weekend?
9. I (take) _am taking_ a train to Avignon.
10. What time (begin) _does_ the film _begin_?
11. Excuse me. What time (arrive) _does_ this train _arrive_ in Barcelona?
12. I (go) _am_ not _going_ out this evening.

I'm on the computer.   I study 4 times during a week

112   **Interactions 1   Integrated Skills**

from 9.00 to 5.00
I study 4 times a week

D. Prepositions of Place and Time

Prepositions of Place

	Examples	Notes
in	Eduardo is **in** the library. Palermo is a city **in** Italy.	Use *in* before buildings, towns, cities, regions, provinces, countries and continents.
on	I live **on** a beautiful street. The boat is sailing **on** the river.	Use *on* before streets and bodies of water.
at	Jen lives **at** 17 Bow Street. I will meet you **at** the corner of Main Street and Elm Street.	Use *at* with street addresses and many specific locations.
between	The video store is **between** the bank and the post office. The house is **between** two big trees.	*Between* describes a location between two points.
near	I hope there is a cash machine **near** the movie theatre. The professor's office is **near** the chemistry laboratory.	*Near* describes something close in distance.
far from	Your house is too **far from** school to walk. The hospital is **far from** town.	*Far from* describes something far in the distance.
next to	Her house is **next to** yours. The restaurant is **next to** the movie theatre.	*Next to* describes something beside something else.
across from	The post office is **across from** the police station. Their house is **across from** a bookstore.	*Across from* describes something opposite something else.
under	The boats pass **under** the bridge. The ball is rolling **under** the car.	*Under* describes something that is below something else.
over *above*	The airplane is flying **over** the ocean. Her office is **over** a café.	*Over* describes something that is above something else.

Prepositions of Time

	Examples	Notes
in	The new post office will open **in** January. Paris is beautiful **in** the springtime.	Use *in* before years, seasons, months, and parts of the day.
on	Some stores are closed **on** Sunday. We'll have a St. Patrick's Day parade **on** March 17th.	Use *on* before days of the week and dates.
at	The laundromat opens **at** 9:00 A.M. I love to walk around the city **at** night.	Use *at* before a specific time of day and with the nouns *noon, night,* and *midnight.*
from . . . to	The library is open **from** 9:30 A.M. **to** 5:00 P.M. The parade will last **from** late morning **to** early afternoon.	Use *from . . . to* with beginning and ending times.
during	The supermarket is open late **during** the week. My town is usually covered in snow **during** the winter.	Use *during* with periods of time.
until	The coffee shop is open **until** 9:00 P.M. I am going to live here **until** I graduate.	Use *until* with ending times.
before	I want to go to the mountains **before** summer is over. Run to the store **before** it closes!	Use *before* to express an earlier event or time.
after	Let's get a bite **after** the movie. I like to meet my friends in town **after** class.	Use *after* to express a later event or time.

5 Use the map and prepositions of place to ask and answer the questions. Answer in as many ways as you can, using as many prepositions of place as possible.

Example: Where is the video store? *The video store is above the health food store. It is next to the bank and across from the florist.*

1. Where is the movie theatre?
2. Where is the dentist's office?
3. Where is the ballet school?
4. Where is the pet shop?
5. Where is the bank?
6. Where is the subway?

7. Where is the bookstore?
8. Where is the café?
9. Where is the health food store?
10. Where is the movie theatre?
11. Where is the florist?
12. Where is the gym?

6 Complete the sentences with prepositions of time from the list below.

   at   in   on   from . . . to   until   during   after

1. City Hall is open ____during____ the week; it opens ____at____ 8:00 A.M.

2. The museum is not open ____during____ weekends, but it is open late.

3. The Old State House is open ____from____ 9:30 A.M. ____to____ 5:00 P.M. ____in____ the summer.

4. The Boston Children's Museum is open ____on____ Friday evenings ____at____ 9:00 P.M.

5. Quincy Market is a good place to shop because many shops are open ____at____ 8:00 P.M. or later.

6. ____During____ the summer there are many firework displays. The biggest one is ____on____ the 4th of July.

beg = please money
begger or beggar

Video Activities: A Homeless Shelter

Before You Watch.   Discuss these questions in small groups.

1.   Are there homeless people in your town? Tell what you know about their lives. For example, where do they get food? Where do they sleep?
2.   Who should help homeless people: their families? the community? the government?
3.   Why do some people become homeless?

Watch.   Discuss these questions in small groups.

1.   Why does Oceanside need a homeless shelter? *concern abat diesaster coming*
2.   What does the proposed shelter look like? *portable, removeable, white, camping*   *cot*
3.   What is the woman in the hat trying to do? *raise money for her course.*

Watch Again.   Fill in the blanks.

1.   There are _____ *1,200* _____ homeless people in Oceanside.
2.   However, now there are only _____ *58* _____ shelter beds.
3.   The Oceanside City Council will give _____ *20,000* _____ dollars for the new shelter.
4.   The new shelter will have _____ *100* _____ beds.
5.   The new shelter will be for single men and women and couples. Families will stay in _____ *hotel* _____.
6.   The city needs to raise money, and it is also asking people in the community to _____ *help* _____.

After You Watch.   Write a letter to your family and friends. Ask them to donate money for a new homeless shelter in your town. In your letter,

■   tell people why you are writing
■   explain the problem — why the town needs a new shelter
■   ask people to give money
■   thank them for helping

You can start your letter like this:

Dear Family and Friends,

I am writing to ask for your help. We have a serious problem in our town. …

Chapter 5

Home

IN THIS CHAPTER

Listening
- Listening for main ideas
- Listening for specific information
- Identifying stressed words and reductions
- Taking notes on apartment information (specific information)

Speaking
- The -ed ending
- Summarizing main ideas
- Making and answering requests

Reading
- Previewing vocabulary
- Reading: A Short History of the Changing Family
- Understanding time order of paragraphs
- Understanding the main idea

- Using punctuation and phrase clues
- Recognizing time details

Writing
- Developing ideas: making a lifeline, limiting information, writing topic sentences
- Using time words and *because*
- Punctuating sentences with dependent clauses
- Writing an autobiographical paragraph
- Editing for content, form, cohesion, style, and grammar
- Editing for punctuation with dependent clauses

Grammar
- The simple past tense: regular verbs
- The simple past tense: irregular verbs

PART 1

Listening to Conversations

Before You Listen

1 **Prelistening Questions.**   Before you listen, talk about your home with a partner.

1. What kind of place do you live in now: an apartment? a house? a student dormitory?
2. How many times in your life have you moved to a new place? What were the reasons?
3. Is it common for young adults in your culture to live by themselves?

2 **Vocabulary Preview.**   Complete the sentences with these words and expressions from the conversation.

[handwritten annotations: worried, bother, anxiety; stressed out about sth; abat; person who own the building; an increase in the money; you earn]

stressed out	landlord	move out *put everthing away* raised
vacancy	studio	furnished/unfurnished
pretty (adv.)	closet	fireplace *an open place in the wall of a room where you can make a fire*

1. Mr. Davis is the owner of the house where I live. He always helps me when something is broken in the kitchen or the bathroom. He is a very good ___*landlord*___.

2. Don't leave your clothes and shoes in the living room. Put them in the
   ___closet___.

3. I only need one room to live because I'm alone and I don't have much
   money. So I will rent a ___studio___ apartment.

4. Jack has to buy a bed, a desk, a table, chairs and some other things because
   his new apartment is ___unfurnished___.

5. My place is ___pretty___ close to campus. It's only a 20-minute
   walk.

6. After two years, the owner of the building ___raised___ my
   rent from $850 to $950 a month.

7. This hotel is full; it has no ___vacancy___. We'll have to look for
   a room at another hotel.

8. I like to use my ___fireplace___ in winter. It makes my apartment
   warm and romantic.

9. If you don't like your apartment, you can ___move out___ and find
   another place.

10. Joanne has to study for two tests tomorrow, and she also has to pick up
    her parents at the airport. That's why she feels ___stressed out___.

Listen

3   **Listening for Main Ideas.**   Ming is talking to her friend Jennifer about apartments.

1. Close your books as you listen to the conversation. Listen for the answers to
   these questions.
   1. Why is Jennifer stressed out? Landlord raised the rent.
   2. What does Ming suggest that Jennifer do? She suggests Ming to look for another place.
   3. Is Jennifer happy in her apartment now? Why or why not? No, she doesn't have enough money
   4. What kind of apartment does Jennifer need? unfurnished apartment, chep
   5. Describe an apartment in Ming's building. one bedroom care with bathroom pretty big closet, kitchen fire place in the living room
   6. What is Jennifer going to do tomorrow? She will call Jerry or stop by at new apartment

2. Compare answers with a partner.

Stress

4   **Listening for Stressed Words.**   Listen to the conversation again.

1.   Some of the stressed words are missing. During each pause, repeat the phrase or sentence. Then fill in the blanks with words from the list.

bad	living	own	studio (2 times)
bathroom	manager's	rent	sure
furnished [t]	move	stop by	ten
interested	moved out	stressed	vacancies
laundry (2 times)			

Jennifer: I'm so __stressed__ out. My landlord just raised my __rent__.
I think I'll have to __move__.

Ming: Really? My building has some __vacancies__. It's a pretty nice
place and it's just __ten__ minutes from campus.

Jennifer: Oh? How much is the rent for a __studio__?

Ming: There're no __studio__ apartments in our building. My
neighbor just __moved__ __out__ of a one-bedroom. He
paid $850 a month, I think.

Jennifer: That's not __bad__. Tell me more.

Ming: Well, one-bedrooms come with a __bathroom__, a kitchen, a
fireplace in the __living__ room, pretty big closets and uh . . .
Are you looking for a __furnished__ or unfurnished place?

Jennifer: Unfurnished. I have all my __own__ stuff. What about
parking and __laundry__?

Ming: There's no garage. You have to park on the street. But there is a
__laundry__ room downstairs.

Jennifer: Hmm. I think I'm __interested__. Could you give me the address?

Ming: Sure. It's 1213 Rose Avenue. The __manager__ name is Jerry
Kohl. Call him up or __stop__ __by__ and talk to him.

Jennifer: Thanks, Ming. I'm going to do that tomorrow for __sure__.

2.   Now read the conversation with a partner. Practice stressing words correctly.

Reductions

5   **Comparing Long and Reduced Forms.**   Listen to the following sentences from the conversation. They contain reduced forms. Repeat them after the speaker.

Reduced form*	**Long form**
1. I think I'll <u>hafta</u> move.	I think I will have to move.
2. <u>Areya</u> looking for a furnished place?	Are you looking for a furnished place?
3. You <u>hafta</u> park on the street.	You have to park on the street.
4. <u>Couldja gimme</u> the address?	Could you give me the address?
5. Call '<u>im</u> up.	Call him up.
6. Stop by '<u>n</u>' talk to '<u>im</u>.	Stop by and talk to him.
7. I'm <u>gonna</u> do that tomorrow.	I'm going to do that tomorrow.

* *Note:* The underlined forms are not acceptable spellings in written English.

6   **Listening for Reductions.**   Listen to the following conversation. You'll hear the reduced forms of some words.

1.   Repeat each sentence during the pause. Then write the long forms in the blanks.

A: Mr. Kohl, I ___have___ ___to___ talk to you. I ___have___ another problem.

B: ___Could___ ___you___ call me later? I'm busy now.

A: No, I need the plumber again. ___Could___ ___you___ call ___him___ right now?

B: I have a ___lot___ ___of___ things to do. I'll call ___him___ tomorrow morning, okay?

A: No, I need ___him___ right now!

B: ___Have___ ___you___ having trouble with the toilet again?

A: Yes. Look, just ___give___ ___me___ the plumber's phone number. I'll call ___him___.

B: All right, all right. Just ___give___ ___me___ a minute and I'll do it.

2.   With a partner, repeat the sentences for pronunciation practice.

After You Listen

7 **Vocabulary Review.**   Discuss the following questions with a partner. Use the underlined vocabulary in your answers.

1. In what situations do you feel <u>stressed out</u>?
2. In your community, can <u>landlords</u> <u>raise</u> the rent any time? Does the government control the rent?
3. Is it <u>pretty</u> easy to find <u>vacancies</u> for apartments in your neighborhood?
4. What are the advantages and disadvantages of a <u>studio</u> apartment?
5. Are you planning to <u>move out</u> of your present home? Why or why not?
6. When you first moved into your present home, was it <u>furnished</u> or <u>unfurnished</u>?

Pronunciation

> ### The -ed Ending
>
> The -*ed* ending is pronounced one of three ways, depending on the sound that comes before -*ed*:
>
> - /id/ after -*d* and -*t* → sound
>   **Examples:** waited, invited, needed
>
> - /t/ after -*p*, -*k*, -*f*, -*s*, -*ch*, -*sh* → sound
>   **Examples:** missed, watched, helped
>
> - /d/ after -*b*, -*g*, -*j*, -*m*, -*n*, -*l*, -*r*, -*th*, -*v*, -*z* → sound
>   **Examples:** lived, showed, listened

8 **Distinguishing between -*ed* Endings.**   Listen and write the following words. Then check the sound you hear at the end of the word.

		/id/	/t/	/D/
1.	turned	☐	☐	☑
2.	rented	☑	☐	☐
3.	mixed	☐	☑	☐
4.	asked	☐	☑	☐
5.	recommended	☑	☐	☐
6.	walked	☐	☑	☐
7.	tested	☑	☐	☐
8.	followed	☐	☐	☑
9.	moved	☐	☐	☑
10.	changed	☐	☐	☑

9 **Using -*ed* Endings.**   With a partner, look at the pictures below. Talk about Jennifer's moving day. Use the past tense of the verbs under the pictures. Pronounce the -*ed* endings carefully.

Example:

Jennifer moved into her new place. First, the movers carried the boxes inside. Then, Jennifer...

1.   move / carry / watch

2.   call / ask / describe

3.   look / decide

4.   unpack

5.   wash / drop

6.   dust / sneeze

7.   paint

8.   work / plant

9.   order

10.   rest

| **PART 2** | # Recalling Main Ideas |

Before You Listen

1 **Prelistening Questions.**   Before you listen, answer these questions with a partner.

1. What do you like and dislike about the home where you live now? Name two good things and two bad things.

2. Who found your current home for you: yourself? your parents? a housing advisor? an agent?

3. In your experience, are apartment managers generally helpful or unhelpful?

2 **Vocabulary Preview.**   You will hear the underlined words below in the conversation. Before you listen, write the letter of the correct definition beside each sentence.

Sentences	Definitions
_D_ 1. My apartment <u>lease</u> says that I have to stay there for one year.	a. able to get, free
_A_ 2. The concert is on May 20th, but the tickets are <u>available</u> at the theater starting in January.	b. to repair, to make something work again
_B_ 3. My shower is broken. Can you <u>fix</u> it?	c. water coming from a broken wall or pipe
_E_ 4. You don't have to sign a lease for this apartment. You can just rent it <u>month-to-month</u>.	d. a contract, a signed agreement to use a home for a period of time
_C_ 5. The boat has a <u>leak</u> and is full of water.	e. monthly

Listen

3 **Listening for Main Ideas.**   Jennifer is looking at an apartment in Ming's building. Listen to her conversation with the manager.

1. To help you remember the main points, take notes on these questions while you listen.   are
    1. Which rooms is the manager showing Jennifer? living room, bedroom, kitchen
    2. Is this a good apartment or not?
    3. What's Jennifer's decision? possibly think more

    _____

    _____

    _____

4 **Taking Notes on Specific Information.** Listen again. Take notes about the good things and the bad things in the apartment. Compare your list with a partner.

Good things	Bad things
1. new paint	1. open window
2. big refrigerator	2. no air-condition
3. good electric	3. noisy
4. new carpet	4. higher rent $ 25
5. classic bedroom	5. small bedroom
6. dishwasher	6. plum (leak)
7. shower bathtub	
8. available 2 days	

After You Listen

5 **Summarizing Main Ideas.** Compare notes with a partner. Together, answer the three questions from Activity 3. As you speak, look at your notes to help you remember.

6 **Vocabulary Review.** Discuss your answers to the following questions with a partner. Use the underlined vocabulary in your answers.

1. What is the advantage of a <u>lease</u> for (a) the renter? (b) the landlord?
2. Why do some people prefer to rent a place <u>month-to-month</u>?
3. Is anything broken in your home now? Who is going to <u>fix</u> it?
4. If you have questions for your English teacher, when is she or he <u>available</u> to talk to you?
5. If your ceiling <u>leaks</u>, what should you do?

Using Language

Making requests	Answering requests	
	Yes	**No**
Polite ↓ **Strong**	Could you...? Can you please...? Would you mind* ____ing...? How about ____ing...? I need you to... I want you to...	Sure, no problem. ⎱ polite I'll be happy to do it. ⎰ I don't mind. Okay, that's no problem. casual	I'm sorry, I can't. I'm sorry, but that's impossible. Absolutely not. No way.

* "Would you mind...?" means "Is it a problem for you?" The answer is negative: "I don't mind." = It's not a problem.

7 **Role-Play.**   Jennifer likes the apartment in Ming's building. However, she wants some of the "bad things" corrected. She decides to ask the manager about.

- changing the wall color
- putting in air conditioning
- fixing the bathroom leak
- lowering the rent
- having some pets

With a partner, role-play a conversation between Jennifer and Mr. Kohl, the manager. Use expressions from the box.

PART 3   # Reading

Before You Read

1 Discuss the pictures in small groups.

1.   Where and when does each scene take place? What are the people doing?
2.   How are these scenes similar to situations in your family or community? How are they different?
3.   How do you think family life is changing? How might it change in the future?

briefcase

2 Think about the answers to these questions. The reading selection answers them.

1. What is the difference between an extended family and a nuclear family?
2. What are some kinds of families in the world today?
3. Why and how did the structure of the family change in the twentieth century?
4. How were the 1930s and 1940s difficult years for most families?
5. How did people's ideas about marriage and family change after World War II?
6. What are the most common family forms around the world today?

3 **Vocabulary Preview.** Learn the meanings of these vocabulary items from the reading.

[handwritten: century = 100 year]

Nouns *[handwritten: 1000 year]*	history	**Verbs**	**Phrases**
the millennium	certainty *[handwritten: (sure)]*	consist of	a social institution
cousins		return	a common ancestor
relatives	**Adjectives**	rise	the extended family
partnerships	biological *[handwritten: science of life]* decline	the nuclear family
couples	adopted	face	foster families
thousands	divorced	support	heads of households
millions	widowed	take in → *[handwritten: bring into]* for life
divorces	perfect	adopt *[handwritten: your family]*	on their own
war	childless		loosely related
widows	traditional		

[handwritten left margin: ตัวอย่างเช่น / divorcee (woman) / คู่หญิง ที่หย่าร้างจาก / แต่ยังไม่ใส่]

[handwritten: widower = man whose wife has died and not married again]
[handwritten: widow = a woman whose husband has died]

Read

[handwritten: divorce man]

4 Read the following material quickly. Then read the explanations and do the exercises after the reading.

[handwritten left margin: folktale → / tall tales →]

A Short History of the Changing Family

A   Like the community, the family is a *social institution*. Long ago, human beings lived in loosely related groups. Each group had a common ancestor (a family member from the distant past). But for over a millennium (a thousand years), there have been two main types of families in the world: the extended form and the nuclear form. The extended family may include grandparents, parents, and children (and sometimes aunts, uncles, and cousins) — in other words, relatives living in the same house or close together on the same street or in the same area. In contrast, the nuclear family consists of only parents and their biological or adopted children. Because of industrialization in the nineteenth century, the nuclear family became the most common family structure.

B   Today there are many different kinds of families around the globe. Some people live in traditional families — that is to say, a stay-at-home mother, a working father, and their own biological children. Others live in two-paycheck families — that is, both parents work outside the home. There are many single-parent families; in other words, only a mother *or* a father lives with the children.

plagarism: copy another's words or work

adopted
keep children a little time

Still others have adoptive or foster families (i.e., adults take care of children not biologically theirs) or blended families — in other words, divorced or widowed men and women marry again and live with the children from their previous, or earlier, marriages. There are also same-sex partnerships — with or without children, childless marriages, unmarried live-in relationships, and so on.

C   What caused the structure of the family to change? In the early 1900s in the United States the divorce rate (i.e., the percent of legal endings compared to the number of marriages) began to rise, and the birthrate (i.e., the number of births per 100 or 1000 people) began to decline; in other words, couples stayed married for fewer years, and they had fewer children. Women often chose to get an education and take jobs outside the home. Decades later, the same changes began to happen in other industrialized countries. Today, they are happening in many of the developing nations of the world as well.

D   The decades of the 1930s and 1940s were difficult years in the industrialized world. Many families faced serious financial problems because the heads of households lost their jobs. During World War II (1939–1945), millions of women had to take care of their homes and their children alone. Because so many men were at war, thousands of these "war widows" — that is to say, women whose husbands were away at war — had to go to work outside the home. Most women worked long hours at hard jobs. There weren't many "perfect families."

E   During the next decade (a period of ten years), the situation changed in many places. There were fewer divorces, and people married at a younger age and had more children than in the previous generation. Men made enough money to support the family, so a mother seldom worked outside the home when her children were small. Children began living at home longer — that is, until an older age, usually after high school or even college. The traditional family was returning in the United States, it seemed — as in many other countries.

F   In the years between 1960 or so and the end of the twentieth century, however, there were many new changes in the structure of the family around the globe. From the 1960s to the 1970s, the divorce rate greatly increased and the birthrate fell by half. The number of single-parent families rose, and the number of couples living together without marriage went up even more.

G   Many people today would like the traditional two-parent family back — that is to say, they want a man and a woman to marry for life; they also think the man should support the family and the woman should stay home with the children. However, very few families now fall into this category. In fact, if more women decide to have children on their own, the single-parent household may become more typical than the traditional family in many countries. Also, unmarried couples may decide to have more children — or they might take in foster children or adopt. And because people are staying single and living longer (often as widows), there may be more one-person households. On the other hand, some people believe similar events happen again and again in history: if this is true, people may go back to the traditional extended or nuclear family of the past. Others think the only certainty in history is change: in other words, the structure of the future family could begin to change faster and faster — and in more and more ways.

After You Read

5 **Recognizing Paragraphs in Time Order (History).** Readings about history (true events or happenings from the past) usually begin with introductory material; these one or two paragraphs may tell the most important ideas and points of the whole selection. The several paragraphs after that may tell about various *periods* of history — probably in time order. The last paragraph or paragraphs may give information about the present or thoughts about the future.

In the reading "A Short History of the Changing Family," there is a capital letter next to each of the seven paragraphs. After its letter, finish the specific topic of each paragraph. Some items are done as examples.

A. definitions of _types of family_
B. the _kinds of families_ around the globe
C. reasons for _present changes in the structure of the family_
D. the typical family _in the 1930s and 1940s_
E. the typical family _in the 1950s_
F. _The changes_ between 1960 and the end of the twentieth century
G. How might family structure _changes in the future._ ?

6 Which phrase best tells the topic or subject of the whole reading "A Short History of the Changing Family"? Circle its letter. Give the reasons for your answer.

a. the advantages of the traditional family form over single-parent or adoptive relationships
b. the effects of World War II on jobs, home, and children in the future
c. reasons for divorce in a changing global community of live-in couples
(d.) changes in the structure of the nuclear family from the twentieth century to the future

7 **Understanding the Main Idea.** What is a simple method to get and tell the point of reading material? You can ask one question about the information in each paragraph — and then a general question about the point of the whole reading. A one- or two-sentence answer to each question gives the main idea.

For each of paragraph topics from the reading "A Short History of the Changing Family," complete a different question about the information. (Write the necessary words on the lines.) Two items are done as an example.

A. _What are the definitions_ of the two main types of families?
B. _What are_ the different kinds of families around the globe today?
C. _What are_ changes in the structure of the family?
D. _What happened to_ families in industrialized countries in the 1930s and 1940s?

E. _What happened to the_ families in the United States in the next decade?

F. In general, how did families change _during the 60s and 70s_ ?

G. _How might family struture change_ in the future?

In what different ways _maye family change_ in the twentieth and twenty-first centuries?

8 In order, here are some false sentences about the information in paragraphs A–G of the reading. The possible statement of the point of the *whole* reading is not right, either. Change the eight wrong sentences to true statements of the point. Then use them as correct answers to the eight questions in Exercise 7.

1. The *nuclear family* is the same as the *extended family*: it consists of many relatives (grandparents, parents, children, cousins, etc.) living in the same house.

2. There is only one kind of family on planet earth today: it is the traditional nuclear family.

3. In the early 1990s in the United States (and later in other countries), the divorce rate went down and the birthrate began to rise; couples were staying married longer and having more children.

4. Before and during World War II, families faced few financial problems in the industrialized world, so women didn't have to work outside the home. Families were perfect.

5. After the war, family structure changed back in the other direction: there were more divorces and fewer stay-at-home mothers; children began to leave home earlier.

6. From the 1960s on, there were few new changes in the structure of the family around the globe.

7. People don't want the traditional two-parent nuclear family—with a working father and a mother at home; however, this structure will probably come back and all other family forms will disappear from the earth.

In the twentieth century, there weren't any changes in the structure of the typical family; in the next century, there won't be any changes either.

9 **Using Punctuation and Phrase Clues.** Short definitions of new vocabulary items, words with similar meanings, and explanations of meaning sometimes appear between or after certain punctuation marks, such as parentheses ( ), dashes (—), or commas (,). They might also be in another sentence part after a semicolon (;) or a colon (:). The phrases *in other words, that is to say,* or the abbreviation *i.e. (that is)* can also be clues to the meaning of vocabulary. So can other words in the sentence or paragraph.

Example: The family is a social institution; in other words, it is an organization with a purpose inside a human community — that is, among the people living together in a certain area. (A definition of a *social institution* is "an organization with a purpose within a community." The word *community* can mean "people living together in a certain area.")

figure out → think, consider
come up with → think
the idea,
the solution

A hyphen (-) between word parts is another punctuation clue to meaning. *Multi-word adjectives* before nouns are usually hyphenated. An example in the previous sentence is the phrase *multi-word adjectives*; it means "adjectives that consist of more than one word."

On the lines, finish the explanations of the words from the reading material. (The letters in parentheses are the letters of the paragraphs.) One item is done as an example.

loosely-related groups: (A): _groups of people that are not close relatives_

___

an ancestor: (A) a family member _from the distant past_

___

the extended family: (A) relatives _living in the same house or close together on the same street or in the same area._

the nuclear family: (A) a living group with only _parents and their biological or adopted children_

a stay-at-home mother: (B) a mother that _stay at home with the children but father works_

single-parent families: (B) families with only _a mother or father lives with the children_

blended families: (B) family groups with _divorced or widowed men and women marry again and live with the children from their_ previous

the divorce rate: (C) the percent of _legal endings compared to the number of marriages._

war widows: (D) women whose _husbands were away at war_

___

a decade: (E) a time period of _ten years_

___

For more practice, look for and explain other vocabulary items with meaning clues, such as *a social institution, a millennium, family structure, two-paycheck families, adoptive or foster families, previous, same-sex partnerships, the birthrate, one-person households,* and others.

10 **Recognizing Time Details (Facts).**   In readings about history, there are often time details. These facts tell when things happened. Some examples of past-time phrases are years such as *1860* or *the year 2000*; centuries, decades or time periods like *the eighteenth century, the early 1930s,* or *the years between 1990 and 2001*. A hyphen (-) between points of time usually means *to*, as in *1925-1955*. Time details also appear with phrases like *long ago, since the beginning of the millennium, for a century, between the 1960s and the end of the 1900s,* and many others.

Column A lists some of the important events in the history of family forms. Match them with the time phrases in Column B, and write the correct letters *a-h* on the lines.

Column A	Column B
E 1. Many families had money problems, so more women began to work outside the home.	a. over a millennium ago
A 2. There have been two main types of families: the extended and the nuclear.	b. since the year 1000 or so
C 3. Industrialization made the nuclear family the most common form.	c. in the nineteenth century
G 4. Many new family forms became common, such as single parenthood and unmarried couples living together.	d. in the early 1900s
D 5. Because women began to get education and work, the divorce rate rose and the birthrate fell in the United States.	e. in the 1930s and 1940s
B 6. People lived in loosely related groups, not in small family units.	f. in the decade after World War II in the U.S.
F 7. Men supported the family, and women stayed home to take care of the children. There were fewer divorces.	g. from the 1960s to the end of the twentieth century
H 8. There are and will continue to be many different family structures: "traditional" two-parent families, families with two working parents, single-parent families, adoptive or foster families, blended families, etc.	h. today and in the future

For more practice, you can turn back to the Before You Read section on page 125 and answer the questions in your own words.

Discussing the Reading

11   In small groups, talk about your answers to the following questions. Then tell the class the most interesting information and ideas.

1. What is the most common family structure in your community?
2. In your opinion, what caused so many changes in the structure of the family after the middle of the twentieth century? Explain your answers.
3. In your opinion, how and why might the structure of the family change in the twenty-first century?

PART 4	# Writing

Before You Write

Exploring Ideas

1   **Using a Lifeline.**   Draw a line down the middle of a piece of paper. The top of the line represents the year you were born, and the bottom of the line is the present time. You can write some ages along the line too, as in the picture below. Think about your life and write some of the important events on the left of the lifeline. Write your feelings about your life on the right. Write in English if possible, but don't worry about correctness. If you can't think of something in English, use your native language. You can use pictures and symbols, and you may also want to look at family photographs. Look at the woman's lifeline on page 132 as an example.

Organizing Ideas

Limiting Information

You can't write about your whole life in one paragraph, so you need to choose one part of your life to write about. You may want to write about your childhood, your school years, or one important event in your life.

2 Look at the woman's lifeline again. Discuss where a paragraph on a part of her life can begin and end. Then look at your own lifeline and choose part of your life to write about. As you think about the different parts, consider the following points.

- Is this part of my life interesting? Often unusual or funny events are more interesting to write about.

- Is this part of my life important?

- Is this part of my life about one topic? Don't try to write about too many events or times. Everything in your paragraph should be about one main subject.

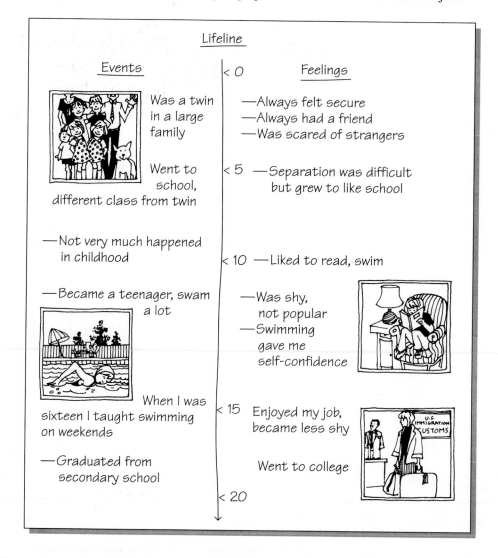

3 Making Paragraph Notes. Look at the part of the lifeline you chose and add information you think is important. Cross out information that is not about the topic of your paragraph. Discuss your decision with some other classmates.

4 **Writing Topic Sentences.** Look at these paragraph notes. For each paragraph, circle the number of the topic sentence that you think gives the main idea. Discuss your choices with your classmates.

Paragraph 1

- Was born a twin—very important to childhood
- Large family
- Always had a friend, felt secure
- Separation from twin sister at school was difficult

Topic Sentences

1. Because I was born a twin, I had a very different childhood from most people. *general idea*
2. Because I had a twin sister, I felt secure.
3. I didn't like school because I was in different classes from my twin.

Paragraph 2

- Teenage years difficult
- Liked to read, was shy, not popular
- Was a good swimmer
- Taught swimming on weekends
- This gave me self-confidence

Topic Sentences

1. I wasn't popular as a teenager.
2. As a teenager, I taught swimming on weekends.
3. My teenage years were very difficult at first, but they ended happily.

5 Write two possible topic sentences for your paragraph. Show the notes for your paragraph and your topic sentences to another student. Which one does he/she think is better? Why? Which one do you think is better? Why?

When I was 27-years-old, I had a lot of things that was wonderful in my life.

Write

Developing Cohesion and Style

Using the Past Tense

Because you are writing about events in the past, most of your sentences will be in the past tense.

6 Look at your paragraph notes and write sentences with past tense verbs about your life. Compare your verbs with those of other students. Be careful to use past tense verbs only for completed events; don't write "I studied English for three years" if you are still studying English.

Combining Sentences with Time Words and because

■ When you write a paragraph that describes events, you can use time words to combine sentences. Some common time words are *before, after, when,* and *as soon as.*

Examples:

> *Before* I started school, I was very happy.
> *After* I left high school, I got a job.
> *When* my family said good-bye, I was sad.
> *As soon as* I came to the United States, I got sick.

■ You can also combine sentences with *because* to show reasons.

Example:

> *Because* she worked hard, my mother was always tired.

---

7 Complete the following paragraph with *before, after, when, as soon as, because, and, but,* or *so.*

I had a typical childhood _____but_____ my life
                                                1

changed _____when_____ I was fourteen. We
                         2

moved from our small village to Karachi, a big city

in Pakistan. ____Before____ we moved, life in
                           3

the country was wonderful for me, but

____as soon as____ I started school in Karachi,
        4

I became shy and nervous. Some of the other girls in my classes were mean

_____and_____ they laughed at my country ways. _____Because_____ I didn't fit in,
5   6

I became more interested in books. I always liked biology, _____so_____ I started
7

to read about medicine. I was very unhappy at the time, _____but_____ I'm glad
8

this happened _____because_____ I finally decided to become a doctor.
9

Punctuating Sentences with Dependent Clauses

■ When you add a time word or *because* to a sentence, it becomes a dependent clause. A dependent clause cannot stand alone — it is a sentence fragment.

Examples: When I was five.   ⎫ sentence
                Because my father had a new job   ⎭ fragments

■ You must combine a dependent clause with an independent clause — a clause that can stand alone.

Example: We moved to Caracas.

■ If the dependent clause appears at the beginning of a sentence, use a comma after it.

Examples: When I was five, we moved to Caracas.
                Because my father had a new job, we moved to Caracas.

■ If the dependent clause appears at the end of the sentence, don't use a comma in front of it.

Examples: We moved to Caracas when I was five.
                We moved to Caracas because my father had a new job.

---

8 Combine the sentences with the word in parentheses. Use correct punctuation. It may be necessary to change the order of the sentences.

1. I was a good student. I got a scholarship. (because)

   _____I got a scholarship because I was a good student._____

2. I graduated from high school. I was sixteen. (before)

   _____Before I was sixteen, I graduated from high school._____

3. My father died. My mother went to work. (after)

   _____After my father died, my mother went to work._____

4. I found a job. I finished high school. (as soon as)

As soon as I finished high school, I found a job.

5. I stopped studying. I was unhappy. (when)

When I stopped studying, I was unhappy.

I stopped studying when I was unhappy.

9 Look at your paragraph notes and use each of the words below to write one sentence about your life. Be sure to use correct punctuation.

because I got sick because the weather was cold.

before Before I came to Houston, I quited my job.

after After I got engaged, I came to the U.S.A.

when When I was a teenager, I had a lot of friends.

as soon as I graduated bachelor degree, my parents gave me a car.

Writing the First Draft

10 Now write your paragraph about a part of your life. Use the topic sentence and the notes you wrote. Combine some sentences with time words and *because, and, but,* and *so.* Remember to use the past tense when you write about completed actions.

Edit and Revise

Editing Practice

11 Edit this paragraph twice and rewrite it correctly. The first time, see where you can combine sentences with *and, but,* and *so.* (Remember to use correct punctuation.) The second time, correct past tense verb forms. Make any other changes you think are necessary.

How I Became a Jazz Musician

I fall in love with jazz when I am five years old. I always heared jazz in the streets but for my fifth birthday my brother tooks me to a concert. There I saw a great saxophonist I decided to learn to play the saxophone. First I need a saxophone, I ask my father. My father say he no have money for a saxophone. I work for my brother, uncles, and cousins. I made a little money then my father see I work hard. He gave me money for a saxophone. I listen to recordings. My brother teach me. I practice every day. Soon I am a good saxophone player.

Editing Your Writing

12   **Editing Using a Checklist.**   Edit your paragraph using the following checklist.

Editing Checklist

1. Content
   a. Is the information interesting?
   b. Is the information important?
   c. Is there an interesting title?
2. Organization
   a. Does the topic sentence give the main idea of the paragraph?
   b. Are all the sentences about one topic?
   c. Should you change the order of any of the sentences?
3. Cohesion and Style
   Did you combine sentences with time words and *because*?
4. Grammar
   a. Are your nouns, pronouns, and articles correct?
   b. Did you use complete sentences?
   c. Did you use the correct past tense verbs?
5. Form
   a. Did you use correct paragraph form?
   b. Did you use correct punctuation?

13   **Peer Editing.**   Exchange paragraphs with another student. Discuss the paragraphs. Are there any other changes you should make?

Writing the Second Draft

14   Rewrite your paragraph using correct form. Then give it to your teacher for comments.

PART 5

Grammar

A. The Simple Past Tense: Statements

Use the simple past tense to talk about completed past events and activities.

	Examples	**Notes**
Affirmative	He **helped** her paint her kitchen. I **stayed up** late last night. We **listened** to music after dinner.	All regular verbs take an *-ed* ending in the past tense. This form is used for all subjects, both singular and plural.
Negative	Her roommate **didn't like** that restaurant. We **didn't order** a pizza last night. I **didn't live** in a dorm last year.	For negative past tense verbs, use *did not* before the simple form of the main verb. The contraction for *did not* is *didn't*.

Note: For spelling rules for the past tense of regular verbs, see Appendix 3, pages 287–288.

Expressions of Past Time

Expressions of past time specify the time in the past when an action was completed. Here are some examples of expressions for past time:

yesterday	in 1998	last year
the day before yesterday	in April 1992	last Monday
yesterday morning	on November 15	last week
yesterday afternoon	on Tuesday	last night
yesterday evening	a year ago	the next day
a week later	a long time ago	a week later
at 3:00	a few minutes ago	then

1 Fill in the blanks with the correct simple past tense forms of the regular verbs in parentheses.

When I was a child, we _____didn't stay_____ inside watching TV in hot weather. We
    1 (not stay)
_____didn't own_____ an air conditioner, so on warm summer evenings, we
    2 (not own)
_____stayed_____ outside on the porch for hours. We children _____played_____ games or
    3 (stay)   4 (play)
_____looked_____ at comic books. My dad _____relaxed_____ in his chair and
    5 (look)   6 (relax)
_____smoked_____ his pipe. Sometimes he _____tried_____ to do a crossword
    7 (smoke)   8 (try)

puzzle in the newspaper. Occasionally some neighbors _____visited_____ us on the
9 (visit)

porch. Then dad _____stopped_____ reading the newspaper and _____discussed_____
10 (stop)   11 (discuss)

current events with them. They _____argued_____ about politics or the economy.
12 (argue)

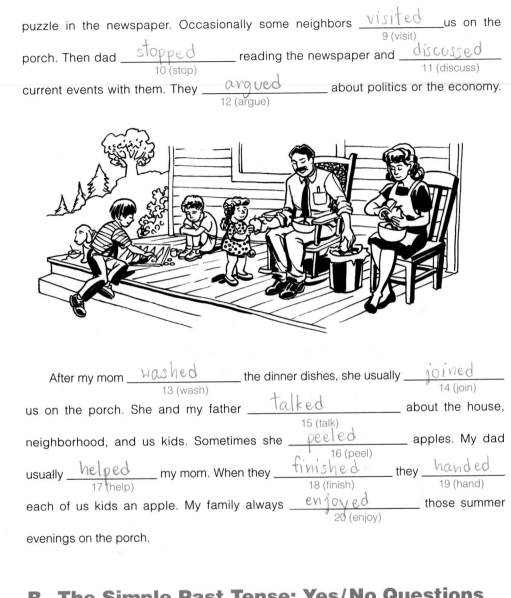

After my mom _____washed_____ the dinner dishes, she usually _____joined_____
13 (wash)   14 (join)

us on the porch. She and my father _____talked_____ about the house,
15 (talk)

neighborhood, and us kids. Sometimes she _____peeled_____ apples. My dad
16 (peel)

usually _____helped_____ my mom. When they _____finished_____ they _____handed_____
17 (help)   18 (finish)   19 (hand)

each of us kids an apple. My family always _____enjoyed_____ those summer
20 (enjoy)

evenings on the porch.

B. The Simple Past Tense: Yes/No Questions and Short Answers

Simple past tense yes/no questions include *did(n't)* before the subject. Note that the main verb in the question is in the simple form: There is no final *-ed* ending in the question form.

	Examples	Possible Answers	
		Affirmative	**Negative**
Affirmative Questions	**Did** your mother **cook** last night? **Did** you **move** to a new apartment?	Yes, she **did**. Yes, I **did**.	No, she **didn't**. No, I **didn't**.
Negative Questions	**Didn't** she **rent** a video last night? **Didn't** he **call** you at home?	Yes, she **did**. Yes, he **did**.	No, she **didn't**. No, he **didn't**.

2 What did you do last weekend? First, Student A asks simple past tense questions using the words below, and Student B gives a short answer. Then, Student B asks the questions, and Student A gives short answers. After you give an affirmative short answer to a question, give additional information with a simple past tense sentence.

Examples: A: Did you clean your room last weekend?
B: No, I didn't.
A: Did you play any sports last weekend?
B: Yes, I did. I played tennis on Saturday afternoon.

1. clean your room?
2. play any sports?
3. listen to the radio?
4. watch TV?
5. cook?
6. telephone anyone? Did you telephone
7. visit your friends?
8. wash your clothes?
9. study at home?
10. finish your homework?
11. receive any letters or packages?
12. mail any letters or packages?
13. use a computer?
14. surf the Internet?
15. stay up late?
16. enjoy yourself?

When you finish, join with another pair of students. Take turns telling the group five things that your partner did (or didn't do) last weekend.

C. The Simple Past Tense: Information Questions

Many simple past tense information questions use *did* before the subject; *why* can also have *didn't* before the subject. Note that when *who* or *what* is the subject of the sentence, the main verb is in the simple past tense and *did* is not used before the subject.

Who call you
subject

object Examples	Possible Answers	Notes
Who did you **call**?	My sister.	In information questions with *did* and *didn't*, the main verb is in the simple form. There is no *-ed* ending.
What did you **do** yesterday?	I cleaned my house.	
Where did your relatives **stay**?	They stayed in the upstairs bedroom.	
What happened last night?	We rented a video.	When *who* or *what* is the subject, the main verb appears in the simple past tense and *did* is not used before the subject.
Who argued a lot?	My sister and I.	

3   The following information questions are missing question words. Fill in the blanks with question words from the list below. Use each question word at least once. Then interview a classmate about his or her childhood, using these questions. Write your classmate's answers on the lines provided below the questions.

What   Where   When   Who   How   Why

1. _____ did you live?

   _____

   _____

2. _____ did you play with?

   _____

   _____

3. _____ games or sports did you play?

   _____

   _____

4. _____ did you start school?

   _____

   _____

5. _____ did you like school?

   _____

   _____

6. _____ did you want to study English?

   _____

   _____

D. Irregular Past Tense Verbs

Many verbs have irregular past tense forms. These verbs do not take an -ed ending in the past form.

Examples				Notes
Simple Form	Past Tense Form	Simple Form	Past Tense Form	
cost cut hit hurt	cost cut hit hurt	let put quit shut	let put quit shut	The simple and the past forms of some verbs are the same.
bend build lend	bent built lent	send spend	sent spent	With some verbs, the simple form ends in -d and the past form ends in -t.
dream have hear	dreamt had heard	lose make	lost made	Some verbs have other consonant changes or add a consonant in the past tense.
begin bleed come choose drink drive eat fall find get give	began bled came chose drank drove ate fell found got gave	grow know ride ring run sing take tear throw win write	grew knew rode rang ran sang took tore threw won wrote	Many verbs have vowel changes in the past tense.
be* bring buy catch creep do fly go keep	was/were brought bought caught crept did flew went kept	leave lie pay say sell sleep teach tell think	left lay paid said sold slept taught told thought	Many verbs have consonant and vowel changes in the past tense.

Note: Irregular past tense verbs follow the same patterns in affirmative statements, negative statements, yes/no questions, and information questions as regular verbs.   * *Be* is the one exception to this rule.

4   In the story below, Yukata tells about leaving Japan and finding a new home in England. Fill in each of the blanks with the past form of the verb in parentheses.

Cambridge University (send) _____ me the letter of acceptance on
₁

May 10th. I (let) _____ my father read the letter first. Then he (read)
₂

_____ it aloud to the whole family. I know he and my mother (be)
₃

_____ proud. I (be) _____ really excited. I (sleep)
4   5
_____ badly that night. The next day I (take) _____ my parents downtown.
6   7
We (have) _____ dinner in a nice restaurant. Two days later, I (go)
8
_____ shopping for some new clothes with my mother. The clothes (cost)
9
_____ a lot of money, but my mother proudly (spend) _____ the money.
10   11
The day before I (leave) _____, my friends (throw)
12

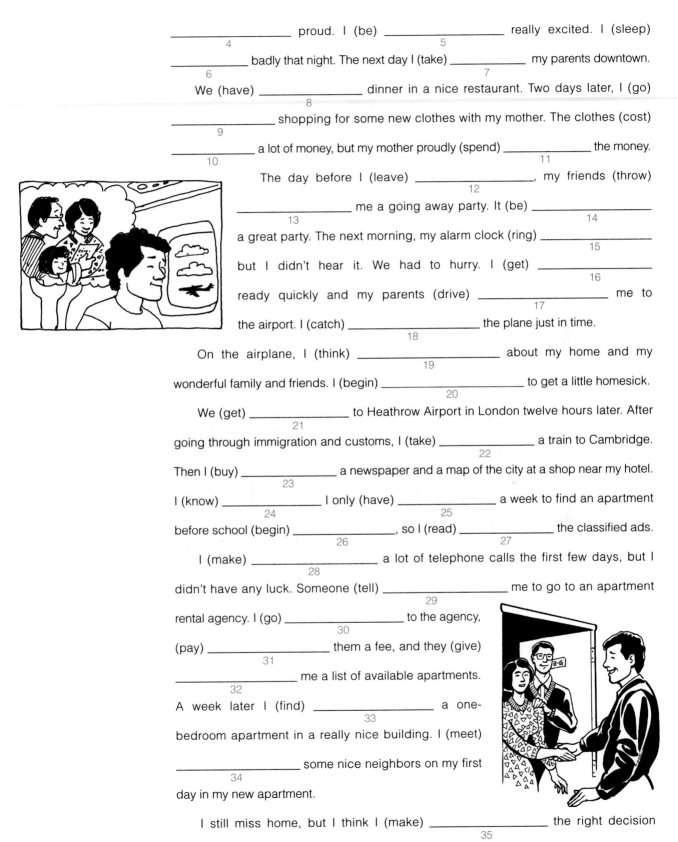

_____ me a going away party. It (be) _____
13   14
a great party. The next morning, my alarm clock (ring) _____
15
but I didn't hear it. We had to hurry. I (get) _____
16
ready quickly and my parents (drive) _____ me to
17
the airport. I (catch) _____ the plane just in time.
18

On the airplane, I (think) _____ about my home and my
19
wonderful family and friends. I (begin) _____ to get a little homesick.
20

We (get) _____ to Heathrow Airport in London twelve hours later. After
21
going through immigration and customs, I (take) _____ a train to Cambridge.
22
Then I (buy) _____ a newspaper and a map of the city at a shop near my hotel.
23
I (know) _____ I only (have) _____ a week to find an apartment
24   25
before school (begin) _____, so I (read) _____ the classified ads.
26   27

I (make) _____ a lot of telephone calls the first few days, but I
28
didn't have any luck. Someone (tell) _____ me to go to an apartment
29
rental agency. I (go) _____ to the agency,
30
(pay) _____ them a fee, and they (give)
31
_____ me a list of available apartments.
32
A week later I (find) _____ a one-
33
bedroom apartment in a really nice building. I (meet)
_____ some nice neighbors on my first
34
day in my new apartment.

I still miss home, but I think I (make) _____ the right decision
35
when I decided to come here.

Video Activities: Asthma and Dust Mites

Before You Watch.   Discuss these questions in small groups.

1. What do you know about asthma? Tell what you know about the causes and the treatment of this condition.
2. Can you guess what a "dust mite" is?
3. How can people reduce the amount of dust in their house?

Watch.

Write words to describe Linda Vine's house. _____
2. How big do you think dust mites are? _____
3. In Linda Vine's house, you won't find _____.
    a. dust   b. dust mites   c. anything made of cloth
4. Write four things Linda Vine does to control dust mites in her house.

    _____
    _____

5. What is an easy way to kill dust mites on bedding?

    _____

Watch Again.   Discuss these questions in small groups.

1. The announcer says, "Asthma is part genetic and part environment." What does this mean? Can you think of other medical problems like this?
2. Did you know about dust mites before you saw this video?
3. If you had asthma, would it be difficult for you to change your house like Linda Vine did?

After You Watch.   Read the paragraphs below and fill in the blanks with one of the following words: *because, before, after, if, when, and, but, or, so.*

Getting Rid of Dust Mites

_____ some children are exposed to dust mites, they get asthma. _____ they already have asthma, dust mites make it worse. Therefore, you should cut down the number of dust mites in the home _____ your child has allergies or asthma. How can you do this?

Dust mites love warm, humid areas filled with dust, _____ pillows, mattresses, carpets, and furniture are great places for them to live. You should wash your sheets and blankets in very hot water every week. If possible, dry them in the sun _____ heat kills dust mites. You should also wash your pillow every week _____ put a plastic cover on it. Vacuuming your carpets every week can help, _____ the best thing to do is to remove all the carpets. Finally, _____ dust mites love warm, humid places, it helps to run your air conditioner and keep the air dry.

Chapter 6

Cultures of the World

IN THIS CHAPTER

Listening
- Listening for main ideas
- Listening for specific information
- Identifying stressed words and reductions
- Taking notes on a lecture (specific information)

Speaking
- Discussing cultural values
- Summarizing main ideas
- Giving opinions about customs

Reading
- Previewing vocabulary
- Reading: Cross-Cultural Conversation
- Reading conversation in paragraph form

- Understanding the point
- Using context clues
- Recognizing details of opinions

Writing
- Developing ideas: using a time sequence, limiting information
- Writing time clauses with *as soon as* and *then*
- Using quotations
- Writing an ending to a folktale
- Using editing symbols

Grammar
- The present perfect tense

PART 1   Listening to Conversations

Before You Listen

1   **Prelistening Questions.**   Before you listen, talk about travel with a partner.

1.   Which countries have you visited? When? Tell your classmates a little about your traveling experience.

2.   How do you feel when you travel to a new place, meet new people, and experience new customs? Circle the words that describe you. Explain or give examples of your feelings.

excited   careful   afraid   shy   nervous
energetic   homesick   worried   interested   curious

3.   Do you know the expression "When in Rome, do as the Romans do?" Tell about a time when you followed this advice.

2   **Vocabulary Preview.**   You will hear the underlined words in the conversation. Before you listen, use the context to guess their meanings. Write your guesses in the spaces.

Contexts	Meanings
1. My first <u>impression</u> of my new boss was not good. He seemed strict and unfriendly. *first judgement*	the opinion or feeling you have about someone or sth because he/she/it seems
2. I don't like getting up at 6 A.M., but I <u>am used to it</u>.	Something do it usually or routine
3. My neighbor is a <u>bizarre</u> person. She rarely leaves her house and she never looks you in the eye when she talks to you. *change* *adj*	abnormal, very unusual and strange
4. Mr. and Mrs. Haley like to travel to <u>exotic</u> places that other tourists rarely visit. *different from far away* *adj* *lian, tiger*	unusual and exciting because of a connection with a foreign country
5. If you don't finish your food in an American restaurant, you can take the remaining food home in a <u>doggie bag</u>.	
6. When I arrived in the U.S., I was <u>amazed</u> at the number of large cars on the road.	
7. Our teacher has not given us a lot of homework <u>so far</u>.	
8. When we finished dinner, we put the <u>leftovers</u> in the refrigerator and washed the dishes.	

exotic breed

Listen

3   Listening for Main Ideas.   Kenji is having lunch with Jennifer and her friend Simone, who is visiting from France.

1. Close your book and listen to their conversation. Listen for the answers to these questions.
    1. What was Simone's impression of American streets and people?
    2. Does Kenji like American food now?
    3. What is a doggie bag?
    4. What was Simone's problem in the Mexican restaurant?
    5. Where did Jennifer tell Simone to smoke?
    6. What does Simone mean when she says "When in Rome, do as the Romans do"?

2. Compare answers with a partner.

Stress

4   Listening for Stressed Words.   Listen to the conversation again.

1. Some of the stressed words are missing. During each pause, repeat the phrase or sentence. Then fill in the blanks with words from the list.

air	else	friendly	love
amazed	exotic	ice	Mexican
bizarre	finish	impression	much
clean	first (2 times)	isn't	salt
cold	food	ketchup	sweater
delicious	France	leftovers	too
doggie	French	like	used
	fried	lot	we

Kenji: Is this your ___first___ trip to the U.S., Simone?

Simone: Yes, it is.

Kenji: What's your ___impression___ so far?

Simone: Well, the streets are very ___clean___, and the people are so ___friendly___. But the ___food___ is not so good.

Kenji: That's what I thought too, when I ___first___ got here. But I'm ___used___ to it now. I really ___love___ hamburgers and french fries.

Simone: _French_ fries? What is that?

Jennifer: You know, _fried_ potatoes. I think you call them "pommes frites" in _France_. But _we_ call them french fries, for some reason. And a _lot_ of people eat them with _ketchup_.

Simone: Ketchup! That is very _bizarre_. We eat our pomme frites with _salt_, or maybe mustard.

Jennifer: Last night I took Simone to a _Mexican_ restaurant. I wanted her to try something _exotic_.

Kenji: Did you _like_ it?

Simone: The food was _delicious_, but it was _too_ _much_. I couldn't _finish_ it all.

Jennifer: Simone was _amazed_ when I said she could take the _leftovers_ home in a doggie bag.

Kenji: Yes, that's funny, _isn't_ it? They call it a _doggie_ bag but it's for people. Was there anything _else_ that surprised you?

Simone: Yes. The restaurant was so _cold_! We don't use _air_ conditioning so much in France. And the water had _ice_ in it too. I had to put on my _sweater_!

2.   Now read the conversation with a partner. Practice stressing words correctly.

Reductions

5   **Comparing Long and Reduced Forms.**   Listen to the following sentences from the conversation. They contain reduced forms. Repeat them after the speaker.

Reduced form*	**Long form**
1. Is <u>thishyer</u> first trip to the United States?	Is this your first trip to the United States?
2. <u>Whatcher</u> impression so far?	What's your impression so far?
3. You call <u>'em</u> *pommes frites* in France.	You call them *pommes frites* in France.
4. I wanted <u>'er ta</u> try something exotic.	I wanted her to try something exotic.
5. If you <u>wanna</u> smoke in someone's house, you'd better ask <u>fer</u> permission first.	If you want to smoke in someone's house, you'd better ask for permission first.

(handwritten note above "wanna": no stress)

* *Note:* The underlined forms are not acceptable spellings in written English.

6   **Listening for Reductions.**   Two women, Anita and Brenda, have just finished eating lunch together. Listen to their conversation. You'll hear the reduced forms of some words.

1.   Repeat each sentence during the pause. Then write the long forms in the blanks.

Anita: Well, it's time to get back to the office. I'll see you soon, Brenda.

Brenda: OK, see you …Wait, Anita, is ____this____ ____your____ cell phone?

Anita: Oh my goodness, yes, thanks. By the way, I almost forgot: My parents are coming ____for____ a visit next week.

Brenda: Really? I'd love ____to____ meet ____them____.

Anita: Well, do you ____want____ ____to____ have lunch with us on Saturday?

Brenda: Saturday? Hmm … I told my roommate I'd go shopping with ____her____ that day. Could we get together ____for____ a drink later in the afternoon?

Anita: I ____don't____ ____know____, they might be busy. I'll ask ____them____ and let ____you____ know.

After You Listen

7   **Vocabulary Review.**   Discuss the following questions with a partner. Use the underlined vocabulary in your answers.

1.   Are you planning to <u>take a trip</u> during your next vacation? Where do you want to go?

2.   Do you remember the first time you saw your university? What was your first <u>impression</u> of it?

3.   Has anything changed in your life in the past year? For example, have you started a new job? Have you had a baby? Are you <u>used to</u> the new situation in your life?

4.   Tell about a <u>bizarre</u> person you know. What is so strange about this person?

5.   What is the most <u>exotic</u> place or exotic food that you have experienced in your life?

6.   What would happen if an American asked for a <u>doggie bag</u> in your country?

7.   How many years of education have you completed <u>so far</u>?

8.   What amazes you about the United States or American people? Finish this sentence: "I am <u>amazed at</u> _____."

9.   Some people hate to eat <u>leftovers</u>. How about you?

<table>
<tr><td>**PART 2**</td></tr>
</table>

Recalling Main Ideas

Before You Listen

1   **Prelistening Questions.**   Before you listen, talk with a partner about coming-of-age in different countries.

1.   At what age does a person come of age, or become a legal adult?
2.   Do you know of any special customs or ceremonies when a person becomes an adult? Is it different for boys and girls?

Coming-of-Age Day in Japan.

2   **Vocabulary Preview.**   You will hear the following words in the lecture. Before you listen, write the letter of the correct definition beside each word.

Words	Definitions
_E_ 1. the woods	a. a formal or traditional way of celebrating an important event in a person's life
_G_ 2. an adult	b. the time of life when a person is not a child
_B_ 3. adulthood	c. to wait for an event with a feeling of pleasure
_A_ 4. a ceremony	d. a change or movement
_F_ 5. (to be) responsible for (something)	e. a forest
_D_ 6. a passage child become adult	f. to be the person who must take care of something
_C_ 7. to look forward to (something)	g. a person who is not a child

Listen

3   **Listening for Main Ideas.**   Listen to a short lecture about becoming an adult in four different cultures. As you listen, list the cultures in the spaces below.

1. North American Indian become 13 years
2. Japan   20 years old special ceremony
3. Jewish   religion   ceremony
4. U.S.A. 16 birth day , legal 18 , 21 can buy alcohol

4   **Taking Notes on Specific Information.**   Listen again. This time, fill in the details regarding each culture or religion.

Culture/religion	Age	Details without food, water safely
1. North American Indian	12–13	A. Boys: go to the wood alone and go back B. Girls: old enough to have a baby
2. Jewish g̊ ăg̊	12 – 13	A. Boys: religion ceremony religio B. Girls: spend y (12) bamith responsible to
3. Japanese	20	A. Boys: attend to special ceremony B. Girls: wean traditional cloths, visit friends
4. American [U.S.] vote 16 get driven license 18 get married work fulltime	21	A. Boys: ___ B: Girls: ___

celebrate birthday with drink and beer,

After You Listen

5   **Summarizing Main Ideas.**   In groups of four, use your notes to summarize the lecture. Each student should speak about one culture. Try to speak in complete sentences.

6   **Vocabulary Review.**   Discuss the following questions with a partner. Use the underlined vocabulary in your answers.

1.   Are you legally an <u>adult</u>?

2.   Which is easier in your opinion: <u>adulthood</u> or childhood? Why?

3.   In your community, is there a <u>ceremony</u> when a baby is born? If yes, describe it.

4.   When you were a teenager, were you <u>responsible for</u> watching your younger brothers and sisters? How did you feel about this responsibility?

5.   What has been the most important <u>passage</u> in your life until now?

6.   Do you enjoy walking in <u>the woods</u>?

7.   Are you <u>looking forward to</u> the end of this English course? Why or why not?

Talk It Over

At What Age…?
Work in small groups. Talk about when you think people should be allowed to do the following activities.

Example:

I think 16 is too young to get a driver's license. Age 18 is better.

Activity	Age	Activity	Age
get a driver's license		join the army	
get married with parents' permission		gamble	
get married without parents' permission		buy alcohol	
vote		buy a handgun	
get a credit card		be the president of your country	
buy cigarettes		retire (with full government benefits)	

PART 3   Reading

Before You Read

1 In small groups, discuss the picture on page 154.

1. What does the scene show? What kinds of people are taking part in a group conversation?

2. In your view, from what cultures are the group members? Why do you think so? Look at their clothing, the space between them, their body language, their facial expressions, etc.

3. What do you think the people are saying about culture?

2 Think about the answers to these questions. The reading selection answers them.

1. What is a "cultural legacy" from the past? What elements might it include?

2. What are some technical or scientific achievements of ancient cultures?

3. In what ways might culture be universal in today's world?

4. In what ways might modern cultures vary around the world?

5. What are some views of the concept or idea of "culture?"

3 **Vocabulary Preview.** Here are some vocabulary items from the reading. You can learn them now or come back to them later.

Nouns		**Adjectives**		**Phrases**
cathedrals	religions	proud	unpleasant	works of art
painters	weapons	magnificent	polite	classical music
sculptors	a concept	world-famous	rude	concert halls
museums		first-class *top*		in a loud voice
literature	**Verbs**	significant	**Adverbs**	one another
theaters	interrupt	ancient	loudly	cultural diversity
discoveries	wave	amazing	pleasantly	and another thing
medicine	object	enthusiastic *very excited*	impolitely	
achievements	invent	pleasant		
	agree			
	irritate			

maximum (handwritten above Adjectives)

enjoyable, friendly, nice (handwritten)

Read

4   Read the following material quickly. Then read the explanations and do the exercises after the reading.

Cross-Cultural Conversation

A   "You want to talk about culture?" Alain began the conversation in a proud voice. "The United States is only a few hundred years old. Americans aren't lucky enough to *have* any culture—they have *zero* culture, I say." He made the sign for "nothing" with his hand.

B   "You are completely correct," interrupted Werner, loudly. He was pointing his finger. "*Old Europe* of the last thousand years—it's easy to tell *that's* where the great culture was! The age of architecture—just look at the magnificent historical cathedrals and castles. Our ancestral art legacy—if you don't know the works of world-famous painters and sculptors from previous centuries, it's *essential* to see them in our excellent museums. And *everyone* has the chance to experience our classical literature and music in first-class theaters and concert halls. I just gave you a logical description of a long and significant cultural history!"

C   "You call a short millennium a cultural history?" Waving his arms, Kamil was objecting strongly to Werner's views. "The *real* beginning of culture— I mean, *significant civilization*—was in the Middle East and Africa over *five thousand* years ago. Ancient communities not only knew how to create magnificent architecture and art; they also made amazing scientific and technological discoveries. They *invented* things. They figured out how to write and do mathematics; they studied astronomy—the science of the skies, the sun, and the planets—and invented the calendar. They even had medicine; it's important to remember that the ancient religions came from that area too. I'm happy to tell you about *their* achievements because they made world civilization possible. *Those* were the civilizations that gave humanity the most meaningful cultural legacy!"

D   With his hands together and his head down, Jade agreed with Kamil. In a soft but nervous voice, he added, "But the *really* important science and technology began to develop in Asia and the Americas. While the ancient Chinese were building walled cities, they organized the first governments. They invented tools for work and weapons for protection. And the native peoples of the Americas had very, very old civilizations and societies. *That* was ancient traditional culture."

E   "Ancient culture? That's a contradiction in definitions!" Grinning, Kevin objected in an enthusiastic way. Going against Jade's views, he said, "It's *impossible* for culture to be old or traditional. The *opposite is* true! Culture isn't dead—it's *alive*. Culture is *modern*! Culture is *now*!"

F   Ken was starting to fall asleep, but suddenly he came alive. "I agree!" he said, interrupting Kevin in a forceful way.

G   "You tell them!" said Kevin, wanting support for his point of view.

H   "Culture is worldwide—it's universal!" answered Ken in his clear speaking style. He had a wide smile on his face. "I mean, like—take today's food culture. With our global fast food, I have to say, everyone eats the same. And because of the worldwide media—movies, TV, CDs (compact disks), the Internet—

everybody knows the same information, plays the same music, enjoys the same stories—even the jokes! And I mean, it's like—people everywhere have a chance to buy the same clothes—all because of advertising. A beautiful young couple in jeans and bright Hawaiian shirts anywhere in the world, eating hamburgers and french fries with their friends from many countries—*finally*, we have a global culture! And *tradition* has nothing to do with it!"

I   However, Monika was of another opinion. "You want to call modern movies, music, food, and clothes *culture*?" she said, beginning to get irritated. "Culture isn't about the *sameness* of people in communities around the world; it's about their *differences*. Like—it's important for people to *greet* one another in various ways, and they need to use different titles and follow a variety of social rules in their relationships. Some societies are formal, while others are informal, or casual. Some groups are friendly, and others aren't. And another example is the diverse use of language—is it direct or indirect? How do communication styles include motions, gestures, facial expressions, and other body language? And *customs* are so interesting! They're what people of different national groups *do* in their everyday lives and on special occasions like holidays or celebrations. Culture means *cultural diversity*. What makes life amusing? It's the *variety* of cultures around the world, its contradictions and opposites!"

J   "Why are you talking so much?" interrupted Alain, impolitely.

K   "Yeah, and why don't you understand what culture is?" said Werner in a loud voice.

L   "And another thing—what's your problem with ancient civilizations and tradition?" disagreed Kamil with an unpleasant expression on his face. He liked to contradict Monika in a rude way.

M   "And why do you always have a *different* view of things?" asked Kevin and Brandon. They weren't smiling either, and they wanted to talk a lot more.

After You Read

5 **Recognizing Conversation in Paragraph Form.** In a selection that explains something, the information appears in paragraphs—with each paragraph about a different topic within the wider subject of the whole reading. Explanatory material can appear in other forms, however. For instance, opinions and views on a topic can be in the form of a conversation—with the words of each speaker between quotation marks (" ") in a different paragraph.

In the reading "Cross-Cultural Conversation," the speakers talk about different definitions or elements (features) of the concept (idea) of "culture." For each section of the reading, check (✓) the topic.

1. A, B

_____✓_____ the long cultural legacy of the arts in European history

_____ the importance of international education through the centuries

2.   C, D

___✓___ humanity's scientific and technological discoveries and achievements

_____ the business practices of cultural groups in Africa and the Americas

3.   E — H

_____ the differences among ancient cultures on various continents

___✓___ the cultural sameness and similarities among modern peoples

4.   I

___✓___ cultural diversity—how groups vary in their styles and customs

_____ attitudes toward nature in a variety of times and places

5.   J — M

_____ definitions of the word *society*—according to various world cultures

___✓___ different cultural ways of discussing ideas and telling opinions

Which phrase best tells the topic or subject of the whole reading "Cross-Cultural Conversation"? Circle its letter. Give the reasons for your answer.

a.   the relationships among human beings in a variety of family structures and forms

b.   education, food, community, family, and other subjects of interest to young people

(c.) various opinions about the meaning and importance of the concept of "culture"

d.   variety in contrast to sameness in the global community of the Internet

6 **Understanding the Point.**   Following are some false statements about the points of the reading selection "Cross-Cultural Conversation." Make true statements by changing the underlined words. No. 5 is about the whole reading. The first item is done as an example.

1.   Some people believe that a country with a ~~short~~ [long] history has more of a cultural legacy than ~~old~~ [young] countries—especially in its ~~communication styles and body language~~ [technology and religion].

2.   For other thinkers, civilization ~~didn't include~~ [include] old architecture and art; it also meant human ~~opinions and statements~~ [invention and discovery] in mathematics, astronomy, medicine, weapons, city building, and the like.

3.   Young people around the world ~~don't want~~ [want] to think about food, media, music, or clothes as culture because those things are ~~ancient,~~ [modern] and ~~nobody~~ [everybody] seems to like the same kinds.

4. According to others, diversity is <u>less significant than</u> sameness in discussions about culture; such speakers say that people should <u>decrease and forget about</u> their differences.

increase and remember

5. People from various <u>cathedrals and castles</u> around the world have <u>exactly the same</u> views on the meaning and importance of the concept "culture." In fact, it's common for them to express their ideas in <u>similar</u> ways.

around the world   *different*

different

7 **Figuring Out New Vocabulary from Context.**   Only occasionally does reading material give clear explanations of vocabulary items that are new or difficult for language learners; there aren't always punctuation or phrase clues to meaning either. Even so, readers may not have to look in the dictionary to understand important words and phrases. Instead, they can *figure out* their general meaning from the context.

In the reading "Cross-Cultural Conversation," the speakers talk about two kinds of culture. One meaning of *culture* is "a society's achievements in the arts, science, or government." Werner has that meaning in mind when he talks about the cathedrals, castles, and museums of Europe. Another meaning of *culture* is "the values, beliefs, and customs of a society." Monika has that meaning in mind when she talks about greetings, titles, and social rules.

Here are some sentences with important vocabulary from the reading selection. From the context, answer the questions about the <u>underlined</u> items. Then circle the letter of the explanation that seems the most logical in the context.

1. Some examples of the <u>architecture</u> of old Europe are the magnificent cathedrals and castles. The design and building styles of modern <u>architecture</u> are excellent too.
   What are some examples of old *architecture*?

   _____

   What are some excellent features of modern *architecture*?

   _____

   What does the noun *architecture* mean in these sentences?
   a. the form and plan of buildings and other structures
   b. the art and science of designing the study of classical literature
   c. people that study the culture of old Europe and other societies

2. Perhaps the real beginning of <u>civilization</u>—with its scientific and technological discoveries and inventions—was in the Middle East and Africa. Over five thousand years ago, ancient <u>civilizations</u> had astronomy, mathematics, medicine, government, and so on.
   Where and when did *civilization* begin?

   _____

   What kinds of things did ancient *civilizations* have?

   _____

Which word is a synonym of the word *civilization*?

a.   astronomy

b.   technology

c.   culture

3.   The cultural <u>legacy</u> of ancient Chinese and Indian peoples included walled cities, the first governments, tools for work, and weapons for protection. Modern peoples built on this <u>legacy</u>.

Does a *legacy* come from the past, the present, or the future?

_____

What kinds of things might a *legacy* include?

_____

What is a possible explanation of the word *legacy*?

a.   a gift of money that somebody gives to another person

b.   ideas and achievements passed from earlier generations to modern society

c.   the state or condition of being legal; not against the law

4.   "For me, the idea of ancient culture creates a <u>contradiction</u> in definitions," said Kevin, going against Jade's views. "Only modern things can be part of culture. Of course, people that like classical art and music will <u>contradict</u> me."

According to Kevin, what kinds of things are part of culture?

_____

Do people that like classical art and music agree with him?

_____

Do Kevin and Jade have the same or very different opinions?

_____

What might the noun *contradiction* and the verb *contradict* mean?

a.   (noun) the opposition of two opinions; (verb) to say that someone's ideas are wrong

b.   (noun) the short forms of two words together; (verb) to put words together

c.   (noun) wearing a Hawaiian shirt in an ancient culture; (verb) to eat hamburgers with french fries

5.   Because of the worldwide <u>media</u>—movies, TV, CDs, the internet, newspapers, magazines—everybody knows same information, plays the same music, and enjoys the same jokes.

What are some examples of "the worldwide media?"

_____

What do the *media* give to people around the world?

_____

How might you define the phrase *the media*?

    a.   events that appear in the daily news and that everyone knows about

    b.   the tradition of being in the middle—not on the extremes of possible views

    c.   the combination of visual, sound, and printed ways to send ideas around the world

For more practice, in the reading material look for and figure out the general meanings of other vocabulary items, such as *in a proud voice, logical, significant, magnificent, essential, amazing, invented, astronomy, tools and weapons, enthusiastic, going against, alive, a wide smile, greet, diverse, cultural diversity, an unpleasant expression,* and so on. For each item, explain the reasoning for your guesses.

8 **Recognizing the Details of Opinions.**   Clearly, the speakers in the "Cross-Cultural Conversation" have diverse opinions and views about the value and importance of their various concepts of culture. Some words in their speeches are in *italics*; this special kind of slanted print can mean the speakers think the words are important to their point, so they say them more strongly than other words. An exclamation point, a punctuation mark that looks like this (!), also shows strong emphasis.

According to their opinions, what do the speakers in the "Cross-Cultural Conversation" value within their concepts of culture? Circle the letters of *all* the correct answers to each question.

1.   Alain and Werner felt that the age of a culture added to the value of its fine arts. Which elements (parts) of culture were essential to them?

    a.   fast food and junk food
    b.   old painting and sculpture
    c.   literature and classical music
    d.   human feelings and emotions
    e.   the architecture of buildings and structures
    f.   things in museums, theater plays, and concerts

2.   Kamil and Jade most valued the ancient civilizations of the Middle East, Africa, and the Americas. What things did they include in "a cultural legacy?"

    a.   international business
    b.   magnificent architecture and art
    c.   scientific discoveries and invention
    d.   writing and mathematics
    e.   the study of astronomy
    f.   protected cities and government structure

3. Kevin and Brandon are happy that modern culture is worldwide and similar all over the planet. Which features did they find the most important?

    a. ancient religions
    b. the historical structure of the family
    c. food from global chains
    d. Indian rock tools and weapons
    e. the media of movies, TV, and the web
    f. advertising for clothes and other things

4. Monika preferred cultural diversity to sameness. What things did she include in her concept of culture?

    a. greetings, including titles and names
    b. relationship and other social rules
    c. formality in contrast to informality
    d. directness and indirectness in language
    e. body language and movements
    f. everyday and special occasion customs

5. In what ways did the group members discuss their ideas and opinions with one another?

    a. proudly and with emphasis
    b. strongly and forcefully
    c. in a loud or a soft voice
    d. grinning or smiling—or not
    e. with a clear speaking style
    f. agreeing or disagreeing

For more practice, turn back to the Before You Read section on page 153 and answer the questions.

Discussing the Reading

9   In small groups, talk about your answers to the following questions. Then tell the class the most interesting information and ideas.

1. In your view of the concept of culture, which elements are essential—or very important? Why?
2. According to your experience, in what ways are world cultures similar or alike? Which features are different? Explain your views.
3. Which is better for humanity and the future of the world—one global culture or cultural diversity all over the planet? Explain your reasoning or logic.

PART 4	# Writing

Before You Write

Exploring Ideas

> ### *Folktales*
>
> Every culture has its own folktales. These stories tell us a lot about the culture in earlier times. Folktales are not written by one person. They are also not written at one time. Each story develops over many years. In this way, folktales come from the imagination of the whole culture.
>
> Folktales are usually told in time sequence. There is not usually a lot of description. Since the stories were told aloud, a simple story line helped the memory of both the storyteller and the listener.

1   Read the beginning of this folktale from Saxony, a part of Germany.

A powerful king was once lost in a forest. It was late at night. He was tired, cold, and hungry. He at last reached the hut of a poor miner. The miner was working and his wife was home alone. She was cooking potatoes on the fire when she heard someone at the door.

The king asked her for help. "We are very poor," she explained, "but we can give you potatoes for dinner and a blanket on the floor for a bed." The king gratefully accepted the kind old woman's offer. He sat down to dinner with her and ate a large plate of potatoes. "These are better than the best beef," he exclaimed. Then he stretched out on the floor and quickly fell asleep.

(Early) the (next morning,) the king washed in the river and then returned to the hut. He thanked the woman for her kindness and gave her a gold coin. Then he left.

(As soon as) the miner returned home, his wife told him about the visitor. (Then) she showed her husband the gold coin. The husband realized that the visitor was the king. (However,) he felt that the gold coin was too generous. He decided to take a bushel of potatoes to the king.

The miner went to the palace to see the king. "Your majesty," he said, "last night you gave my wife a gold coin for a hard bed and a plate of potatoes. You were too generous. (Therefore,) I have brought you a bushel of potatoes, which you said were better than the best beef. Please accept them."

The miner's words pleased the king. He wanted to reward him for his honesty, so he gave him a beautiful house and a small farm. The miner was very happy and he returned to tell his wife the news.

The poor miner had a brother. His brother was rich but greedy and jealous of anyone who had good luck. (When) he heard his brother's story, he was very upset.

2   Look at these pictures and choose the ending of the story. (If you want, you can make up your own ending.)

3   Make notes for an ending for the story, but do not write it yet. Use these questions as a guide.

1.   What did the brother decide to give the king? *horse*
2.   Was the king happy with the brother? *No.*
3.   What did the king do? *refuse*
4.   How did the brother feel? *angry*

Organizing Ideas

Using a Time Sequence

Writers use time words such as *before, after, as, when, while, then,* and *as soon as* to organize the information in a story.

4 Look at the story again. Make a list of the time words. Compare your list with another student's. Are there any words you missed?

Limiting Information

Remember that it is important to limit what you say. If you include many unnecessary details, your reader or listener will lose interest in your story.

5 Look at your notes. Tell your story to another student, and discuss these questions.

1. Is my ending too complicated or difficult for the reader to understand?
2. Did I include too much description?
3. Can I fit everything into one paragraph?

Write

Developing Cohesion and Style

Using *as soon as*

Use *as soon as* to emphasize that one action happened immediately after another.

Examples:

As soon as the miner got home, his wife told him the story.

The miner ran home to tell his wife *as soon as* he received the gift from the king.

6 Combine these sentences with *as soon as.*

1. The brother heard the story. He decided to give the king a better gift.
    As soon as the brother heard the story, he decided to give the king a better gift.

2. The king talked to the brother. He knew that he was a liar.
    The king talked to the brother as soon as he knew that he was a liar.

3. The king ate dinner. He fell asleep.
    As soon as the king ate dinner, he fell asleep.

4. The miner got the farm. He quit his job.
    As soon as the miner got the farm, he quit his job.

7   Look at the notes for your story and write two sentences with *as soon as*.

Using then

You can use *then* when you are narrating a story: By using *then*, you can make the time sequence clear and not repeat the same words. Compare:

Examples:
I ran out of the house. After I ran out of the house, I saw a man in the street.
I ran out of the house. *Then* I saw a man in the street.

---

8   Rewrite these sentences using *then*.

1. The king washed in the river. He thanked the woman and left.
   The king washed in the river. Then he thanked the women and left.

2. The woman gave the king a plate a potatoes. She gave him a blanket.
   The woman gave the king a plate a potatoes. Then she gave him a blank and a fan.

3. The king gave the woman a coin. He gave the miner a house and a farm.
   After the king gave the woman a coin, he gave the miner a hase and a farm.

4. The brother found a bushel of potatoes. He took them to the king.
   The brother fand a bushel of potatoes. Then he took them to the king.

Using Quotations

A good story tells the reader what the characters are thinking and saying.

- When you write exactly what someone said or thought, you use quotation marks. Use quotation marks in pairs. Use one set at the beginning of the quotation and one at the end.

- A quotation is always set off from the rest of the sentence by a comma, a question mark, or an exclamation point.

- The first word of a quote always starts with a capital letter.

Examples:
"It's not fair that he had such good luck," thought the miner's brother.
"We are very poor," the woman said, "but we can give you potatoes for dinner."
"I am lost and hungry. Can I have dinner and a place to sleep?" asked the king.

---

she said, "It is getting dark because the sun is setting."
"It is getting dark," she said, "because the sun is sitting"
"It is getting dark because the sun is setting," she said.

9 Underline the sentences in the story that tell you what people are thinking and saying. Then look at the notes for your paragraph again. Write the conversation between the king and the brother.

Writing the First Draft

10 Now write your ending to the folktale. Remember to follow these three guidelines:
1. Use time words where they are necessary.
2. Limit the information. Your story should be one paragraph of 100 to 150 words.
3. Use quotations.

Edit and Revise

Editing Practice

Using Editing Symbols

There are some common editing symbols that your teacher or your classmates may use. In Chapter 1 you learned about the caret (^). Here are some other symbols and examples of how they are used.

sp   wrong spelling

      sp

      He is a studint in Texas. → He is a student in Texas.

sf   sentence fragment

      sf

      When I was ten. We moved to New York. →

      When I was ten, we moved to New York.

/   use lowercase (small letters)

      The

      ^ Thief ran out the door. → The thief ran out the door.

  take out this word, letter, or punctuation

      Sylvia sang a song, while she washed the dishes. →

      Sylvia sang a song while she washed the dishes.

○   add punctuation here

      The doctor arrived at ten o'clock○ →

      The doctor arrived at ten o'clock.

11 Edit the following paragraph twice. The first time, check that all the information is really important. The paragraph has about 230 words. It should have about 150 to 170 words. Are there any sentences you can take out? The second time, check that the writer has used time expressions correctly. Make any other changes you think are necessary.

When he was riding home through the forest, he thought of a plan. "I'll give the king my best horse, he thought, then he will have to give me an even better gift!" As soon as breakfast the next day, he went to the palace. The palace was not far from his house. When he got to the palace. He asked to see the king. Tell him I have a present for him, he said. The guard immediately took him to see the king. Your majesty," he said, you know I have the best horses in the land. As king, you should have the best of my horses. If you look out the window, you will see my finest horse in your courtyard." The horse was magnificent. It was a big, black stallion. The king knew that this was not an honest gift. He smiled and said, "Thank you my friend. I accept your kind gift. Now I am going to give you a gift in return. Do you see that bushel of potatoes in the corner? Well those potatoes cost me a house and a farm. I am sure that they are the most expensive potatoes in the land. I would like you to have them." What could the greedy brother do? He lifted the heavy bushel and sadly left the room. As he was leaving, he heard the king laughing.

Editing Your Writing

12   **Editing Using a Checklist.**   Edit your paragraph using the following checklist.

Editing Checklist

1. Content
   a. Is the story clear?
   b. Is all the information important?
2. Organization
   a. Did you use time words when necessary?
   b. Did you add a title?
3. Cohesion and Style
   a. Did you vary the time words and expressions?
   b. Did you include enough description?
   c. Did you use quotations?
4. Grammar
   a. Did you use the correct forms of the past tense?
   b. Did you use the correct forms of the present continuous tense?
   c. Did you use good sentence structure (no fragments)?
5. Form
   a. Did you use commas correctly?
   b. Did you use quotation marks correctly?

13   **Peer Editing.**   Exchange paragraphs with another student. Use editing symbols to edit each other's paragraphs. Discuss your paragraphs. Are there any other changes you should make?

Writing the Second Draft

14   Write the second draft of your paragraph using correct form. Then give it to your teacher for comments.

PART 5	# Grammar

A. The Present Perfect Tense

The present perfect tense is formed with *have/has* + the past participle form of the verb. The present perfect tense often refers to an event that happened at an unknown or unspecified time in the past. It also refers to repeated past actions. Time expressions often used with this meaning of the present perfect include *already, ever, just, recently, still, yet, so far, up to now, once, twice, three times*, etc. No specific time is given in a past perfect statement or question. (If we use past time expressions such as *yesterday* or *last week*, we use the past tense.)

Statements

Purpose	Examples		Notes
	Affirmative	**Negative**	
Actions or situations at an unspecified time in the past	My parents **have** just **returned** from there. I**'ve been** to Canada.	I **have never traveled to** the Taj Mahal. I **have not been** to India.	For regular verbs, the past participle is the same as the simple past tense (verb + *-ed*).
Repeated actions at unspecified times in the past	I**'ve been** to Canada twice. My parents **have visited** there many times.	I **haven't eaten** Indian food more than once or twice. I **haven't played** tennis many times.	For irregular verbs, the past participle often changes spelling and/or pronunciation. See Appendix 2, page 286.

Note: The present perfect can be contracted with subject pronouns: *I've, we've, you've, they've, he's, she's*, and *it's*. The negative contractions are *haven't* and *hasn't*.

Yes / No Questions

	Examples	Possible Answers	
Affirmative	**Have** you ever **been** to New York? **Have** you ever **seen** the Empire State Building?	Yes, I have. Yes, I have.	No, I haven't. No, I haven't
Negative	**Haven't** you ever **been** to New York? **Haven't** you ever **seen** the Empire State Building?	Yes, I have. Yes, I have.	No, I haven't. No, I haven't.

Information Questions

	Examples	Possible Answers
Affirmative	Who **has lived** abroad? Why **have** you **come** here? How many times **have** you **been** here? How much money **have** you **spent**?	Juan has. To learn about other cultures. Twice. A lot!
Negative	Who **hasn't taken** any pictures? Why **haven't** you **brought** a map?	They haven't. I don't need one.

1   Fill in the blanks with the present perfect tense of the verbs in parentheses.

Queridos mamãe and papai,

I'm sorry I (not, write) ___haven't written___ sooner, but I (not, have) ___haven't had___
                          1   2
a free moment! There (be) ___has been___ so much to do here in London.
                            3
I (meet) ___have met___ some great people and I am having a wonderful time.
            4

    There's so much to tell you, I don't know where to begin. I'll start by telling

you about some of the things that I (do) ___have done___ here. I (be)
                                            5
___have been___ to Westminster Abbey, which is the most famous church
    6
in England. Also, I (visit) ___have visited___ Buckingham Palace, which is
                               7
where the queen lives! I've (ride) ___ridden___ double decker buses
                                       8
a few times and I (eat) ___have eaten___ traditional English foods like
                          9
Yorkshire Pudding and Steak and Kidney Pie. (I'm not crazy about the food, so I

(lose) ___have lost___ some weight!).
          10

    I (speak) ___have spoken___ with some English people and they (teach)
                 11
___have taught___ me a few things about British culture. I (learn) ___have learned___
    12   13
that pubs are where people go to meet friends and relax. I (go) ___have gone___
                                                                    14
to pubs a few times, and I really like them! In the pubs, I (play) ___have played___
                                                                       15
a few games of darts, a popular English bar game. I (watch) ___have watched___
                                                                16
a few soccer matches on TV at the pubs. I (discover) ___have discovered___
                                                          17
that soccer is almost as popular here as it is back home in Brazil!

I (be) ___have been___ amazed at how much tea people drink
<u>18</u>

here. I (try) ___have tried___ the coffee, but it's usually very weak. I (not, be)
<u>19</u>

___haven't been___ able to find really strong coffee like we drink in Brazil.
<u>20</u>

Unfortunately, the weather (not, be) ___haven't been___ very good. It's
<u>21</u>

often rainy and foggy here. I (not see) ___haven't seen___ sunshine since I left
<u>22</u>

Brazil. With all of this rain, I (catch) ___have caught___ a little cold.
<u>23</u>

I can't wait to tell you more about my trip. I (take) ___have taken___ many photos
<u>24</u>

to show you and I (buy) ___have bought___ many souvenirs for everyone at home.
<u>25</u>

I really like it here, but I think I'd better leave soon — my friends (tell) ___have told___
<u>26</u>

me that I (begun) ___have begun___ to speak with a British accent!
<u>27</u>

Besos,
Alex

2 Write present perfect questions for the following answers. Be careful to use the correct
question form (yes/no questions *or* information questions) as appropriate.

Example: 1. Q: ___Has he eaten Indian food?___

A: Yes, he has eaten Indian food.

2. Q: ___How many times has he eaten Indian food?___

A: Only once or twice.

3. Q: ___Where has he eaten Indian food?___

A: In London.

A.

1. Q: _____?
   A: Yes, she has taken a lot of photographs.

2. Q: _____?
   A: Probably about 6 or 7 rolls.

3. Q: _____?
   A: Mostly of churches and castles.

B.

1. Q: _____?
   A: Yes, I've spent a lot of money on transportation.

2. Q: _____?
   A: About £40.

3. Q: _____?
   A: Double decker buses, the tube, and a few taxi rides.

Video Activities: Chinese New Year

Before You Watch.   Discuss these questions in small groups.

1. Have you ever seen a Chinese New Year celebration? Describe this experience.
2. Talk about your New Year celebration last year. Where were you? Who was with you? How did you celebrate? Was it a happy time for you?

Watch.   Write answers to these questions.

1. In which season is the Chinese New Year? ___ winter ___
2. Who is the blond woman? ___ tourist ___
3. Which Chinese customs did you see in the video? ___ lion dancing ___ fire cracker ___

Watch Again.

1. How is the man going to celebrate the Chinese New Year? Place a check next to the things he says.

   _____ eat
   _____ drink alcohol
   _____ buy gifts for his children
   _____ see dancing
   _____ light firecrackers

2. Complete this paragraph: "Some men are doing the Red Lion Dance. They dance for _____. If the _____ likes the dance, he gives them _____ envelopes with lucky _____ inside."

3. Why do people light firecrackers on the New Year?

4. The New Year celebrations will continue for _____ days.

After You Watch.   There are many words for describing noises. In the video, you learned that the noise of firecrackers is called a "bang." Below are some more "noise words." With the help of a dictionary, match them with the items on the right that make that noise.

_____	1. boom	a. a door closing loudly
_____	2. crash	b. a baby
_____	3. cry	c. a lion or a waterfall
_____	4. jangle	d. a car accident
_____	5. purr	e. a chicken
_____	6. ring	f. something falling into water
_____	7. roar	g. keys
_____	8. slam	h. a happy cat
_____	9. splash	i. a bell
_____	10. squeak	j. thunder
_____	11. squawk	k. a metal object that needs oil (like the hinges of an old door)

Chapter 7

Entertainment and the Media

IN THIS CHAPTER

Listening
- Listening for main ideas
- Listening for specific information
- Identifying stressed words and reductions
- Taking notes on a news report
  (specific information)

Speaking
- Expressing opinions, agreeing, and disagreeing
- Summarizing a news report

Reading
- Previewing vocabulary
- Reading: Media Stories
- Classifying stories
- Putting events in order

- Summarizing a plot
- Explaining reasons for choices

Writing
- Developing ideas: categorizing, summarizing,
  writing a title
- Using adjectives
- Using the historical present
- Writing a summary about your favorite movie
- Editing for use of two or more adjectives

Grammar
- The past continuous tense
- The simple past versus the past continuous
- *When* and *while*

PART 1	# Listening to Conversations

Before You Listen

1 **Prelistening Questions.**   Before you listen, talk about television with a partner.

1. How many hours of TV do you watch a week?
2. How many television sets do you have in your house? Where are they?
3. In your opinion, what's the best way to get the news: from television, a newspaper, or the Internet? Why?
4. Say two good things and two bad things about television.

My favorite series is friend
It's comedy

2   **Vocabulary Preview.** Complete these sentences about TV-watching habits. Use each expression only once.

I'm not a channel surf

<u>g</u>   1.   As soon as I get home from work, I

a.   a couch potato.

<u>F</u>   2.   When friends come to visit, we usually

b.   channel surf. *I like channel surfing*

c.   turn down the volume.

<u>I</u>   3.   When I don't like a TV show, I

d.   the TV on.

<u>C</u>   4.   The commercials are very loud, so I

e.   a waste of time.

<u>D</u>   5.   I prefer to study in a quiet room, without

f.   turn the TV off.

<u>B</u>   6.   To find a good program on TV, I
   don't look in the newspaper. I
   usually just

g.   turn on the TV.

h.   an average week.

i.   change channels.

<u>A</u>   7.   I don't like to exercise or go out;
   I prefer to stay home and watch
   TV. I guess I am

j.   remote control.

<u>J</u>   8.   It's easy to change channels with a

<u>E</u>   9.   I think TV is very entertaining and
   educational, but other people think it's

<u>H</u>   10.   I watch 20 hours of TV during

Listen

3   **Listening for Main Ideas.**   Ming is visiting Jack. They are talking about television.

1.   Close your book and listen to their conversation. Listen for the answers to these questions.

   1.   What are Jack and Ming discussing? *Watching T.V.*

   2.   Why does Ming call Jack a "couch potato"? *Jack always has the TV on*

watching TV. is a waste of time
   3.   What is Ming's opinion about watching TV? Does Jack agree or disagree? *disagree*

   4.   What do they both think about TV commercials? *They both hate TV commercials.*

   5.   What does Jack suggest at the end? *Jack lets Ming has the remote control*

   6.   What is Ming's idea? *When she comes over ∧turn the TV off* *just*

2.   Compare answers with a partner.

Stress

4   **Listening for Stressed Words.**   Listen to the conversation again.

1.   Some of the stressed words are missing. During each pause, repeat the phrase or sentence. Then fill in the blanks with words from the list.

always	disagree	mean	soap
average	hate	news (2 times)	some
better	information	newspaper	turn
channels	Internet	off	TV
control	joking	over	waste
couch	listen	read	you're
crazy	magazine	six	

Ming: Hey, ____listen____ to this. The ____average____ American family watches __six__ hours of TV a day.

Jack: A day? You're ____joking____.

Ming: No, it says so right here in this ____magazine____. Hmm, I guess ____you're____ an average American, Jack. When I come over to your place, you ____always____ have your ____TV____ on.

Jack: Come on. Are you saying I'm a ____couch____ potato?

Ming: Yeah. I really think watching TV is a ____waste____ of time.

Jack: Well, I ____disagree____. ____Some____ programs are silly, like those ____soap____ operas. But what about sports or the ____news____? You watch those sometimes, don't you?

Ming: Well, actually, for the ____news____, I prefer the ____newspaper____. Or the ____Internet____.

Jack: Why?

Ming: First, because they give you a lot more ____information____. And I can ____read____ them any time I want. Plus, I ____hate____ all the TV commercials.

Jack: I know what you ____mean____. That's why, when the commercials come on, I just ____turn____ down the volume or change ____channels____.

Ming: Yeah, I noticed that. Channel surfing drives me ____crazy____.

The sky is falling → boring, bad

proud [adj]
pride [n]

Jack: Well, then next time you come_____over_____, I'll let you have the remote ____control____.

Ming: That's so sweet. But I have a _____better_____ idea. Next time I come over, let's just turn the TV____off____.

2. Now read the conversation with a partner. Practice stressing words correctly.

Reductions

5 **Comparing Long and Reduced Forms.** Listen to the following sentences from the conversation. They contain reduced forms. Repeat them after the speaker.

Reduced form*	**Long form**
1. <u>Areya</u> saying I'm a couch potato?	Are you saying I'm a couch potato?
2. You watch those sometimes, <u>doncha</u>?	You watch those sometimes, don't you?
3. I know <u>whatcha</u> mean.	I know what you mean.
4. I'll <u>letcha</u> have the remote control.	I'll let you have the remote control.

_____
* *Note:* The underlined forms are not acceptable spellings in written English.

6 **Listening for Reductions.** Listen to the following sentences. You'll hear the reduced forms of some words.

1. Repeat each sentence during the pause. Then write the long forms in the blanks.

B: ___Are___ ___you___ ___calling___ the movie theater?

A: Uh-huh. Why, what's wrong? ___Don't___ ___you___ ___want___ ___to___ go to the movies tonight?

B: To tell ___you___ the truth, I'm pretty tired. But we ___can___ go to an early show. ___Do___ ___you___ know ___what___ ___you___ ___want___ ___to___ see?

A: Not really. I'll ___let___ ___you___ choose. Terminator III is playing at 8:00 and James Bond is at 10:00.

B: Let's see Terminator. I'm tired now and by 10 o'clock I'm ___going___ ___to___ be dead.

After You Listen

7   **Vocabulary Review.**   Look at the ten statements in Activity 2. Check [✓] the sentences that are true for you. Discuss the sentences that are <u>not true</u> for you. Use the new vocabulary in your discussion.

Example:

> Number 6 is not true in my case. I don't like to <u>channel surf</u>. Before I <u>turn on</u> the TV, I always choose a program from the TV guide. But my brother <u>channel surfs</u> all the time.

Using Language

> ### *Expressing Opinions, Agreeing, and Disagreeing*
>
> When Ming and Jack had different opinions about television, they used the following language:
>
> > *Ming:* **I really think** watching TV is a waste of time.
> > *Jack:* Well, **I disagree.**
>
> There are many other expressions English speakers use to express opinions, to agree and to disagree.

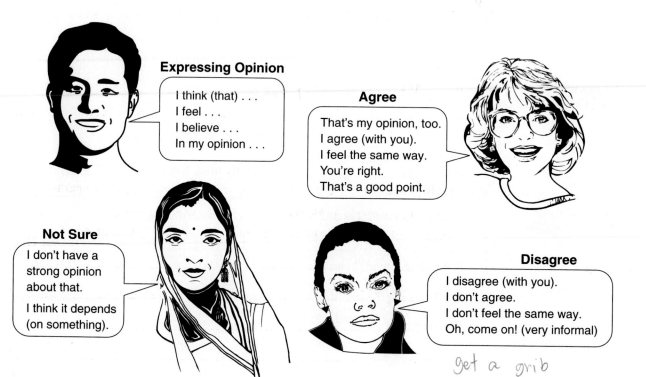

Expressing Opinion

I think (that) . . .
I feel . . .
I believe . . .
In my opinion . . .

Agree

That's my opinion, too.
I agree (with you).
I feel the same way.
You're right.
That's a good point.

Not Sure

I don't have a strong opinion about that.

I think it depends (on something).

Disagree

I disagree (with you).
I don't agree.
I don't feel the same way.
Oh, come on! (very informal)

get a grib

8   **Expressing Opinions.**   Work in groups of three. Look at the ten topics below. Play the role of A, B, and C. Change roles with each topic.

Student A: Give your opinion about the topic. Give reasons.
Student B: Agree or disagree. Give reasons.
Student C: Agree or disagree with A or B. Give reasons.

Example:

Ming: I think watching TV is a waste of time. Most programs are stupid or boring.

Jack: I disagree with you. Many programs are useful — if you choose them carefully.

Peter: I agree with Ming. There are so many better things to do than sit and watch TV.

1. violence on television
2. cigarette advertisements on the street (billboards)
3. magazine stories about private lives of famous people
4. high salaries of superstar athletes
5. high salaries of movie stars
6. low salaries of teachers
7. government control of television programs (censorship)
8. high price of rock concert tickets
9. rap music
10. age limit for drinking alcohol

PART 2

Recalling Main Ideas

Before You Listen

1   **Prelistening Questions.**   Before you listen, talk about accidents with a partner.

1. Have you ever seen a traffic accident? Describe what happened.
2. Imagine a news report about an airplane crash. Ask four questions about it:

What _happened_ ?

Where _did an airplane crash_ ?

When _did the accident occur_ ?

How many / who _people got injured_ ?

Who is responsible?
Who made the mistake?

back seat driver

2 Vocabulary Preview.   You will hear the underlined words in a news report. Before you listen, write the letter of the correct definition beside each sentence. Note: two of the words have very similar meanings!

	Sentences		Definitions
E	1.	What was the <u>top story</u> on the evening news last night? *most important*	a. rider, person in the car besides the driver
G	2.	The airplane left Chicago at 3:00 and <u>landed</u> in San Francisco at 8:00.	b. have no more
A	3.	My sports car is so small, I can only take one <u>passenger</u>.	c. person who saw what happened
F	4.	He had two serious <u>injuries</u>: a broken arm and a broken knee.	d. damage to the body
D	5.	She had to go to the hospital because she was <u>hurt</u> in the accident.	e. the first story in a news program
C	6.	The police talked to a <u>witness</u> who saw the accident.	f. damage to the body
B	7.	I <u>ran out of</u> money, so I asked my parents for $100.	g. arrived, touched the ground

Listen

3 Listening for Main Ideas.   Listen to a news report about an airplane crash.

1. As you listen, write the key words in the space provided.

_____

_____

_____

_____

2.   Which of the following is the main idea of the story?

   a.   An airplane crashed onto the highway and everyone died.

   b.   Two people saw the airplane crash and called the police.

   c.   An airplane landed on the highway, but nobody died.

4   **Taking Notes on Specific Information.**   Listen again. This time, take notes about the following details.

1.   Location of the plane: _highway 1_

2.   Number of passengers: _6 passengers_

3.   Number of passengers injured: _three of the passengers injured_

4.   Type of injuries: _1 broken leg, 2 back hurt_

5.   Number of people injured on the ground: _no one_

6.   Possible cause of crash: _run out of gasoline could cause this accident_

After You Listen

5   **Summarizing Main Ideas.**   Compare notes with a partner. Together, summarize the news report. Use your notes from Activities 3 and 4.

6   **Vocabulary Review.**   Discuss your answers to the following questions with a partner. Use the underlined vocabulary in your answers.

1.   Did you watch the news on TV last night? What was the <u>top story</u>?

2.   If an airplane can't <u>land</u> because of bad weather, what can the pilot do?

3.   On a long car trip, do you prefer to be the <u>passenger</u> or the driver? Why?

4.   Tell about some <u>injuries</u> you received when you were a child. Were you <u>hurt</u> while playing or while doing sports? Were you seriously <u>hurt</u>?

5.   If you <u>run out of</u> money while on vacation, what can you do?

6.   Have you ever been a <u>witness</u> to a crime? Did you report it to the police?

Talk It Over

Summarizing News Reports.

1.   Watch a news program the day before your class.

2.   Choose one of the reports.

3.   Tell the class a short summary of the report. Use simple words and focus on the key ideas only. Talk about *who, what, where, when,* and *why.*

PART 3   Reading

Before You Read

1 Vocabulary Preview.   Here are some vocabulary items from the reading. You can learn them now or come back to them later.

Nouns *order*	a motel	singles	transfer *offer*	halfway
a sequence *step by step*	a swamp *brown water*	roommates	propose *to make a suggestion*	neat
fiction	an investigator	characters		optimistic
a series *continue*	a skeleton *bone of the whole body*		**Adjectives**	
an adventure	a murderer	**Verbs**	animated *happy excited*	**Phrases**
a drama	a hunter	stab	musical	science fiction
a comedy	explorers	investigate	run-down	get the best of *bother*
an episode	gorillas	sink	spooky *a little scary*	a rocking chair
plots *story*	imagination	kill	bloody* *scary*	the shower curtain
an enemy	a vehicle	raise	shadowy	
a bank	galaxies *star, planet*	capture	suspenseful	
temptation	a shutdown	recover		

Handwritten annotations: Don't let the get best of you → don't worried about

* This is a swear word in British English; it should be used with caution.

Read

2 Classifying Stories and Putting Events in Order.   Most kinds of programs in the media include stories — sequences of events that are fact or fiction — true or untrue. Like real history (the study of past events), media stories tell what happened, most often in time order. Here are the kinds of stories that most often appear in movies.

_____ adventure or action	_____ comedy
_____ crime or mystery story	_____ suspense or horror
_____ story based on history	_____ science fiction
_____ serious drama	_____ animated cartoon
_____ musical	

Following are four story plots—that is, they are present-time descriptions of the actions or events of a real movie or TV show that is or was well known worldwide. On the lines before some of the listed story types write the paragraph letters A, B, C, and D. (You can write the same letter more than once, but you will not find stories of all nine types.) After you skim each plot description, circle the number 1, 2, or 3 of the movie title or the name of the TV show that—in your opinion or experience—best fits the events.

Media Stories

In what movie does this sequence of events occur?

1. *Psycho* (a psychological suspense film directed by Alfred Hitchcock in 1960)

2. *The Public Enemy* (a drama about the social forces that cause violent crime)

3. *Gone with the Wind* (a world-famous 1939 American Civil War drama)

terrific → good
terrible → bad

not consistent
emotion

A

Marion, who works in a real-estate office, is depressed about her life — especially her unhappy love relationship. Because she is feeling ill, her supervisor lets her leave early; he gives her $40,000 in cash from a house sale to put in the bank on her way home. However, temptation gets the best of the moody young woman. With the cash in an envelope, she packs her bags and drives out of town. On a dark lonely road, a severe thunderstorm forces her to stop at the run-down Bates Motel. There is a spooky old house high on a hill behind the motel, with the form of an old woman in a rocking chair at the window. Norman Bates, the motel owner, is happy to sign in a guest, but his mother shouts at him angrily. After a conversation with Norman, Marion goes to her room. When she is in the shower, the bathroom door opens. In a very famous, very bloody murder scene, the shadowy figure of an old woman pulls aside the shower curtain, and stabs the motel guest to death. Horrified, Norman cleans up the room, puts Marion's body in her car, and pushes the car into the swamp.

Worried about her and the stolen money, Marion's sister, lover, and boss send out a detective, who finally arrives at the Bates Motel. Suspicious of Norman's strange behavior, the investigator goes into the scary house, where the dark shape of an old "woman" at the top of the stairs kills him too — with a long knife. Others come to investigate. After many suspenseful scenes, they discover that Norman's "mother" is a skeleton. The murderer in the old woman's clothes was Norman Bates himself, who has turned more and more into his mother.

rocking chair

In what movie (produced in many versions) do these events happen?

1. *Robinson Crusoe* (an adventure story about a man who lives alone on an island)

2. *A Night to Remember* (the film about the sinking of the ship *Titanic*)

3. *Tarzan, the Ape Man* (the first of a series based on the "Lord of the Jungle" characters)

B | After a hurricane sinks their ship to sink off the coast of Africa, a British couple finds their way to land with their baby son. However, the parents are killed by a wild animal. A gorilla (the largest of the humanlike monkeys) finds the baby, brings him home to her mate, and raises the helpless human in the jungle. As a result, he grows to adulthood in the natural ape community. Nevertheless, the young man's peaceful life in the jungle soon changes. To study African wildlife in its natural environment, Professor Porter arrives with his daughter Jane and a hunter named Clayton. When the explorers meet the jungle man, at first they think he is "the missing link" (a being halfway between an animal and a human being). Therefore, they are surprised to discover that he is as human as they are. When he begins to feel strange, unfamiliar emotions toward Jane, the man that grew up in the jungle becomes very confused. He wants to be with his own kind but doesn't want to leave to the gorilla family that raised him—especially since Clayton sees the apes not as friends but as animals to hunt and kill. When Jane has to leave with her father, the ape-man is very sad and upset. Even so, he saves the white people when they are captured, and Jane stays with him in the jungle.

What popular American TV series are these events from?

1. *The Twilight Zone* (amazing stories about the effects of the human imagination)

2. *Superman* (the adventures of a being from another planet with superhuman powers)

3. *Star Trek: The Next Generation* (futuristic adventures of travelers in space)

c | The star ship *Enterprise* (a flying vehicle that travels to other galaxies at amazing speeds) stops at a space station for repairs. The four Bynars (beings with computerized brains) that are doing maintenance seemed worried. Suddenly, they realize the ship is about to explode and order evacuation. Everyone leaves except Picard, the captain, and Riker, the second man in command, who don't hear the alert. After everyone else reaches the starbase (the space station), the problem mysteriously corrects itself, and the ship disappears. As the crew on the starbase try to figure out a way to recover the *Enterprise*, the captain and his helper discover what has happened. They instantly transfer themselves to the bridge, where they find the Bynars unconscious, dying, and asking for help.

The ship reaches Bynarus, the Bynars' planet. Because of an exploded star that destroyed the planet's center computer, Bynarus is dead too. The Bynars needed the *Enterprise* to store the data from the planet during the shutdown time. Picard and Riker manage to get into the Bynarus file and restart the computer. The Bynars come back to life. Undamaged, the ship returns to the starbase.

In what well-known TV series — especially popular with young people — do these characters play roles?

1. *All in the Family* (a funny show about a working-class man and his wife and their daughter and son-in-law—all in the same house)

2. *Friends* (a popular show, known worldwide, about the relationships and situations of a group of friends in New York)

3. *The Brady Bunch* (a series about a widower with three sons who marries a widow with three daughters)

D | Three men and three women frequently get together at one another's apartments and at a New York cafe. Monica is a restaurant cook who wants everything in order. Her roommate Rachel is her best friend from high school. Ross, Monica's older divorced brother, has long been interested in Rachel. Living across the hall are roommates Chandler, who works in an office, and Joey, who wants to be a successful actor; Joey loves New York, sports, women, and — most of all — himself. The other main character is Phoebe, a strange and very funny folk singer.

In one typical episode, after a romantic dinner Chandler is going to ask Monica to marry him. But Richard, an older man who used to date Monica, happens to come into the restaurant with his date. Chandler feels so uncomfortable that he doesn't propose that night. So he can surprise her later, he pretends that he is not interested in marriage at all. The next day, Richard goes to Monica's workplace to propose. She packs her bags and goes home to her parents—so she can decide what to do. Chandler goes after her, and she accepts his marriage proposal. Meanwhile, the other main characters promise to marry one another if they are still single at age forty.

After You Read

3   **Learning to Summarize.**   A reading selection or paragraph that describes a *plot* (a sequence of events in a story) is most often organized in time order — that is, one event follows another. To prepare to summarize a plot, you might number the main events in the reading material. Then after an introduction to set the scene, you tell the most important things that happened. Here is an example of possible event numbering from plot description A of "Media Stories."

Marion, an employee in a real estate office, is depressed about her life — especially her unhappy love relationship. 1. Because she is feeling ill, her supervisor lets her leave work early; he gives her $40,000 in cash from a house sale to put in the bank on her way home. 2. However, temptation gets the best of the moody young woman. With the cash in an envelope, she packs her bags and drives out of town. 3. On a dark lonely road, a severe thunderstorm forces her to stop at the run-down Bates Motel. There is a spooky old house high on a hill behind the motel, with the form of an old woman in a rocking chair at the window. 4. Norman Bates, the motel owner, is happy to sign in a guest, but his mother shouts at him angrily. 5. After a conversation with Norman, Marion goes to her room.

Work in groups of four. Choose a plot description A – D from "Media Stories." Read it carefully. After a short introduction, list the main events needed to understand the story in as few words as possible. Then tell or read your plot summary to your group.

Discussing the Reading

4   In small groups, talk about your answers to these questions. Then tell the class the most interesting information or ideas.

1.   Of the nine media story types listed in Exercise 2 on page 182, tell which is your favorite, your second favorite, and so on. Give reasons for your preferences.

2.   For several of the kinds of stories, tell the titles of some well-known movies or television series. Working together, how many of each media type can your group name within a time limit?

Choose one of your preferred kinds of media stories. In short form, describe the plot of your favorite story.

Talk It Over

What are your favorites and preferences in the area of media entertainment? On the lines, number your choices 1 through 3 or 4. Then explain the reasons for the order you chose. Compare your choices with those of your classmates.

Media

___ television

___ prerecorded videotapes or DVDs

___ feature films in theaters

___ media on the Internet

___ radio programs

___ other kinds of media

Movies

___ comedies or animated features

___ romance

___ action or thrillers

___ horror or suspense

___ serious drama

___ other kinds of movies

TV Series

___ situation comedies

___ science fiction

___ crime or detective shows

___ law or hospital dramas

___ soap operas

___ other kinds of series

Music

___ classical music

___ jazz or blues

___ popular singers and groups

___ country music or dancing

___ international folk music

___ other kinds of music

Other Programming

___ news or current events

___ talk shows

___ quiz shows

___ educational programs

___ travel shows

___ other kinds of programs

Other Entertainment

___ live theater (plays)

___ cabarets or dinner theater

___ stand-up comedy clubs

___ dance clubs or discos

___ casino gaming

___ other _____

PART 4	# Writing

Before You Write   genre ชนิด

Exploring Ideas

1 **Describing and Categorizing Movies.**   Look at the photos from these six movies and match them with the movie categories below.

<table>
<tr><td>musical
science fiction</td><td>comedy
drama</td><td>horror
action</td></tr>
</table>

1.

Mission Impossible

Category: _action_

2.

Chicken Run

Category: _animation_

3.

Star Wars

Category: _science fiction_

4.

Evita

Category: _drama / musical_

5.

Life is Beautiful

Category: ____drama____

6.

Category: ____horror____

Scream

2   Discuss these questions in small groups.

1.   What kind of movie do you like best?

2.   What kind of movie do you like least?

3.   What is your favorite movie? Who are the stars of that movie? Who are the main characters? What type of movie is it? When and where does it take place?

3   **Building Vocabulary.**   Circle the adjectives that describe your favorite movie.

exciting	realistic	action-packed
funny	sad	well-written
fascinating	imaginative	well-directed
horrifying	touching	frightening
interesting	entertaining	heart-warming

Organizing Ideas

Summarizing a Movie Plot

When you write about your favorite movie, you will include a summary of the plot. A good way to do this is to first write a list of events from the movie and then to choose the most important and interesting events to include in your summary.

4   Look at the following list of events from the movie *Titanic*. Then write a similar list of events in your favorite movie. Don't worry about grammar or form. If there are any words you don't know in English, write them in your native language. You can look them up in a dictionary later if you choose to include the event in your summary.

1. Jack wins a ticket on the Titanic in a card game.
2. Jack sees Rose on the ship.
3. Rose tries to commit suicide and Jack saves her.
4. Rose invites Jack to dinner.
5. Rose's fiancée Cal Hockley gives her a diamond necklace.
6. Rose and Jack go dancing with his friends.
7. Cal's friends tell him that Rose and Jack were together.
8. Cal gets angry with Rose.
9. Jack steals a coat and goes to find Rose.
10. Jack draws Rose's picture. They put the picture in the safe.
11. Jack and Rose see the iceberg that hits the ship.
12. Cal's friends put the diamond necklace in Jack's pocket. Then they accuse him of being a thief.
13. Jack is arrested and locked in a room.
14. The ship begins to sink.
15. Rose helps Jack escape.
16. Jack and Cal put Rose onto lifeboat.
17. Rose jumps back onto ship to be with Jack.
18. Rose and Jack jump into the water.
19. They find something to float on but it won't hold both of them.
20. Jack dies in the water. Rose is saved.

Including Important Information in a Summary

A good movie summary should be more than a list of events. It also tells the problem and events leading to a solution. In addition, a good movie summary includes only important events—the ones that relate the problem and the solution. Finally, a good movie summary shows the relationship between important events.

You can show the relationship between two events by using words such as *when, while, so, but, and, because* and so on.

Examples:

While Rose and Jack are together, an iceberg hits the ship.

Rose is very grateful, *so* she invites Jack to dinner.

Cal accuses Jack of stealing the necklace *and* he is arrested.

Rose gets into a lifeboat *but* she can't leave Jack.

5 Read the following two summaries of *Titanic*. Which is the better summary of the movie? Why? Think about these questions:

■ What is the problem in the movie *Titanic*? What is the solution?

■ Which paragraph includes the important events that show the problem and the solution?

■ Which paragraph explains the story more clearly?

-an interesting title

-include

- title of movie

-actors, genre, setting

plotsummary

- why do you like it so much

imdb . com

The movie, *Titanic,* is a love story which takes place in the middle of a disaster. Rose DeWitt Bukater is a beautiful young woman. She is returning to the United States with Caledon Hockley and her mother. Rose is engaged to Hockley. Her mother wants her to marry him because he is rich. Rose is very unhappy because she doesn't love Hockely. One night, she gets upset and tries to commit suicide. Jack Dawson, a poor young artist, saves her life. Rose is very grateful, so she invites Jack to a formal dinner. After dinner, he takes her dancing in the part of the ship where all the poor people are. Rose has a wonderful time. She and Jack fall in love. The next day they meet in secret. While they are together, an iceberg hits the ship. Meanwhile, a friend of Cal's puts a diamond necklace in Jack's pocket. Cal accuses Jack of stealing the necklace and he is arrested. The ship begins to sink. Rose fights her way down to Jack and helps him to escape. There are not enough lifeboats. Rose gets onto a lifeboat but she can't leave Jack. She jumps back onto the ship. Right before the ship sinks, Rose and Jack jump into the water. They find a piece of wood that is floating but it is not large enough for both of them. Jack stays in the water. He dies from the cold. Rose is saved.

The movie, *Titanic* is basically a love story. The main characters are Rose, a beautiful upper class young woman and Jack, a poor young artist. Rose is on the Titanic with her mother and her fiancée, Cal. By chance, Rose and Jack meet and fall in love. Then the ship begins to sink. Rose saves Jack's life. Then they jump off the ship together. Unfortunately, Jack dies but Rose survives.

6 Look at the list of events you wrote from your favorite movie. Work in groups or pairs. Which events are the most important? Are there any events that you can combine to show their relationship?

Writing a Title

If you give your paragraph an interesting title, people will want to read it. Titles of movies are underlined (or put in italics in printed material). Important words begin with a capital letter. Small words such as *and, in, a, the, to, at,* or *with* do not begin with a capital letter unless they are the first words in the title.

Examples: The Story of Qui Ju

Dona Flor and Her Two Husbands

7 Punctuate the titles in parentheses and capitalize words that need capital letters. Then write a title for your paragraph.

1. You should see (the seven dwarfs), a classic Disney film.

   You should see The Seven Dwarfs, a classic Disney film.

2. The Spanish actor Chow Yung Fat was in (anna and the king)

   _____

3. The Italian movie (life is beautiful) won several awards.

   _____

4. Sandra Bullock starred in (while you were sleeping).

   _____

5. One of the most famous horror movies of all time is (the exorcist).

   _____

Write

Developing Cohesion and Style

Using Adjectives

One way to make a movie summary interesting is to add adjectives that describe characters and events.

8 Look at the adjectives that describe movies on page 190. The carets mark places to add adjectives. Think of appropriate adjectives and use them to rewrite the sentences.

1. *Star Wars* is a ∧ science-fiction movie.

   Star Wars is a realistic science fiction movie.

2. *Dracula* is a ∧ horror movie about a ∧ vampire.

   _____

3. *Titanic,* is a ∧ love story about a couple on a sinking ship.

   _____

4. *Schindler's List* is a ∧ drama about a German who saved the lives of many Jews.

   _____

9 Write a similar sentence about your favorite movie.

Using the Historical Present Tense

You can use the present tense to talk about movies that describe events in the past. This is the "historical present."

---

10   Look at the following paragraph and complete it with the correct forms of the verbs in parentheses. Use the historical present.

It's a Wonderful Life _____is_____ (be) a heartwarming drama. In this movie,
                   1

James Stewart _____ (play) an ordinary family man who _____
                 2   3

(live) in a small American town. When he is about to lose his business because of

a serious mistake, Stewart _____ (become) very depressed. He (try)
                                               4

_____ to jump off a bridge, but an angel _____ (show) him
         5   6

how important he _____ (be) to his friends, family, and the community.
                        7

He then _____ (decide) not to kill himself.
        8

Writing the First Draft

11   Write the paragraph about your favorite movie. Use important events and information, and combine sentences to show the relationship between events. Also include adjectives and appositives to describe the movie and characters. Use the title you wrote. You can write the paragraph in the historical present tense.

Edit and Revise

Editing Practice

Using Two or More Adjectives

■   Sometimes you may want to use more than one adjective. You can separate two or more adjectives with a comma.

    Examples:

        E. T. is a friendly, lovable creature from outer space.
        In the movie *Rocky*, the main character is a handsome, determined boxer.

■   When there are two contrasting adjectives, you can separate them with *but*.

    Example: In *Star Wars*, Han Solo is a brave but egotistical pilot.

12 Look at these sentences. Put a comma between the two adjectives.

1. *Gandhi* is the story of a wise kind man who leads India to freedom.
2. In *It's a Wonderful Life*, James Stewart plays a hard-working ordinary man.
3. *The 400 Blows* tells the story of a lonely unhappy boy.
4. *Women on the Verge of a Nervous Breakdown* contains many colorful comic characters.

13 Put the word *but* in the appropriate places in the sentences.

1. *Gandhi* is about a gentle powerful leader.
2. *Frankenstein* is the story of a destructive tragic monster.
3. *The Godfather* is about an evil loyal man.
4. The lead characters in *Thelma and Louise* are vulnerable brave.

Editing Your Writing

14 **Editing Using a Checklist.** Edit your paragraph using the following checklist.

Editing Checklist

1. Content
   a. Is the title interesting?
   b. Would others want to see the movie because of your summary?
   c. Did you present the problem and the events leading to the solution?
   d. Does your summary include the type of movie, when and where the movie takes place, and the main characters?
2. Organization
   a. Is all the information in the paragraph important?
   b. Does the topic sentence give a general idea of what kind of movie you're writing about?
3. Cohesion and Style
   a. Did you combine sentences to show the relationship between events?
   b. Did you use appositives correctly?
   c. Did you use adjectives to describe the characters and the movie?
   d. Did you use the historical present tense?
4. Grammar
   a. Are the present tense verbs correct?
   b. Are the count and noncount nouns correct?
   c. Did you combine sentences correctly?
5. Form
   a. Did you underline the title of the movie?
   b. Did you use commas with appositives and adjectives correctly?
   c. Did you punctuate combined sentences correctly?

15 **Peer Editing.**   Exchange papers with another student and edit each other's paragraphs.

Writing the Second Draft

16 After you and another student edit your paragraph, rewrite it using correct form. Then give it to your teacher for comments.

| PART 5 |

Grammar

A. The Past Continuous Tense

The past continuous tense describes activities happening or in progress at a specific time or during a period of time in the past.

<table>
<tr><th colspan="3">Statements</th></tr>
<tr><th></th><th>Examples</th><th>Notes</th></tr>
<tr><td>Affirmative</td><td>I was watching the news at 6:00. The anchorman was telling about a robbery.</td><td>Past continuous statements consist of a past form of be before the -ing form of a verb.</td></tr>
<tr><td>Negative</td><td>He wasn't telling about a murder. The bank tellers weren't screaming.</td><td>Negative statements include not after the be verb.</td></tr>
</table>

Note: For the spelling rules for verbs with *-ing* endings, see Appendix 3, pages 287–288.

<table>
<tr><th colspan="4">Yes / No Questions</th></tr>
<tr><th colspan="2">Examples</th><th colspan="2">Possible Answers</th></tr>
<tr><th></th><th></th><th>Affirmative</th><th>Negative</th></tr>
<tr><td>Affirmative</td><td>Was the manager working?
Were the police investigating the robbery?</td><td>Yes, he was.
Yes, they were.</td><td>No, he wasn't.
No, they weren't.</td></tr>
<tr><td>Negative</td><td>Wasn't the policeman running after the suspect?
Weren't the customers screaming?</td><td>Yes, he was.

Yes, they were.</td><td>No, he wasn't.

No, they weren't.</td></tr>
</table>

<table>
<tr><th colspan="3">Information Questions</th></tr>
<tr><th colspan="2">Examples</th><th>Possible Answers</th></tr>
<tr><td>Affirmative</td><td>What were the suspects wearing?
Who was carrying weapons?</td><td>They were wearing masks.
All of them.</td></tr>
<tr><td>Negative</td><td>Why weren't the tellers screaming?
Who wasn't paying attention?</td><td>They weren't scared.
The guard.</td></tr>
</table>

1   Fill in the blanks in the interviews below, using the verbs in parentheses to form past continuous verb phrases.

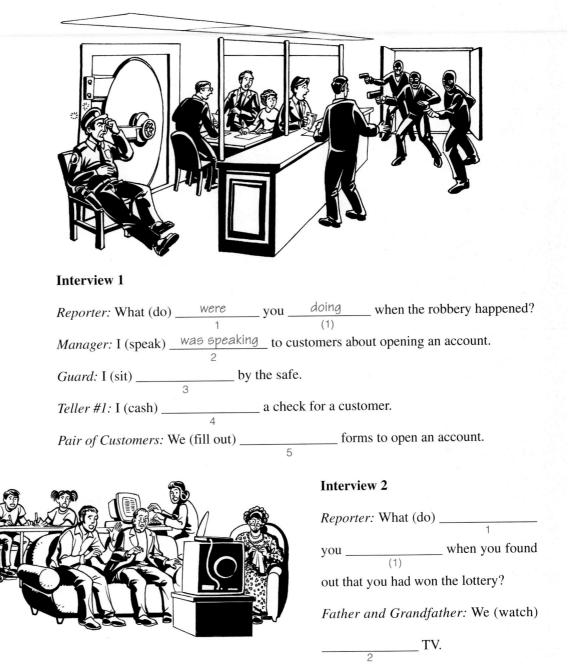

Interview 1

Reporter: What (do) _____were_____ you _____doing_____ when the robbery happened?

          ₁   ₍₁₎

Manager: I (speak) __was speaking__ to customers about opening an account.

                    ₂

Guard: I (sit) _____ by the safe.

                ₃

Teller #1: I (cash) _____ a check for a customer.

                    ₄

Pair of Customers: We (fill out) _____ forms to open an account.

                              ₅

Interview 2

Reporter: What (do) _____

                          ₁

you _____ when you found

      ₍₁₎

out that you had won the lottery?

Father and Grandfather: We (watch)

_____ TV.

      ₂

Mother: I (work) _____ on the computer.

                  ₃

Mother: (*pointing to her children*) They (do) _____ their homework.

                                                  ₄

Grandmother: I (knit) _____ a sweater.

                        ₅

B. The Simple Past Versus the Past Continuous

	Examples	Notes
Simple past	I **read** the newspaper. She **didn't use** the computer last night. Did you **see** the movie?	Use the simple past tense to talk about events and activities that began and ended in the past.
Past continuous	I **was reading** the newspaper when I fell asleep. She **wasn't using** the computer at 8:00 last night. **Were** you **watching** the movie when I called?	Use the past continuous tense to describe activities that were happening or in progress at a specific time or during a period of time in the past.

2 Choose between the simple past and the past continuous form of the verb in each set of parentheses.

A: What (did you do / were you doing) yesterday?
                    1

B: Let's see. I (woke up / was waking up) at around 10:00 yesterday. It (rained / was
                    2   3
raining), so I (stayed / was staying) home and (read / was reading) the newspaper.
                    4   5

A: I called you at around 11:00. (Did you read / Were you reading) the newspaper then?
                                          6

B: Yes, I (did / was).
              7

A: What (did you do / were you doing) after we hung up?
                    8

B: I (watched / was watching) TV for a while.
          9

A: (Didn't you go / Weren't you going) outside at all yesterday?
              10

B: Sure I did. I wasn't home between 5:00 and 6:00.

A: Why not? What (did you do / were you doing)?
                        11

B: I (returned / was returning) the video I (watched / was watching) last night.
          12   13

A: So, what (did you do / were you doing) last night?
                  14

B: I (played / was playing) video games. I called to ask you to come over, but you
          15
weren't home. What (did you do / were you doing)?
                          16

A: What time (did you call / were you calling)?
                  17

B: About 8:00.

A: At 8:00 I (walked / was walking) my dog in the park. I (didn't want / wasn't
                  18   19
wanting) to stay home on such a beautiful night.

C. *When* and *While* with the Simple Past and Past Continuous Tenses

When and *while* are used to introduce time clauses. They can relate two events or activities that happened (simple past) or were happening (past continuous) at the same time in the past. *When* can also relate events that happened in a sequence.

	Examples	Notes
when	**When** the movie **ended,** we **went** home.	Clauses with *when* are most often in the simple past tense. If both verbs are in the simple past, the action in the *when* clause happened first.
while	She **was watching** TV **while** her husband **was using** the computer. **While** she **was watching** TV, her husband **was using** the computer.	Clauses with *while* are most often in the past continuous tense. If both verbs are in the past continuous, it means the two actions were going on at the same time. In these sentences, *while* can go at the beginning or in the middle of the sentence.
when or while	My mother **was listening** to the radio **when** she got the call. My mother **got** the call **while** she **was listening** to the radio.	The simple past and the past continuous can appear in the same sentence. In these cases, *while* begins clauses with the past continuous and *when* begins clauses with the simple past. One event began before the other one and was in progress when the second event interrupted it.

3 Fill in the blanks with either *when* or *while*.

1. I was reading a magazine _____when_____ my friends arrived.

2. _____ it was time for the movie to start, we turned on the TV.

3. My roommate was listening to the stereo _____ we were watching the movie.

4. _____ a commercial came on, we ordered a pizza.

5. The pizza came _____ we were watching the movie.

6. The telephone rang _____ we were watching the last scene of the movie.

7. I tried to listen to the movie _____ I was speaking with my mother.

8. _____ I got off the phone, the movie was over.

Video Activities: Quiz Shows

Before You Watch.

1. Circle the kinds of TV show you like to watch.
   a. comedies   b. dramas   c. quiz shows   d. soap operas

2. Do you like watching quiz shows on TV? Discuss with a partner.

3. Describe your favorite TV quiz show to your partner.

Watch.   Discuss the following questions with your classmates.

1.   On all the game shows you saw in the video, what must contestants do in order to win money?
2.   Why do television networks like to make game shows?
3.   The contestants on today's game shows are

    a.   millionaires   b.   ordinary people   c.   scholars

Watch Again.   Write *T* if the statements below are true or *F* if they are false. Then correct all the false statements.

_____   1.   In the United States, you can watch a game show on TV almost every night of the week.

_____   2.   Quiz shows are a new idea.

_____   3.   The first game show in America was called "Who Wants to be a Millionaire?"

_____   4.   If a television show is successful, other networks hurry to copy it.

_____   5.   Game shows are cheaper to make than sitcoms.

_____   6.   In the short term, American TV networks will stop making game shows.

_____   7.   The questions on the new "Twenty-One" show are called "relatable." This means they are about families.

After You Watch.   Complete the following sentences with the correct tense of the verb in parentheses. Then check the video to see if your answers are correct.

1.   "Who Wants to be a Millionaire" _____ (start) the current quiz show craze last summer.

2.   Other networks quickly _____ (jump) on the bandwagon.

3.   Television networks always _____ (clone) shows that are popular, and now they _____ (do) it again.

4.   Their motivation _____ (be) greed.

5.   In the short term the networks _____ (make) more game shows, more quiz shows.

6.   Game shows _____ (be) not a new idea.

7.   In the late 50's, the audience _____ (find out) the show "Twenty-One" was rigged, and quiz shows _____ (lose) popularity. Now NBC _____ (bring) back "Twenty-One."

8.   On the new quiz shows, you _____ (have to, not) be a scholar in order to be a millionaire.

9.   The sixty-four thousand dollar question is, how long _____ the craze _____ (last)?

Chapter 8

Social Life

IN THIS CHAPTER

Listening
- Listening for main ideas
- Listening for specific information
- Identifying stressed words and reductions
- Taking notes on a phone conversation (specific information)

Speaking
- Intonation with exclamations
- Discussing dating customs
- Making a videodating presentation

Reading
- Previewing vocabulary
- Reading: Meeting the Perfect Mate
- Recognizing the structure of conversations
- Understanding the main idea
- Supplying left-out words and references

Writing
- Developing ideas: interviewing, writing topic and concluding sentences, organizing information in a paragraph
- Making transitions with *in fact, however, in addition,* and *also*
- Writing a biographical paragraph
- Editing for long forms and capitalization

Grammar
- Time expressions with the present perfect: *for, since, all, always*
- Time clauses with *since*
- The present perfect continuous tense
- The present perfect continuous versus the present perfect

PART 1   # Listening to Conversations

Before You Listen

1 **Prelistening Questions.**   Before you listen, talk about your friends with a partner.

1. How long have you known your closest friends: since elementary school? middle school? high school? college? after college?

Tug of War → ชักเย่อ

2. Have you ever had a *reunion* with old friends? What did you talk about? Did you stay in touch after that?

social life → fun no study

3. Have you ever run into an old friend by accident? Tell where and when this happened.

2 **Vocabulary Preview.**   Complete the sentences with these words and expressions from the conversation. Then go back and write the meaning of the expressions in the chart.

	Expressions	Meanings
graduation		finish some level from school
be up to *(What have you been up to)*		What have you been doing
make(s) sense		easy to understand, logical
terrific	positive	very good, great, wonderful
(to be) good at	He's good at math.	to be able sth have still
sales rep *(representative)*	He's a sales rep	*Someone part of company* salesperson who is represent
on the road	I'm on the road	traveling
nurse		assistance of doctor with patience
keep in touch	keep in touch calling	keep in relationship

take care and keep in touch keep in toch calling.

salesperson → try to make people convince

1. I love your new haircut. It really looks _____terrific_____.

2. *Yolanda:* Hi Peter. I haven't seen you in a while. What have you
    ____been up to____?

    Peter: Not much. Just studying and going to school.

3. David plans to become a doctor because he has always been ____good____
    _____at_____ science.

4. I'm ____on____ ____the____ ____road____ most of the time
    my company needs me to travel a lot.

5. Karen helps sick people get well; she works as a ____nurse____ in a hospital.

6. I send e-mail to my friends every week because I want to ____keep____
    ____in____ ____touch____ with them.

7. To celebrate my ____graduation____ from college, my parents bought
    me a new computer.

8. It doesn't ____make sense____ to buy a car if you live five minutes
    from your university.

9. *Karen:* I took this job because I am really good at selling things!

    Peter: Oh! So, you're a ____sales rep____?

Listen

3 **Listening for Main Ideas.**   Peter is visiting his hometown. He runs into two of
his high-school classmates walking down the street.

1. Close your book and listen to the conversation. Listen for the answers to
    these questions.

    1. What is the main thing the three friends discuss?

        a. the fun they used to have

        b. what they are doing now

        c. how many children they have

    2. When was the last time Peter saw Karen and Yolanda? since graduation night

    3. Peter says he's been studying hard. What do the women think? They don't believe that

    4. What is Peter's major? computer science

    5. Yolanda is a sales rep. Where does Karen work? nurse in a hospital

    6. At the end of the conversation, what do the friends say they will do?
        keep in touch from now on.

2. Compare answers with a partner.

Stress

4   Listening for Stressed Words.   Listen to the conversation again.

1.   Some of the stressed words are missing. During each pause, repeat the phrase or sentence. Then fill in the blanks with words from the list.

believe	graduation	love	sales	studying	up
body	great	math	science	sure (2 times)	were
computer	kidding	nurse	seeing	terrific	you (3 times)
good	like	really	so far	that	

seen ออกเสียง ซีน
publishing
hóspital
compú ter

Karen: Yolanda, look! I can't ___believe___ it! It's Peter Riley. Hey Peter! How are you?

Peter: Karen? Yolanda? Wow! I haven't seen you guys since ___graduation___ night!

Yolanda: I know. You look ___great___!

Peter: Thanks. So do ___you___!   ออกเสียง *ben*

Yolanda: So what have you been ___up___ to?

Peter: Well, I go to Faber College.

Karen: ___Really___? Do you ___like___ it?

Peter: Yeah, ___so___ ___far___. But I've been ___studying___ really hard.

Yolanda: ___Sure___ you have . . .

Karen: What's your major—___body___building?

Peter: No, actually it's ___computer___ science.

Yolanda: Ah-h-h. ___that___ makes sense. You always ___were___ good at ___math___ and ___science___.

Peter: Thanks. Anyway, what have ___you___ guys been up to?

Yolanda: Well, I'm a ___sales___ rep for a publishing company.

Peter: No ___kidding___! How do you like that?

Yolanda: Oh, I ___love___ it! I'm on the road a lot, but I get to meet some interesting people.

Peter: That's ___terrific___. And how about ___you___, Karen?

Karen: I'm a ___nurse___ in a hospital.

Peter: You always were ___good___ at science too. Well, it was great ___seeing___ you both. We should be ___sure___ to keep in touch from now on.

2. Now read the conversation with a partner. Practice stressing words correctly.

After You Listen

5 **Vocabulary Review.** Discuss the following questions with a partner. Use the underlined vocabulary in your answers.

1. What have you <u>been up to</u> — besides studying English?
2. Was your high school <u>graduation</u> a special occasion? In what way?
3. Tell about a restaurant that has <u>terrific</u> food in your opinion.
4. Tell about something you are very <u>good at</u>.
5. Do you <u>keep in touch</u> with all your teachers from high school?
6. Would you like a job that required you to be <u>on the road</u> 50% of the time?
7. Give several reasons why it <u>makes sense</u> for students to wear uniforms in high school.

Pronunciation

Intonation with Exclamation

To express strong feelings (surprise, anger, happiness), we use exclamations. These are expressions that we pronounce with especially strong emphasis and with falling intonation at the end.

Examples:

Wow!   I can't believe it! *go down*   That's great!   That's awful!

6 **Pronouncing Exclamations.** Repeat the following exclamations from the dialogue. Follow the stress and intonation patterns carefully.

1. Yolanda, look!
2. I can't believe it!
3. Wow! I haven't seen you guys since graduation night!
4. You look great!
5. So do you!
6. No kidding!
7. That's terrific!

7   **Matching Statements and Responses.**   Listen to these eight statements or questions. Choose the appropriate responses from the box and write their letters in the spaces below. Use a different exclamation each time.

> a.   That's amazing! How's she doing?
> b.   Congratulations!
> c.   That's great! I knew you could do it.
> d.   That's disgusting!
> e.   No way!
> f.   You're kidding! What did you talk about?
> g.   Not again!
> h.   Oh no! That's awful!

1.   _A_   3.   _E_   5.   _H_   7.   _D_
2.   _B_   4.   _C_   6.   _F_   8.   _G_

8   **Practicing Exclamations.**   Work in pairs. Each student looks at a different box. Read your partner one statement or question in your box. Your partner should respond with an appropriate exclamation. Then your partner will read one of his or her statements and you should respond with an appropriate exclamation. Take turns.

Student A

1.   I got 100% on the last grammar test.

2.   Do you like my new haircut?

3.   Yesterday my dog was hit by a car.

4.   I got free tickets to the _____ concert. *(name of a rock group)*

5.   _____ *(choose your own)*

Student B

1.   Somebody stole my brand-new bicycle.

2.   I got accepted for next year at _____.
     (name of an excellent university)

3.   What do you think of the food at _____ ?
     (name of a terrible restaurant or eating place)

4.   Today is my birthday.

5.   _____ *(choose your own)*

PART 2	# Recalling Main Ideas

Before You Listen

1   **Prelistening Questions.**   Before you listen, talk about dating with a partner.

1.   Have you ever had a blind date?

2.   Who arranged it?

3.   Where did you go?

4.   Did you enjoy the date?

5.   Did you go out with the person again after the first date?

Listen

2   **Listening for Main Ideas.**   Karen wants to arrange a blind date for Beverly. As you listen to their conversation, answer the following questions.

1.   What does Karen want to do for her friend Beverly?

2.   What is the surprise at the end of the conversation?

3   **Taking Notes on Specific Information.**   Listen to the conversation again. This time, take notes about Franco.

Appearance:
dark hair , green eyes, wonderful smile, beard

Job:
Import - Export

Interests:
He loves jazz , travel , play piano , dance

Age:
almost 30 years old.

Problems:
Franco doesn't speak English.

After You Listen

4   **Summarizing Main Ideas.**   Describe Franco to a partner. Use your notes from Activity 3 to help you.

5 **Discussing Dating Customs.**   Work in small groups. Talk about dating customs and your personal experiences.

1. What age do you think is appropriate for young people to start dating? How old were you?

2. Is it OK to ask someone you have just met out on a date?

3. Where do couples of different ages go on dates: to a movie? a restaurant? a nightclub? a concert?

4. When a couple goes out, who usually pays?

5. Do you think it is OK for a person to date more than one person during the same period of time?

6. Do you think it is a good thing to date many different people before you get married?

7. Tell about an enjoyable date you went on, or describe your imaginary perfect date.

Talk It Over

Videodating

Some countries have videodating services to help people find interesting dates. These services have become more and more common everywhere. To use this service, you must first fill out an application like the one on page 209. Then you make a short video in which you talk about yourself and the kind of person you would like to meet. If two people see each other's videos and want to meet, the dating service "matches" them. Then they meet and decide if they want to go out on a date together.

Pretend that you are going to sign up with a videodating service and follow these instructions.

Cross-Cultural Note

When two people who have romantic feelings for each other go out together, their meeting is called a date. In the United States and Canada, boys and girls start dating around age 15. Often, they meet at school, at work, at a sports event, or at a concert. Once in a while, a friend or relative arranges a date, and people meet for the first time at the time of the date. This is called a "blind date."

1. Fill out the application, but don't write your real name at the top. Use an imaginary name. Your teacher will collect all the applications and put them on the board or wall.

2. The women in the class will read the applications from the men, and the men will read the applications from women.

3. Choose the application of the person that looks the most interesting to you.

4. The teacher will hold up each application and ask, for example, "This application is from Mr. Cool. Who would like to see his video?" The women who chose him will raise their hands.

5. Finally, "Mr. Cool" will stand up and reveal his identity.

6. Repeat steps 4 and 5 for all the applications.

Note: If you have a video camera, make individual videos in a separate room. Be sure to talk about yourself, your likes and dislikes, and the kind of person you want to meet. Then, instead of students revealing their identities in Step 5, have the class watch the chosen video!

Role-Play

Rose is a businesswoman who doesn't have time to look for a boyfriend. Richard, a divorced teacher, is ready to start dating again.

Rose and Richard decide to sign up with a videotaping service. To begin, each of them must make a videotaped presentation about themselves. Pretend that you are Rose or Richard and give a short presentation in which you describe yourself and the person you're looking for.

The videodating application can give you ideas of what to say. You can also talk about what you like and don't like.

Name ___Linsey Lohan___   Age ___24___   ☐ Male ☑ Female

Address _____   Occupation ___dentist___

_____   Work hours _____ Work phone _____

THE PERSON I AM LOOKING FOR:

Age from ___28___ to ___32___

Education	☐ high school	☐ 2-year school	☐ some college	☑ college degree
Occupation	☐ clerical	☐ technical	☐ managerial	☑ professional
Marital status	☑ never married	☐ divorced	☐ widowed	☐ doesn't matter
Interests	☑ sports	☑ music	☑ movies	☑ dancing ☐ nature

ABOUT MYSELF:

Situation
- ☐ new in town
- ☐ very busy
- ☐ shy
- ☑ interested in marriage

Marital Status
- ☑ never married
- ☐ divorced
- ☐ widowed

Plans
- ☑ not planning to move
- ☐ planning to move soon

Interests
- ☑ sports
- ☑ music
- ☑ movies
- ☑ dancing
- ☐ nature

Children
- ☐ have
- ☑ don't have
- ☐ want
- ☐ don't want
- ☐ doesn't matter

| **PART 3** | # Reading |

Before You Read

1   Discuss the pictures in small groups.

1. Who are the people?
2. What are they talking about? How are the three people different from one another?
3. Do you agree with any one of them? Why or why not?
4. How do young people in your country often meet their boyfriends/girlfriends?

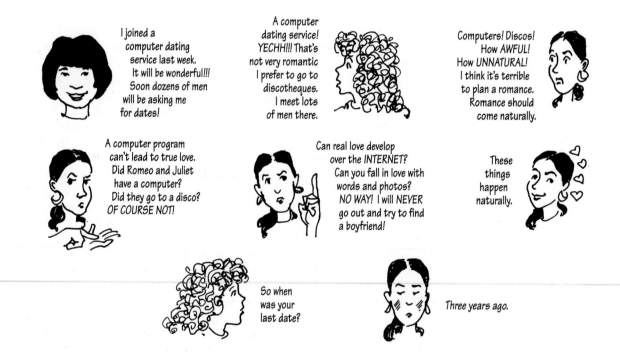

2   Think about the answers to these questions. The reading selection answers them.

1. What was a common kind of marriage in Korea in the past?
2. How do some young people around the world meet the people who become their boyfriends or girl friends?
3. What is an advantage to each method (way) of meeting people? What is a disadvantage?

3 Vocabulary Preview. Here are some vocabulary items from the reading. You can learn them now or come back to them later.

pub , bar American

Nouns	Verbs *to look at closely*	Adjectives	Adverbs
photos	examine	popular	fortunately
mates *couple*	interview	potential	
a guy	reply	aggressive	
a search	match	discouraged	
a match	accept		
cyberspace [internet]			
cafes			

Read

Read the following material quickly. Then read the explanations and do the exercises after the reading.

Meeting the Perfect Mate

For the past month I've been taking a university graduate course called "Social Structure." It's a very popular class. We've been discussing friendship, social life, dating, marriage, and other relationships—through the generations and throughout the world. One of our assignments is to examine the ways that people meet potential husbands and wives. I've been interviewing students on campus all week as part of my study.

First, I talked with my roommate in the dormitory, Sook In, an international student from Korea.

"What's one way to meet a possible mate?" I asked her.

"Well," she said, "one method in my country is to have a matched marriage."

"A what?" I asked. "I know you can match a tie to a shirt—or two socks after you do the laundry. Then they're a match. But people?"

"Sure," she replied. "There aren't many arranged marriages these days, but there were a lot not too long ago. My parents, for example, met each other for the first time on their wedding day. My grandparents chose their children's mates and arranged the wedding."

"Do you mean that they weren't in love? That sounds awful! Weren't they worried?"

"Maybe a little bit," Sook In said, "but they accepted each other. Then, fortunately, they grew to love each other. They've had a good, successful marriage for the past thirty years. This happens in a lot of arranged marriages."

I shook my head. "Amazing!" I said.

The next person that I interviewed was Bill, a guy in my business management class. "I meet a lot of women in dance clubs—at least more than I do on campus," he said. "The environment is exciting and I go every weekend, if possible, to dance or talk or just listen to music."

"That seems great," I said.

"I thought so, too, at first," he said a little sadly. "But on the other hand, very often the women in those places are unfriendly. A lot of men are too aggressive, and as a result the women are very cold. So I tried the Internet—you know, the World Wide Web."

You meet potential girlfriends on the Web? On your computer?" I asked, even more amazed.

"Yeah, there are plenty of people to communicate with in cyberspace—at home, at cafes, in the library... But who knows what is real there and what isn't? Who knows who might be dangerous?" asked Bill, discouraged. It seemed he was talking more to himself than to me. I continued my search for the perfect way to find the perfect mate.

"The Internet? Never!" said Julie, a student who works part time in the campus bookstore. "I prefer to make new friends at places where people have interests in common. I met my boyfriend at the health club, for example, and it seems that the healthy atmosphere of the gym is continuing into the relationship that I have with him."

"That sounds wonderful," I said.

"Yes," she said, "I guess so. But to be honest, there's one problem with this arrangement."

"What?" I asked.

"The truth is that I really hate to exercise, so I don't want to go to the gym anymore. What's my boyfriend going to think when he finds this out?"

After You Read

5 **Recognizing the Structure of Conversations.** Even in conversational form— with the words of each speaker between quotation marks (" "), some reading selections may follow the organization of an outline. The main parts, or topics, can appear after numbers like I, II, III, IV, etc. The ideas of each part can follow capital letters like A, B, C, and so on.

The following outline shows the organization of the parts (main topics) and important ideas of the reading selection "Meeting the Perfect Mate." First, on the numbered lines, arrange these phrases in the same order as in the reading. Items I and IV are done as examples.

2 ■ Arranged marriages

3 ■ Meeting people in dance clubs

4 ■ Finding friends in cyberspace

5 ■ Meeting in health clubs or the gym

1 ■ Introduction: reasons for interviewing people

Next, write the following ideas in sentence form on the correct lettered line under each topic. Be sure to put them in the right order. Items IIIA and VB are done as examples.

■ I'm studying "Social Structure" in a graduate seminar.

■ I'm interviewing people about ways to meet potential mates.

- You can talk or just listen to music.

- Husbands and wives may learn to love each other.

- Mates may meet for the first time on their wedding day.

- The women act unfriendly because a lot of men are too aggressive.

- You can go online at home, in cafes, and in other places.

- People with a common interest in physical exercise meet here.

- You don't know what is unreal or dangerous about people you meet on the Web.

- If you're not really interested in exercise, there might be a problem.

Meeting the Perfect Mate

I. Introduction: reasons for interviewing people
   A. I'm studying "Social Structure" in a graduate seminar.
   B. I'm interviewing people about ways to meet potential mates.

II. Arranged marriages
   A. Husbands and wives may learn to love each other.
   B. Mates may meet for the first time on their wedding day.

III. Meeting people in dance clubs
   A. You can talk or just listen to music.
   B. The women act unfriendly because a lot of men are too aggressive

IV. Finding friends in cyberspace
   A. You can go online at home, in cafes, and in other places.
   B. You don't know what is unreal or dangerous about people you meet on the Web

V. Meeting in health clubs or the gym.
   A. People with a common interest in physical exercise meet here.
   B. If you're not really interested in exercise, there might be a problem.

To tell the main (the most general) idea of the reading, finish this sentence.

There are ____advantages____ and disadvantages to the various

ways __to meet the perfect mate__.

6   Understanding the Main Idea. The main idea of the reading selection is in the first sentence of the following paragraph, but it is not quite true. Change the underlined words in the topic sentence and the important supporting details that follow so that the paragraph correctly tells the point of the reading.

---

advantages and

There are ~~only~~ disadvantages to the various possible ways of meeting potential

mates   *disadvantage*

~~classmates or roommates~~. (1) An ~~advantage~~ of arranged marriages is that mates

may not meet until their wedding day; even so, through the years they may learn

love each other   *dance*

to ~~take graduate courses~~ anyway. (2) At ~~stand-up comedy~~ clubs, you can talk

women

or just listen to music; on the other hand, the ~~men~~ in such places are often cold

men

and unfriendly because the ~~children~~ act too aggressive. (3) Meeting people in

convenient   *anywhere / everywhere*   *difficult*

cyberspace is ~~inconvenient~~ because computers are ~~nowhere~~; however, it is ~~easy~~

to know what is unreal or unsafe about the people online. (4) If you meet potential

something

dates at a place where you have ~~nothing in common~~, like the gym, you can share

isn't interested

your interest, but what happens if one person ~~gets interested~~ in the activity?

---

7   Supplying Left-Out Words and References. Often a writer leaves out words because information in other sentences or in another part of the sentence makes them unnecessary. The reader figures out the missing information from the context.

Examples:

"What's one way to meet a possible husband or wife?" I asked.
"Well," she said, "one method in my country is to have a matched marriage."
(Method for what? For meeting a possible husband or wife.)

"I know you can match socks. But people?"
(But can you match people?)

In the following sentences there are missing words that readers can figure out from the context. Which words are understood in these sentences? Write them in the blanks, as in the examples.

1.   "What's one way to meet a possible mate?" I asked my roommate, Sook In.

"Well," she said, "one method ___*for meeting a possible mate*___ in my

country is to have a matched marriage."

2. "I know you can match a tie to a shirt — or _____*match*_____ two socks, too, after you do the laundry. But _____*Can ya match*_____ people?"

3. "Sure," she replied. "There aren't many arranged marriages these days, but there were a lot _____*arranged marriages*_____ not too many years ago."

4. "Do you mean that they weren't in love? That sounds awful! Weren't they upset? "Maybe _____*there were upset*_____ a little bit," Sook In said. "But they've had a successful marriage for thirty years."

5. "I meet a lot of women in nightclubs," Bill said. "At least more _____*women*_____ than I do on campus. The nightclub environment is exciting. I go _____*to nightclub*_____ every weekend."

Some words refer to ideas that came before them in the reading.

Example:

"My parents have had a good marriage for the past thirty years. This happens in a lot of arranged marriages."
(What does *this* refer to? Having a good marriage.)

In each of the following sentences, circle the words that the underlined word refers to. The first one is done as an example.

1. I've been taking a graduate (seminar) in social structure for the past month. It's a very popular course.

2. "One method is to have a (matched marriage)," Sook In said. "A <u>what</u>?" I asked.   *matched marriage*

3. "My grandparents chose (their children's) mates and arranged <u>their</u> wedding," she explained. "Do you mean <u>they</u> weren't in love?"

4. "I (meet) a lot of women in dance clubs—at least more than I <u>do</u> on campus," said Bill.

5. "Dance clubs (seem great)," I said. "I thought <u>so</u> too at first," he said a little sadly.

6. "Yeah, there are plenty of people to communicate with in (cyberspace)—at home, at cafes, in the library . . . But who knows what is real <u>there</u> and what isn't?"

7. "It seems that the healthy (atmosphere in the gym is continuing into) our relationship," Julie said. "<u>That</u> sounds wonderful," I said. "Yes," she said. "I guess <u>so</u>."   *sounds wonderful*

8. "But the truth is that I (hate to exercise.) What's he going to do when he finds <u>this</u> out?"

Now turn back to the Before You Read section on page 210 and answer the questions.

Discussing the Reading

8   In small groups, talk about your answers to the following questions. Then tell the class the most interesting information or ideas.

1. Do you know anyone who has had an arranged marriage? Are there arranged marriages in your country or culture? What is your opinion of this way to meet potential mates?

2. Do you like to communicate with potential friends in cyberspace? How do you do it?

3. Where might people with common interests usually meet in your community?

PART 4	# Writing

Before You Write

Exploring Ideas

1   **Interviewing Someone.**   In this chapter you are going to interview a classmate about his or her life in the past year. In groups, think of different topics to ask about. Add to the list below.

■   Family life

■   Social life

■   Professional life

■   Student life

■   Hobbies life

■   _____

2   Write questions about the topics in Activity 1. Think of other questions you could ask a student in your class. Your teacher will list them on the board.

3   You have prepared to interview a classmate. Now prepare for someone to interview you by making a list of the things you have done in the past year. Think about the questions in Activity 2.

4   Use the questions from Activity 2 to interview a student about his or her life in the past year. Take notes on the information your partner gives you. When your partner interviews you, try to give him / her as much information as you can.

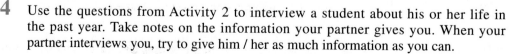

5 **Building Vocabulary.** The chart below has vocabulary you can use to talk about life events. What other words can you add from your discussions and interview? In small groups, discuss of any words you do not understand.

Nouns	Verbs	Adjectives	Other
career	accomplish	exhausted	be interested in
hobby	attend	fascinating	be used to
recreation	enjoy	surprising	_____
_____	_____	responsible	_____
_____	_____	difficult	_____
_____	_____	_____	_____
_____	_____	_____	_____

Organizing Ideas

You are going to write a paragraph about a student in your class for a class newsletter. The paragraph will say what the student has been doing for the past year.

Writing Topic Sentences

Topic sentences about what someone has been doing for the past year are often in the present perfect tense (*have/has* + past participle) or the present perfect continuous tense (*have/has* + *been* + verb + *ing*).

Examples:

June Nomura *has lived* in Texas since April.

Ben Rodriguez *has been working* in a hospital.

A Juggler

6 Which of these sentences are good general topic sentences for a paragraph about someone's life during the past year? Circle the numbers of those sentences. Which sentence do you think is the most interesting? Put a check by it.

1. Tony Prado has had been busy this year.
2. Reiko Suzuki has been married since June.
3. Vega has had so much to do he has felt like a juggler.
4. Hilda Bronheim has learned a lot of English this year.
5. During the past year Li Yun Wen has gotten married, worked at two jobs, played soccer, and studied English.
6. During the past year Ana Leone has had a full but happy life.

7 Write a topic sentence for your paragraph. Use the present perfect or the present perfect continuous tense. Then show the sentence to the person that you interviewed. Does he / she agree with your topic sentence?

Organizing Information in a Paragraph

There are two ways to organize your paragraph:

1. You can begin with more important activities such as work, and you can end with less important activities such as hobbies or interesting events.
2. You can begin with difficult activities and end with more enjoyable activities.

8   Look at the following notes about one student's life. Work in small groups and arrange them in order. Use one of the two types of organization above.

> goes to English classes — has no time to study
>
> works in uncle's factory — makes him tired
>
> got married in June — a lot of responsibility
>
> goes biking with his wife
>
> works evenings in gas station
>
> plays soccer with friends

9   Look at your notes from your interview and arrange them in the order you think you are going to write about them. Discuss the order with your partner.

Writing a Concluding Sentence

The final sentence in this kind of paragraph can summarize the paragraph or indicate some future action. The following are good concluding sentences.

- David hopes to use his new language skills to get a job in Europe this summer.

- All in all, Sandra thinks it has been a busy but a productive year.

These sentences are not good concluding sentences. Why not?

- Nancy has also learned to swim.

- Philip has moved three times this year.

- Ken wanted to get a job in a bakery but he couldn't find one, so he went to work in a restaurant.

10   Write a final sentence you could use in your paragraph.

_____

_____

Write

Developing Cohesion and Style

Using Transitional Words and Phrases

■ *However, in addition, also*
The expressions *however, in addition,* and *also* help unify the sentences in a paragraph.

■ *In fact vs. however*
We use *however* to give contrasting information. We use *in fact* to give facts that show that the sentence before is true. Use a comma to separate *in fact* from the rest of the sentence.

Example:
Tony has been very busy. *In fact,* he's been working at two jobs.

---

11   Add *in fact* or *however* to these sentences. Use commas where necessary.

1. Tony has been working very hard. He works from 8:00 in the morning until 9:00 at night.

   Tony has been working very hard. In fact, he works from 8:00 in the morning until 9:00 at night.

2. Tony has been working very hard. He still finds time to play soccer every week.

   Tony has been working very hard. However, he still finds time to play soccer every week.

3. Raúl has been doing well, and he likes his English class a lot. He's been studying so much that he isn't sleeping well.

   Raúl has been doing well, and he likes his English class a lot. In fact, he's been studying so much that he isn't sleeping well.

4. Raúl has been doing well in his English class. He went from level 2 to level 4 last month.

   in fact

   _____

   _____

5. Patricia enjoys going to school. *however* She doesn't like going at night.

   _____

   _____

6. Patricia has been exercising a lot. *in fact* She now runs about 30 miles a week.

   _____

   _____

12 Look at your notes and write some pairs of sentences for your paragraph. Begin the second sentence of each pair with a transitional phrase: *however, in fact, also,* or *in addition.*

Writing the First Draft

13 Now write your paragraph about a classmate. Use your topic sentence and notes. Also use transitional expressions to unify your paragraph.

Edit and Revise

Editing Practice

Using Long Forms in Formal Writing

When English speakers write formally, they don't use as many contractions as when they speak—instead, they use long forms. Here are some examples of long forms and their contractions:

he has → he's	he has not → he hasn't
they have → they've	they have not → they haven't
it is → it's	it is not → it's not, it isn't

14 Write these sentences without contractions.

1. He's been playing in a band.

   <u>He has been playing in a band.</u>

2. They haven't moved yet.

   _____

3. They're not having problems with Canadian customs.

   _____

4. Recently she's been planning a party.

   _____

5. It's difficult work.

   _____

15 Edit the following paragraph twice and rewrite it correctly. The first time, see if the ideas are well organized. Do you need to rearrange any sentences? The second time, correct any problems with verb tenses and form. Make any other changes you think are necessary.

Marta Duarte has have a very interesting year. Last June she graduated from a tourism

development course in Mexico. She received a scholarship to study English and has been

attending classes here at the University of Ottawa since September. marta is twenty-five years old. She's also been traveling in Canada and the United States. She love dance and goes dancing at least two nights a week. She visits hotels to study the different management systems and has learned a lot. In fact, she says that one day in a hotel is better than ten days in a classroom. However, Marta hasn't spend all her time in Canada at work. She also find time to develop a close friendship with the manager of a big hotel here in Ottawa. She is hoping to get to know him better.

Editing Your Writing

16   **Editing Using a Checklist.**   Edit your paragraph using the following checklist.

Editing Checklist

1. Content
   a. Is the information interesting?
   b. Is all the information in the paragraph important?
2. Organization
   a. Does the topic sentence give the main idea of the paragraph?
   b. Are the sentences well organized?
   c. Does the paragraph have a good concluding sentence?
3. Cohesion and Style
   Did you use transitional expressions correctly?
4. Grammar
   Did you use correct verb forms?
5. Form
   a. Did you use commas correctly?
   b. Did you spell the verb forms correctly?
   c. Did you use correct capitalization?

17   **Peer Editing.**   Exchange papers with a classmate and discuss the changes you made.

Writing the Second Draft

18   Write the second draft of your paragraph using correct form. Then give it to your teacher for comments.

| PART 5 | **Grammar** |

A. Time Expressions with the Present Perfect: *for, since, all, always*

In Chapter 6, you learned that the present perfect tense refers to actions that occurred at an unspecified time in the past, or to repeated past actions. The present perfect also describes actions or situations that began in the past and continue to the present. This tense tells how long something has lasted up to this point.

This meaning of the present perfect usually appears with a time expression. A phrase with *since, for, all,* or *always* can answer the questions "*How long…?*" or "*Since when…?*"

	Examples	**Notes**
for	I have played soccer **for** 5 years.	Use *for* with the amount of time an activity or state has lasted. Examples: *for* an hour, *for* a week, *for* five years, *for* a long time.
since	They have been married **since** January.	Use *since* with a time or point that shows when an activity or state started. Examples: *since* 7:00, *since* Monday, *since* May 15th, *since* my birthday
all	She has been at her friend's house **all** week.	Use *all* to express a time period. Examples: *all* day, *all* night, *all* week, *all* my life all + day/month, year, morning
always	We have **always** wanted to · for a very long time	Use *always* to show that an action or state began in the past and continues to the present. *Always* comes between the auxiliary verb and the main verb.

I have liked pizza for as long as I can remember.

1   Fill in the blanks in the following sentences with *for, since, all,* or *always*.

Example: They have been at the beach _____ all _____ day.

1. Sarah has _____ always _____ been my best friend.

2. I have known her _____ since _____ nursery school.

3. I have _____ always _____ told her all of my secrets.

4. We have lived in this town _____ all _____ our lives.   for our whole lives.

5. We have _____ always _____ wanted to travel.

6. We've talked about it _____ for _____ years.

7. She's been on summer vacation with her family _____ for _____ three weeks.

8. She has been gone _____ since _____ May.

9. I've been lonely and bored _____ since _____ she's been gone.

2   Combine each pair of sentences using the present perfect and *for* or *since*.

Example: She joined the soccer team last year. She is still a member of the soccer team.
She has been a member of the soccer team for a year.

1. Juanita liked Daniel three years ago. She still likes him.
   Juanita has liked Daniel for three years.

2. Adrian moved to Mexico last year. He still lives there.
   Adrian has lived to Mexico since last year.

3. Angela was tired this morning. She's still tired.
   Angela has tired since this morning.

4. Jong got a cell phone in 1998. He still has a cell phone.
   Jong has had a cell phone since 1998.

5. They woke up at 8:00. They are still awake.
   They have been wake up since 8:00

6. She turned the stereo on an hour ago. The stereo is still on.
   She has been on for an hour.

7. I wasn't hungry last night. I'm still not hungry.
   I haven't been hungry since last night.

8. My visitors arrived a week ago. They are still here.
   My visitors have been here for a week.

B. Present Perfect: Time Clauses with *Since*

Sentences in the present perfect (or present perfect continuous) tense often have a time clause with *since*.

Examples	Notes
They've been in love **since** the first time **they saw** each other	The main clause must be in the present perfect (continuous) tense.
	The clause with *since* is usually in the simple past tense. A *since* clause can come at the beginning or at the end of a sentence.
Since I joined the gym, I've had more energy.	A comma is used after the clause when it comes at the beginning of the sentence.

3   Combine each pair of sentences into one sentence using *since*. Combine the sentences in the order in which they appear. Use correct punctuation.

Example: Young went on a diet. He has lost a lot of weight.
Since Young went on a diet, he has lost a lot of weight.

1. Hanna has met a lot of new people. She joined the tennis club.
   Hanna has met a lot of new people since she joined the tennis club.

2. Alfonso went to the concert last night. He has had a headache.

Since Alfonso went to the concert last night, he has had a headache.

3. Taro went on vacation. He has been much more relaxed.

Since Taro went on vacation, he has been much more relaxed.

4. I haven't seen Reiko and Yoko. They moved to an apartment off campus.

I haven't seen Reiko and Yoko since they moved to an apartment off campus.

5. Patrick hasn't been in school. He broke his leg.

Patrick hasn't been in school since he broke his leg.

C. The Present Perfect Continuous Tense

The present perfect continuous tense consists of *have/has been* before the *-ing* form of a verb. When the present perfect continuous is used with time expressions, it stresses the duration or repetition of an action or situation that began in the past and continues to the present. It often implies that the action or situation will continue in the future.

Time expressions often used with this tense include *for, since, all (day, week, etc.), today,* and *this (week, summer, etc.).* Questions with *How long* are frequently used with this tense. When the tense is used without mention of specific time, it is used to talk about a general activity that has been in progress recently. This meaning of the present perfect can be used with inexact time expressions such as *recently, lately,* and *these days.*

Statements		
Purpose	**Examples**	
	Affirmative	**Negative**
To emphasis duration of an activity that started in the past and continues to the present	It**'s been raining** for an hour. She**'s been talking** on the phone all evening.	We **haven't been living** here for more than a month. I **haven't been playing** soccer this week.
To express a general activity that has been in progress recently	I**'ve been going** to a lot of parties recently. He**'s been reading** a good book.	He **hasn't been sleeping** well recently. I **haven't been doing** much.

Present Perfect Con → talk about time but if present progressive → no time.

guinea pigs.

Questions			
	Examples	**Possible Answers**	
		Affirmative	**Negative**
Yes / No questions	**Have** you **been seeing** a lot of movies? **Has** she **been living** here long?	Yes, I have. Yes, she has.	No, I haven't. No, she hasn't.
Information questions	Where **have** you **been living**? Who**'s been playing** music?	London. My neighbors have.	

Notes: 1. See Appendix 3 for spelling rules for the *-ing* ending. 2. Some verbs are not normally used in the continuous tense. These nonaction verbs include verbs which express feeling and thought, possession, and sensory perception.

4   Form present perfect continuous sentences with the cue words below. Add a time expression (*since, for,* or *all*) to each.

Example: I / preparing for the party / 2:00 this afternoon
<u>I have been preparing for the party since 2:00 this afternoon.</u>

1. I / look forward to this party / weeks
<u>I have been looking forward to this party for weeks.</u>

2. the music / play / night
<u>The music has been playing all night.</u>

3. everyone / dance / hours
<u>Everyone has been dancing for hours.</u>

4. that woman / flirt with that man / the party began
<u>That woman has been flirting with that man since the party began.</u>

5. that couple / fight / the party began
<u>That couple have been fighting since the party began</u>

5   Form present perfect continuous questions beginning with *How long* for each of the following sentences. Then answer the questions.

Example: A: He is saving money for a sports car.

     B: <u>How long has he been saving money for a sports car?</u>

     A: <u>He's been saving for about six months.</u>

1. A: Oscar and Melina have been arguing a lot.
   B: <u>How long have Oscar and Melina been arguing</u> ?
   A: <u>They have been arguing for three hours.</u>

2. A: She's been flirting with Felipe!
   B: <u>How long she has been flirting with Felipe</u> ?
   A: <u>She's been flirting him since they studied the same class in the university.</u>

3. A: She dyes her hair.
    B: How long has she been dying her hair ?
    A: She has been dying since she was a teenager.

ยายเพราะทำ ใช้บอกปัจจุบันแต่กริยาสั้นหน่อยให้ เหมือนเป็นตลาดแต่ง ตม

4. A: He wears a hairpiece.
    B: How long has he been wearing a hairpiece ?
    A: He has been wearing for two years.

5. A: He's dieting.
    B: How long has he been dieting ?
    A: He has been dieting since he became a movie star.

6. A: Felipe lives downtown.
    B: How long has Felipe been living downtown ?
    A: He has been living downtown since he got a new job.

D. The Present Perfect Continuous Versus The Present Perfect

The present perfect continuous and present perfect tenses both describe actions or situations that began in the past and continue to the present.

	Examples	**Notes**
Present perfect continuous	We've **been talking** for hours. How long **has** it **been** raining?	The present perfect emphasizes the duration or repetition of the activity or situation.
present perfect	She **has been** in London all summer. She**'s liked** him for years. I **have known** him for six years.	The present perfect emphasizes the length of time the activity or situation has lasted. The present perfect is used with verbs that are not usually used in the continuous tense (nonaction verbs). (NOT: ~~I have been knowing him for six years.~~)
Present perfect continuous OR present perfect	I **have lived** here since 1993. = I **have been living** here since 1993.	With certain verbs (such as *live*, *work*, and *teach*), there is little or no difference in meaning between the present perfect and the present perfect continuous when a time expression is used.

6 Circle the correct verb choice in each set of parentheses.

A. A: You look worried. Is anything wrong?

B: Well . . . I've (thought / (been thinking)) about asking out a girl in my English

class.

A: What's the problem?

B: I don't think she has ((noticed) / been noticing) me since the class began.

B. A: Rahim, wake up.

B: How long have I (slept / (been sleeping))?

A: You've (snored / (been snoring)) almost since we started the video. I thought

that you liked horror movies.

B: I haven't ((liked) / been liking) them since I was a kid.

C. A: My boyfriend has (acted / (been acting)) strange lately.

B: What has he (done / (been doing))?

A: Well, he hasn't ((had) / been having) much time for me for weeks now. He also

hasn't ((been), been being) home for the last few nights. I have ((called) / been

calling) him, but nobody ever answers.

B: Hasn't he (studied, (been studying)) for final exams? Maybe he's been at the

library.

D. A: Hey, it's time to get ready for the party. We've got to clean up this

apartment.

B: Can't you see that I've (cleaned up / (been cleaning up)) the

apartment all morning? Why haven't you two ((helped) / (been

helping)) me?

C: I've (thought / (been thinking)) about the refreshments and the

music for hours. Someone has to make the plans.

Video Activities: Online Love Story

Before You Watch.   Discuss these questions in small groups.

1.   What is a "chat room"? Have you ever visited one?
2.   Do you think the Internet is a useful way to meet new people?
3.   How do you usually meet people?
4.   Do you believe that there is only one man or woman in the world who is exactly "right" for each person?

Watch.   Number the following events in the order that they happened.

___2___   Patrick and Vesna chatted online.

___5___   They got married.

___1___   Patrick came home from work late and couldn't sleep.

___4___   Patrick and Vesna got engaged.

___3___   Vesna came to Patrick's house.

Watch Again.   Discuss these questions in small groups.

1.   Patrick asked Vesna, "What do you look like?" Her answer was "You won't run from me." What did she mean?
2.   Why was it easy for Patrick and Vesna to meet?
3.   How soon after they met did Patrick and Vesna get engaged?
4.   How soon after that did they get married?
5.   What did Patrick and Vesna's friends predict about their relationship?
6.   What do Patrick and Vesna say about one another?
7.   What is the "Romance Network"?

After You Watch.

Work with a partner. One student is "Vesna" and the other is "Patrick." You meet in a chat room for the first time. Patrick begins by introducing himself. Then Vesna reads what he wrote and responds. Continue "chatting" until your teacher tells you to stop. You may write on paper or a computer. Be sure to ask each other questions in order to keep the conversation going.

Chapter 9

Customs, Celebrations, and Holidays

IN THIS CHAPTER

Listening
- Listening for main ideas
- Listening for specific information
- Identifying stressed words and reductions
- Taking notes on the history of a holiday (specific information)

Speaking
- Dropping the /h/ sound
- Taking about holidays
- Summarizing main ideas
- Making and responding to invitations

Reading
- Previewing vocabulary
- Reading: A Traditional Holiday

- Making inferences
- Summarizing

Writing
- Developing ideas: making an outline, prioritizing information
- Listing information
- Unifying a paragraph with pronouns
- Using nonrestrictive relative clauses
- Writing about holidays using an outline
- Editing for punctuation of nonrestrictive relative clauses

Grammar
- Gerunds and infinitives as subjects
- Verbs followed by gerunds and infinitives

PART 1

Listening to Conversations

Before You Listen

1 **Prelistening Questions.**   Before you listen, talk about holidays with a partner.

1.   Name two or three holidays that are celebrated around the world.
2.   In what situations do people in your culture usually give gifts?
3.   Do you know of any other romantic holidays?

2 **Vocabulary Preview.**   Complete the sentences with these words from the conversation. Then go back and write the meaning of the words in the chart.

Words	Definitions
cologne	perfume, more expensive than perfume *(concentrate than perfume / more)*
jewelry	rings, bracelet, earing, necklace, watch
elegant	sth nice, beautiful, formal dress, classic
romántic	kiss, flower, special thing of love
bracelet	jewelry that put on the wrist
(What) else	something more

1.   A: What's that smell?

     B: It's my new ___cologne___. Do you like it?

     A: Yeah, it smells like flowers.

2.   A: What kind of gift should I get Mary for her birthday?

     B: Don't get ___jewelry___. She's got a box full of rings and earrings and necklaces, and she never wears any of them.

Cross-Cultural Note

February 14th is Valentine's Day in the United States. On this holiday, people give people they love greeting cards and romantic gifts such as flowers or candy.

3.   The president's wife is a very ___elegant___ woman. Everything she wears is fashionable and in good taste.

4.   We went to Hawaii for our honeymoon. We had a beautiful hotel room right on the beach. It was so ___romantic___!

5.   My boyfriend gave me a gold ___bracelet___ for my birthday. I wear it on my left arm.

6.   We're having pasta and salad for dinner. What ___else___ would you like?

Listen

3   **Listening for Main Ideas.**   Kenji has just started dating a young American woman he met in class.

1.   Close your book and listen to the conversation between Kenji and the gift shop clerk. Listen for the answers to these questions.

   1.   What is Kenji looking for? *a gift for American girl on Valentine's day*

   2.   Why doesn't he want to buy any chocolate? *That girl is on a diet.*

   3.   Why doesn't Kenji want to buy jewelry? *it's expensive. He can't not spend much money.*

   4.   What else does the saleswoman recommend? *cologne, bracelet*

   5.   What does Kenji finally decide to do?
        He'll bring a nice card with flowers is red rose.

2.   Compare answers with a partner.

Stress

4 **Listening for Stressed Words.**   Listen to the conversation again.

1.   Some of the stressed words are missing. During each pause, repeat the phrase or sentence. Then fill in the blanks with words from the list.

bracelet	expensive	hope	perfume	told
card	flowers	idea	pretty	unusual
chocolate	get	jewelry	romantic	whatever
cologne	girlfriend	money	rose	worry
diet	guess	perfect	sure	yet
else	help (2 times)		that's	

Clerk: Hello. Can I ___help___ you with anything?

Kenji: I'm looking for a Valentine's Day gift for my ___girlfriend___. Well, actually, she's not my girlfriend ___yet___, so I really don't know what to ___get___ her.

Clerk: How about some ___chocolate___?

Kenji: Well, I think she's on a ___diet___.

Clerk: Hmm, then how about some ___jewelry___?

Kenji: Like what?

Clerk: Well, look at this ___bracelet___. It's simple but very elegant, don't you think?

Kenji: It's ___pretty___, but I really can't spend that much ___money___.

Clerk: Okay. Let's see . . . What ___else___? . . .Well, here's a nice bottle of ___cologne___. I'm ___sure___ she'll like that.

Kenji: Actually she once ___told___ me that she doesn't like any kind of ___perfume___. And anyway, I really wanted to give her something ___unusual___.

Clerk: I'm afraid something unusual might be ___expensive___. Look, I have an ___idea___. Why don't you get her a nice ___card___ and give it to her with one ___perfect___ red ___rose___. Most women love to get ___flowers___. Doesn't that sound ___romantic___?

Kenji: Yeah, I ___guess___ so. Okay, ___that's___ what I'll do.

Clerk: Don't ___worry___. I'm sure she'll like ___whatever___
you give her.

Kenji: Oh, I ___hope___ so. Thanks for your ___help___.

2.   Now read the conversation with a partner. Practice stressing words correctly.

Reductions

Dropping the /h/ sound

The /h/ sound is not pronounced when it is

- unstressed
- in the middle of a phrase
- at the end of a sentence

This happens very often with pronouns.

For example:
Long: I don't know what to get her.
Short: I don't know what to get 'er.

Long: Has he arrived yet?
Short: Has 'e arrived yet?

In the following examples, the /h/ is not dropped because it is in a stressed word.

Can I help you?
I hope so.

5   **Comparing Long and Reduced Forms.**   Listen to the following sentences.
They contain reduced forms. Repeat them after the speaker.

Reduced form*	**Long form**
1. I don't know what to get 'er.	I don't know what to get her.
2. Give it to 'im.	Give it to him.
3. Is 'e ready?	Is he ready?
4. What's 'is name?	What's his name?
5. Where 'uv you been?	Where have you been?
6. Susan 'as finished her homework.	Susan has finished her homework.
7. He helped 'er with the housework.	He helped her with the housework.

* *Note:* The underlined forms are not acceptable spellings in written English.

6   **Listening for Reductions.**   Listen to the following conversation between two roommates. You'll hear the reduced forms of some words.

1.   Repeat each sentence during the pause. Then write the long forms in the blanks.

Jane: Hi Helen. Are ___you___ going out?

Helen: Yeah, I'm going downtown. It's my brother's birthday tomorrow, ___and___ I ___want___ ___to___ buy ___him___ a gift. ___Do___ ___you___ ___want___ ___to___ come with me?

Jane: I really can't . . . I ___have___ ___to___ study for a big test. But ___Can___ ___you___ do me a favor?

Helen: OK.

Jane: ___Could___ ___you___ buy me some film? My sister just had a baby boy . . .

Helen: Really? Congratulations! What's ___his___ name?

Jane: Jeremy. He's *so* cute, but my poor sister is *so* tired. I'm ___going___ ___to___ visit ___her___ this weekend and give ___her___ a hand. ___And___ while I'm there, I'm ___going___ ___to___ take some pictures of the baby.

Helen: OK, no problem.

Jane: Thanks. See ___you___ later.

After You Listen

7   **Vocabulary Review.**   Discuss the following questions with a partner. Use the underlined vocabulary in your answers.

1.   Which of the following gifts have you received or given in the last year?
   a.   candy   c.   flowers
   b.   jewelry   d.   cologne

2.   Where would you go if you wanted to spend a romantic evening?

3.   Do you like to wear bracelets?

4.   Are you an elegant person? Why or why not?

5.   You are studying English in school. What else are you studying?

Talk It Over

American Holidays

Below is a calendar with some major holidays that are celebrated in the United States.

Jan **January** 1 New Year's Day	**Feb** **February** 14 Valentine's Day	**Mar** **March**	**Apr** **April** Easter (date changes every year)
May **May** 30 Memorial Day	**Jun** **June**	**Jul** **July** 4 Independence Day (the 4th of July)	**Aug** **August**
Sept **September**	**Oct** **October** 31 Halloween	**Nov** **November** 4th Thursday: Thanksgiving	**Dec** **December** 25 Christmas 31 New Year's Eve

1. Divide the class into teams of eight. Each student should pick one holiday to report on.

2. Turn to pages 284-285 and read the information about your holiday.

3. Give a short presentation to your group about this holiday.

Talking about Holidays

Tell the class about your favorite holiday. Give the following information:

- the date
- why you celebrate this holiday
- special foods
- special customs
- the symbols of this holiday

PART 2	# Recalling Main Ideas

Before You Listen

1   **Prelistening Questions.**   Before you listen, talk about holidays for giving thanks.

1. In your community, do you have a holiday for giving thanks? If so, tell your classmates about it.
   - When is this holiday?
   - Whom do you thank on this holiday?
   - Do you eat special foods on this day?
   - What are some customs that people observe on this day?

2. Review what you have learned about Thanksgiving.

2   **Vocabulary Preview.**   You will hear the following underlined words in the conversation. Before you listen, write the letter of the correct definition beside each sentence.

Sentences	Definitions
_F_ 1. This cake is <u>delicious</u>. May I please have another piece?	a. people who come to live permanently in a new country
_D_ 2. We <u>planted</u> tomatoes last month. They grew very quickly, and now they're ready for eating.	b. the total amount of fruit or vegetables that is collected from the fields when they are ready
_E_ 3. We can <u>pick</u> some for dinner, if you like.	c. types of vegetables
_B_ 4. We didn't have much rain this year, so our apple <u>harvest</u> was smaller than usual.	d. to put vegetable or fruit seeds in the earth so that they can grow
_A_ 5. Each year the United States and Canada receive thousands of <u>immigrants</u> from hundreds of different countries.	e. to remove a fruit or vegetable from the plant when it is ready to eat
_C_ 6. My family eats a lot of <u>corn</u>, <u>squash</u>, and other vegetables.	f. appealing to taste and smell

Listen

3   **Listening for Main Ideas.**   Kenji is having Thanksgiving dinner with Peter and his family. Listen to the conversation. As you listen, answer these questions.

1. Who were the two groups of people to first celebrate Thanksgiving in the United States?
2. What did the first Thanksgiving celebrate?

Cross-Cultural Note

The first Europeans to settle in North America came from England. In 1620 they built a town called Plymouth in the area that today is the state of Massachusetts.

Today we call these early immigrants Pilgrims. They came here because they wanted a place where they could practice their religion freely.

Taking Notes on Specific Information.   Listen to the conversation again. This time, take notes in the spaces below.

The first Thanksgiving: who? _Pilgrims & Indian [native American]_
why? _Thanks for the harvest._
when? _400 years ago_

Special foods: _Turkey, corn, squash_
Thanksgiving today: when? _the 4th Thursday of November_
customs: _the family gets together._

After You Listen

5   **Summarizing Main Ideas.**   Work with a partner.

1. Student A: Imagine that you were at the first Thanksgiving. Use your notes from Activity 4 to tell your partner what you saw and experienced at this event.
2. Student B: Imagine that you were invited to Thanksgiving dinner with an American family. Use your notes to tell your partner about your experience.

6   **Vocabulary Review.**   Discuss the following questions with a partner. Use the underlined vocabulary in your answers.

1.   In your opinion, which foods are the most <u>delicious</u> in the following categories:

    fruit   drink

    vegetable   dessert

    meat

2.   Have you ever <u>planted</u> or <u>picked</u> vegetables? Did you enjoy it?

3.   Does your country receive many <u>immigrants</u>? From where?

4.   Do you like to eat <u>corn</u> and <u>squash</u>?

5.   In your culture, do you have a holiday or special customs to celebrate the picking of the <u>harvest</u>?

Using Language

Inviting	Accepting Invitations	Refusing Invitations
Would you like to...?	I'd love to ...	I'd love to, but ...
Do you want to...?	I'd be delighted to ... _happy_	I'm sorry but ...
Why don't you (we)...?	That sounds great!	I wish I could, but ...
Are you free...? _to go to dinner_	Thank you for the invitation.	Thanks, but
		Thanks for asking, but…

7   **Making Invitations.**   Use the expressions in the explanation box to role-play making and accepting invitations. Perform one of the role-plays in front of the class — without reading!

Example:

    A: My dad is barbecuing tonight.

            <u>Would you like to come over for dinner?</u>

    B: <u>Sure, I'd love to. What time?</u>

    A: <u>Around seven o'clock.</u>

    B: <u>Great! I'll see you then.</u>

1.   *A:*   My family is getting together for Thanksgiving dinner.

            Do you want to enjoy with us? ?

    B: _Sure, I'd love to. What time?_

    A: _six o'clock exactly_

    B: _See you later._

2.   *A:*   I know about a Halloween party on Saturday.

Are you free to go to a Halloween party on Saturday?

B: Of course. That sounds great! Where is it?

A: At my house at 8:00 pm.

B: I'll be there.

3.   *A:*   What are you doing on New Year's Eve?

Do you want to see fireworks with me?

B: I'd love to. What time is it?

A: Around 9 o'clock

B: _____

4.   *A:*   There's a new movie at the Fox Theater.

_____?

B: _____

A: _____

B: _____

 **8**   **Refusing Invitations.**   With a partner, take turns inviting and refusing the following invitations. To be polite, you should try to explain why you can't accept. You might suggest getting together another time.

Here are some more ways to refuse an invitation:

Thanks, but I can't. I have to work.
Thanks for asking, but I have other plans.
I'd love to, but I'm busy. Maybe some other time.

1.   *A:*   Would you like to go swimming this afternoon?

B: I'm sorry but I'm sick.

2.   *A:*   Why don't you have a cup of coffee with us?

B: Thanks, but I drank already at my house.

3.   *A:*   Do you want to go to the ball game tomorrow? I have an extra ticket.

B: I'm sorry but I'm supposed to help my friend.

4.   *A:*   We're going dancing Saturday night. Would you like to come?

B: Thanks for asking, but I don't know how to dance.

| PART 3 | # Reading |

Before You Read

1   **Vocabulary Preview.**   Learn the meanings of these vocabulary items from the reading.

(handwritten left margin) parslay

Nouns	a symbol	coffins	**Phrases**
a god *male*	broomsticks	graves	hold on (to)
a goddess *female*	devils	cemeteries	dress up (as) *← costume/fa*
ghosts	gum		ring doorbells *party*
spirits	mixture	**Verbs**	"trick or treat"
saints	costumes	celebrate	light candles
the harvest *bring the*	disguises *ล้อเลียน*	rule	baked goods
gardens *feed at of*	skulls *costume*	chase	
witches *the field*	skeletons *not much fun*		

(handwritten) hold on do ya hat → sth ya don't believe

Read

(handwritten) connecting idea→not true or false

Making Inferences. The first time readers skim a piece of information, they usually read for *literal* meaning — that is to say, they find out quickly what the material says. After this quick reading, they can usually tell the topic of the material and the main idea or point. On a second, more careful reading, readers often infer (recognize and understand) thoughts that the writer did not state directly.

After you read each of the following five paragraphs for literal (basic) meaning, complete the possible title on the line before the material. On the line that follows the information, finish the possible statement of the main idea or point. Then to better understand the writer's meaning, read the material a second time.

A Traditional Holiday

A   *Title: The First Halloween*

Hundreds of years before the birth of Christ, the Celts—the inhabitants of parts of France and the British Isles—held a festival at the beginning of every winter for the Lord of the Dead. The Celts believed that this god ruled the world in winter, when he called together the ghosts of dead people. On October 31, people believed these spirits of the dead came back to earth in the forms of animals. They thought that very bad ghosts came back as black cats. At their festival on this day, the Celts used to make big fires to frighten the ghosts and chase them away. This celebration was the beginning of the holiday of Halloween.

Main Idea: _*The begining of the celebration*_ in the Celtic culture, centuries ago in areas of France and the British Isles.

B   *Title: A Mixture of ___ *customs* *

The Romans, who ruled the British Isles after the birth of Christ, also held a celebration at the beginning of winter. Because this was harvest time, the Romans brought apples and nuts for the goddess of gardens. Later, the Christians added their customs to those of the Celts and the Romans. They had a religious holiday on November 1 for the saints (the unusually good people in Christianity), which they called All Hallows' or All Saints' Day. The evening before this day was All Hallows' Even ("holy evening"); later the name of this October 31st holiday became Halloween.

Main Idea: Through the centuries, Halloween added customs from ___Celts___ ___Romans and Christians___ .

C

Title: ___Witches___ *: A Symbol of Halloween*

Long ago in Britain, people used to go to wise old women called "witches" to learn about the future. They believed that these witches had the power to tell the future and to use magic words to protect people or change them. There were many beliefs about witches, who are now a symbol of Halloween. For example, people believed witches flew on broomsticks to big, secret meetings, where they ate, sang, and danced. The Christians tried to stop people from believing in witches, but many uneducated people, especially in the countryside, held on to their beliefs. · _believe (v)_

Main Idea: ___Belief___ associated with witches, a common symbol of Halloween.

D

Title: Halloween in ___North America___

When people came to North America from the British Isles, they brought their Halloween customs with them. Today, Halloween is a night when children dress up in costumes—like ghosts, witches, devils, and so on. They go from house to house in their disguises, ring doorbells, and shout, "Trick or treat!" People give them candy, apples, gum, and nuts, and the children have a good time. But most children have no idea that their holiday has such a long history.

Main Idea: Today in North America, Halloween is ___a night when children dress up in costumes___

E

Title: ___Halloween___ *in Latin American Culture*

Today, Halloween is celebrated—mostly by children—not only in the British Isles and the United States but in other areas of the world as well. Related to this holiday are the "Days of the Dead," a traditional Latin American celebration with a mixture of pre-Hispanic and Roman Catholic customs. In many towns of Mexico, November 1 (All Saints' Day) is a time to remember the "little angels"—babies and children that have died; November 2, or All Souls' Day, is a day in honor of people that died as adults. Neither occasion is meant to be sad or scary; instead, their purpose is to welcome back the souls of the dead. Sweets (candy and baked goods) in the shape of skulls, skeletons, and coffins are available everywhere; families get together at the graves of their relatives in cemeteries, where they light candles, have picnics, make music, and tell stories.

Main Idea: In contrast to Halloween, the Days of the Dead ___is to welcome back the souls of the dead.___ .

After You Read

3 Often a reading selection gives information from which the reader can infer (figure out) other information. Write an *X* on the line in front of the ideas that the author stated (clearly said) or implied (suggested) in the reading selection. Write an *O* before the ideas that the writer did not state or imply—even if the ideas are true.

_____X_____ 1. Halloween began a long time before the birth of Christ.

_____O_____ 2. People today put candles in pumpkins (jack-o'-lanterns) to scare away ghosts.

_____X_____ 3. Ideas about ghosts, black cats, and witches are part of the celebration of Halloween.

_____O_____ 4. The early Romans were Christians.

_____O_____ 5. People associated apples and nuts with Halloween because they were symbols of the harvest in Roman times.

_____X_____ 6. One of the origins of Halloween was religious.

_____O_____ 7. The belief in witches came from Christianity.

_____O_____ 8. Witches could really fly and had the power of magic.

_____X_____ 9. Halloween customs came to the United States from Britain.

_____O_____ 10. The custom of trick-or-treating in costumes comes from the days of the Celts.

_____O_____ 11. If people do not give treats to children on Halloween, they might play tricks; thus, Halloween is a very dangerous holiday.

_____X_____ 12. People in many countries of the modern world celebrate Halloween.

_____O_____ 13. The "Days of the Dead" in Latin American culture have no relationship to Halloween.

_____X_____ 14. All Saints' Day and All Souls' Day are meant to be happy celebrations.

4 **Learning to Summarize.**   In a summary, paraphrase the important information in as few words as possible. Leave out minor details and combine items into a series.

Example:

> Some Halloween symbols are ghosts, black cats, jack-o'-lanterns, and witches.

You can combine short sentences with connecting words.

Example:

> Because the Celts believed the Lord of the Dead called ghosts together on October 31, they made fires to scare away the ghosts.

Work in groups of five. Each student chooses a different paragraph from the reading "A Traditional Holiday." Summarize the information in your paragraph. Then take turns sharing your summary with your group.

PART 4	# Writing

Before You Write

Exploring Ideas

1 **Describing Holidays.**   What are the most important holidays that you celebrate? When do you celebrate these holidays? How do you celebrate them? Complete the following chart.

Holiday	Time of Year	Activities	Description of Activities
Makha Bucha day			
Mother's day	August 12	give some presents (eat)	
Father's day	December 5		
King Rama IV's day	October 23		
Chinese New Year			

2 Work in groups. Look at your list of holidays. How could you divide them into groups? Try dividing them by seasons first (winter holidays, summer holidays). Then suggest other ways to group them (by activity, purpose, etc.).

3 **Building Vocabulary.**   The following chart has examples of vocabulary you can use to talk about holidays. What other words did you use to describe holidays? Add your words to the list. Discuss any words you do not understand.

Nouns	Verbs	Adjectives	Other
celebration	celebrate	traditional	_____
commemoration	commemorate	joyous	_____
parade	_____	_____	_____
fireworks	_____	_____	_____
tradition	_____	_____	_____
joy	_____	_____	_____

Organizing Ideas

Categorizing and Making an Outline

You can organize ideas in outline form. First write notes about the topic. Then divide the notes into categories. Finally, write an outline.

Here is an example of the notes that one student made about holidays in the United States.

Christmas	Independence Day	Memorial Day	Easter
New Year's	Presidents' Day	Labor Day	Passover
Ramadan	Valentine's Day	Halloween	Hanukkah

She decided to divide the holidays into three categories.

1. Civic holidays   2. Religious holidays   3. Traditional holidays

Before the student began to write her paragraph, she made an outline:

I. Holidays in the United States
   A. Civic holidays
      1. Independence Day
      2. Presidents' Day
      3. Memorial Day
      4. Labor Day

   B. Traditional holidays
      1. New Year's
      2. Halloween
      3. Valentine's Day

   C. Religious holidays
      1. Christian holidays
         a. Christmas
         b. Easter
      2. Jewish holidays
         a. Passover
         b. Hanukkah
      3. Muslim holidays
         a. Ramadan

4   You are going to write about holidays in one country. Choose a country, then make an outline like the one above.

Ordering Information According to Importance

When you expand an outline, you usually put the items in order of importance.

5   This student is writing about civic holidays. Some information is missing from her outline. Read her outline, and then read the paragraph that follows. Complete the outline with the missing information.

I.   Holidays in the United States

A.   Civic holidays

  1.   Independence Day

   a.   Fourth of July

   b.   _____

   c.   Picnics, barbecues

   d.   Fireworks

  2.   _____

   a.   Last weekend in May

   b.   Commemorate soldiers who died in all wars

   c.   Parades

   d.   Put flags and flowers on graves

   e.   _____

  3.   Labor Day

   a.   _____

   b.   Honor workers

   c.   Parades

   d.   Picnics, beach

   e.   _____

  4.   _____

   a.   _____

   b.   Honor George Washington's and Abraham Lincoln's birthdays

Holidays in the United States

There are three types of holidays in the United States: civic holidays, traditional holidays, and religious holidays. There are more civic holidays than any other type. The most important civic holiday is Independence Day, the Fourth of July.

On this day we celebrate our independence from Great Britain. Most people spend the day with their family and friends. Picnics and barbecues are very popular. In addition, almost every city and town has a fireworks display at night. Another very important civic holiday is Memorial Day, which falls on the last weekend in May. On this holiday we commemorate all the soldiers who died for our country. Many towns and cities have parades, and some people go to cemeteries and put flowers or flags on the soldiers' graves. A third important civic holiday is Labor Day, which we celebrate on the first Monday in September. This is the day when we honor the workers of the United States. People watch parades, go on picnics, or go to the beach.

For students, Labor Day is a bittersweet holiday, because when it is over they must begin school again. Besides these three civic holidays, we also celebrate Presidents' Day on the third Monday in February. On this day we commemorate the birthdays of George Washington and Abraham Lincoln.

6 Make an outline for the type of holiday you are going to write about.

Write

Developing Cohesion and Style

beside same meaning
        in addition to

Listing Information with in addition to, besides, another, *and* the first, second, third, last

You can use these transitional words to add information:
in addition to, besides, another, and *the first, second, third, last*

Examples:

- *In addition to* watching parades and going on picnics, some Americans go to the beach on Labor Day.
- *Besides* Thanksgiving and New Year's Day, there are other traditional holidays in the United States such as Halloween and Valentine's Day.
- The *first* holiday of the year is New Year's Day.

---

7 Look at the paragraph about holidays in the United States on page 246. Underline the transitional words that are used for adding information.

8 The following paragraphs contain no transitional words. Complete them with the appropriate transitions. More than one answer may be correct.

Paragraph 1

Salvadorans celebrate several civic holidays each year. The most important one is

Independence Day on September 15. On this day, people parade in the streets, sing

songs, and recite poems. _____Another_____ important civic holiday is
                                        1

Labor Day. Labor Day is the first day in May. ___Besides | In addition to___
                                                              2

Labor Day and Independence Day, Salvadorans also celebrate the birthday of

José Matias Delgado, the "father of the country."___In addition to___
                                                            3

these holidays, there are other minor holidays such as *Dia de la Raza.*

Paragraph 2

A groundhog

There are some traditional holidays in the United States that no one celebrates seriously. The _____first_____ one is Ground
₄
Hog Day. Ground Hog Day is February 2. On this day, people look for ground hogs coming out of their nests in the ground. Traditional belief says that if the ground hog sees his shadow, there will be six more weeks of winter. _____Another_____ silly holiday is April
₅
Fool's Day. This holiday falls on April first. On this day, people play tricks on each other. _____Besides_____ Ground Hog Day
₆
and April Fools Day, there is Sadie Hawkins Day. Sadie Hawkins Day is on November 13th. On this day, tradition says that women can ask men to marry them.

Unifying a Paragraph with Pronouns and Pronominal Expressions

You can use pronouns to refer to things you have already mentioned so that you don't have to repeat the same words again and again.

9 Here is a list of the pronouns and pronominal expressions in the paragraph about holidays in the United States on page 246. Tell what each one refers to.

1. on this day (line 4)   Independence Day

2. on this holiday (line 8)   Memorial Day

3. this is the day (line 12)   Labor Day

4. it (line 14)   Children Day

5. they (line 14)   Student

6. these three civic holidays (line 15)   Independence Day
                                  Memorial Day
                                  Labor Day.

The arepas were delicious. Maria made the arepas.

The arepas, which Maria made, were delicious.

The arepas, which were delicious, were made by Marie.

Using Nonrestrictive Relative Clauses

■ A restrictive relative clause tells you which person or thing the writer is referring to.

Examples:
Christmas is the Christian holiday *that children like best*.
Children *who have been good* get many presents on this day.

■ A nonrestrictive relative clause gives additional information. In nonrestrictive clauses, use *which* instead of *that*. Use commas to separate a nonrestrictive clause from the rest of the sentence.

Examples:
Thanksgiving, *which falls in November*, is a time for families.
Another traditional holiday is Halloween, *which is mainly for children*.

■ The information in a nonrestrictive relative clause is not necessary. You can omit a nonrestrictive relative clause, but you cannot omit a restrictive relative clause.

Examples:
Thanksgiving, *which falls in November*, is a time for families to get together. (nonrestrictive)

Notice that you can omit the clause *which falls in November*: Thanksgiving is a time for families to get together.

Christmas is the holiday *that I like best*. (restrictive)

Notice that if you omit the clause *that I like best*, the sentence is incomplete:
Christmas is the holiday.

---

10 Combine these sentences with *which* and a nonrestrictive relative clause. Insert a clause at the ∧ mark.

1. Easter ∧ is a happy holiday. Easter comes in the springtime.

   Easter, which comes in the spring time, is a happy holiday.

2. The Fourth of July ∧ is a time for big parades and fireworks. The Fourth of July is Independence Day.

   The Fourth of July, which is Independence Day, is a time for big parades and fireworks.

3. Martin Luther King Day ∧ comes in January. Martin Luther King Day is our newest holiday.

   Martin Luther King Day, which comes in January, is our newest holiday.

I.D. is an important day. There is a parade on ID.

On ID, which is an important day, there is a parade.

4. Halloween ∧ is a favorite children's holiday. Halloween is an ancient British tradition.

    Halloween which is an acient British tradition, is a favorite children's holiday.

5. On New Year's Day ∧ there is a famous parade in Pasadena, California. New Year's Day is the first holiday of the year.

    On New Year's Day, which is the first holiday of the year, there is a famous parade in Pasadena, California.

6. Ground Hog Day ∧ is not a serious holiday. Ground Hog Day is in February.

    Ground Hog Day, which is in Feb, is not a serious holiday.

11 Write three sentences using nonrestrictive relative clauses about the holiday in your outline. Use correct punctuation.

Writing the First Draft

12 Write your paragraph about holidays in the country you have chosen. Use your outline and the sentences you wrote using nonrestrictive relative clauses.

Edit and Revise

Editing Practice

Punctuating Nonrestrictive Relative Clauses

■ Use commas to separate a nonrestrictive clause from the rest of the sentence. If the clause comes in the middle of the sentence, use two commas.

Example:

Valentine's Day, which falls on February 14, is a holiday for lovers.

■ If the clause comes at the end of the sentence, use only one comma.

Example:

Memorial Day is in May, which is almost the beginning of the summer in the United States.

13   Add commas where necessary in these sentences.

1. Songkran which is the Thai New Year is on April 13.
2. Eid-e-Ghorbon is a religious holiday in Iran which is a Muslim country.
3. Christmas which is an important holiday in Christian countries is usually a happy time.
4. Bastille Day which is on July 14 is a very important holiday in France.
5. My birthday which is February 24th is a holiday in Mexico.
6. Labor Day is the first weekend in September which is also the beginning of school in the United States.
7. Day of the Dead which is an important holiday in many Christian countries is not celebrated in the United States.
8. Groundhog Day which Americans celebrate on February 2nd is not an official holiday.

Editing Your Writing

14   **Editing Using a Checklist.**   Edit your paragraph using the following checklist.

Editing Checklist

1. Content
   a. Is the information interesting?
   b. Is there enough information?
2. Organization
   a. Did you list the holidays from most important to least important?
   b. Did you give the same type of information about each holiday?
3. Cohesion and Style
   a. Did you use expressions such as *in addition to, besides, another, the first (second*, etc.)?
   b. Did you use pronouns and pronominal expressions appropriately?
   c. Did you use relative clauses correctly?

15   **Peer Editing.**   Exchange papers with a classmate and discuss the changes you made.

Writing the Second Draft

16   Write the second draft of your paragraph using correct form. Then give it to your teacher for comments.

PART 5

Grammar

A. Gerunds and Infinitives as Subjects

Gerunds and infinitives can appear as subjects of sentences. Their meaning is identical.

Examples		Notes
Infinitive	**Gerund**	
It's fun **to get** presents.	**Getting** presents is fun.	A sentence with an infinitive subject begins with the impersonal *it;* the infinitive follows the adjective or noun.
Is it universal **to celebrate** birthdays?	Is **celebrating** birthdays universal?	A gerund is formed by putting an *-ing* ending on a verb. A gerund or a gerund phrase can be used as the subject of a sentence.

Note: Not is placed in front of a gerund to make the gerund negative.

1 Make an equivalent sentence, with a gerund or an infinitive, for each of the following sentences.

Example: Guessing what's in the box is hard.
  <u>It's hard to guess what's in the box.</u>

1. It's hard to blow up balloons.
  <u>Blowing up balloons is hard.</u>

2. It's fun to make a birthday cake.
  <u>Making a birthday cake is fun.</u>

3. Decorating the house with balloons and colored streamers takes time.
  <u>It takes time to decorate the house with balloons and colored streamers</u>

4. Singing "Happy Birthday to You" is traditional.
  <u>It's a traditional to sing "Happy Birthday to You"</u>

5. It's not easy to blow out all the candles.
  <u>Blowing out all the candles isn't easy.</u>

6. Making a wish before you blow out the candles is very important.
  <u>It's very important to make a wish before you blow out the candles.</u>

7. Opening the presents is exciting.
  <u>It is exciting to open the presents.</u>

8. It's great to be with all of your friends.
  <u>Being with all of your friends is great.</u>

9. It's sad to say goodbye to your guests.
  <u>Saying goodbye to your guests is sad.</u>

10. Washing the dishes after the party isn't fun.
  <u>It's not fun to wash the dishes after the party.</u>

B. Verbs Often Followed by Gerunds or Infinitives

Either a gerund or an infinitive can follow these verbs with little or no difference in meaning.

Examples	Verbs		
I **hate celebrating** my birthday.	begin	hate	love
	can't stand	intend	prefer
I **love to shop** for my friends.	continue	like	start

2 Circle the letter of the correct answer to fill in each blank. If both the gerund and the infinitive are possible, circle both letters.

1. In some Latin cultures, children avoid _____ directly in the eyes of their elders while the elder is speaking to them.
    a. looking
    b. to look

2. In many Asian cultures, people dislike _____ touched by someone they do not know well during a conversation.
    a. being
    b. to be

3. In Russia, people risk _____ a cook if they do not have a second helping of food.
    a. insulting
    b. to insult

4. In Spain, many people prefer _____ dinner after 8:00.
    a. having
    b. to have

5. In Bulgaria, people understand _____ the head from side to side to mean "yes." In most European cultures, it mean "no."
    a. shaking
    b. to shake

6. In the United States, many people don't mind _____ interrupted while they are speaking. In many other countries, this is considered very rude.
    a. being
    b. to be

7. In many Arab and Asian cultures, people avoid _____ physical affection in public.
    a. showing
    b. to show

Video Activities: Puerto Rican Day Parade

Before You Watch.   Discuss these questions in small groups.

1. What is a parade?
2. What kinds of things and people can you see in a parade?
3. What do you know about Puerto Rico?

Watch.   Discuss these questions in small groups.

1. What does the Puerto Rican Day Parade commemorate?
2. Which of the following things or people were part of the parade?

   spectators   a marching band   floats
   a fire truck   clowns   police
   a queen   flag wavers   the mayor of New York

Watch Again.   Fill in the missing information.

1. Columbus discovered Puerto Rico _____ years ago.
2. The queen says she feels _____ of her people.
3. The kind of music that Tito Puente plays is called _____.
4. _____ people traveled from Puerto Rico to New York
   for the parade.

After You Watch.   Work in small groups. Imagine that you are on the planning committee for the _____ Day Parade. Discuss the questions below to help you plan your parade. Then share your idea with the class.

1. What will you name your parade? Fill in the blank: The _____
   Day Parade. (You may choose the name of a national, ethnic, special
   interest, or religious group.)
2. What is the purpose of your parade? In other words, what do you want to
   celebrate?
3. Who will walk in your parade? Which people will you invite?
4. Where will you have this parade? In which city or area?
5. What kind of food do you want to sell during the parade?
6. What kind of music, or which musical group(s), do you want to include?
7. Will you have any animals in your parade?
8. Will you have floats? What kind?

Chapter 10

Science and Technology

IN THIS CHAPTER

Listening
- Listening for main ideas
- Listening for specific information
- Identifying stressed words and reductions
- Taking notes on a speech (main ideas)
- Outlining notes

Speaking
- The American /t/
- Discussing technology in the home
- Summarizing main ideas

Reading
- Previewing vocabulary
- Reading: Everyday Uses of Technology

- Reviewing outline organization
- Understanding the main idea
- Special uses of italics and quotation marks

Writing
- Developing ideas: supporting opinions, writing e-mail subject lines
- Unifying writing with synonyms and pronouns
- Giving opinions and suggestions
- Writing a persuasive e-mail message
- Editing spelling and grammar in computer messages

Grammar
- The passive voice

PART 1

Listening to Conversations

Before You Listen

1   **Prelistening Questions.**   Before you listen, talk about computers with a partner.

1. Do you have a computer in your home? If so, what do you use it for?
2. In what way do people in your family use computers? Who in your family uses computers the most?

2   **Vocabulary Preview.**   Complete the sentences with these words from the conversation. Change the grammar if necessary.

online ^{internet}	research	software $^{program \,\leftarrow\, inside\ the\ computer}$	typewriter	out of date $^{old-fashion}$
laptop	hardware	plug in $^{\rightarrow connect}$ tricks		broke down

1. For listening to music, records and cassettes are ___out of date___. Almost nobody uses them anymore. CDs are much more popular now.

2. I can't watch the news because my TV ___broke down___. I have to call a repairman to fix it.

3. Terry uses his computer for everything: he shops, pays his bills, reads the newspaper, uses a dictionary, and talks to his friends ___online___.

4. Do you know why your stereo isn't working? It's very simple: you forgot to ___plug___ it ___in___ the wall!

5. I asked my professor a question, but he didn't know the answer. He told me to ___research___ the answer in the library or on the Internet.

6. Before I bought a computer, I used my old ___typewriter___ to write letters and school compositions.

7. Carol uses a desktop computer at her office, but takes her ___laptop___ when she travels.

8. Don is a ___software___ engineer. He designs computer programs.

9. You can buy a computer for $500. But that only includes the ___hardware___. You have to buy the programs separately.

10. My dog is very smart. I taught him five ___tricks___ in just one week.

Listen

3 **Listening for Main Ideas.** Ming is talking to her father about computers.

1. Close your book and listen to the conversation. Listen for the answers to these questions.
   1. What is Ming's problem? Her computer was broke down and wants to buy *a new one.*
   2. What does Ming need a computer for? schoolwork, research & writing
   3. What does her father think about computers? *electronic toy* He thought that the computer wasn't necessary.
   4. Can Ming's mother and father use e-mail now? No.
   5. What does Ming suggest to her father at the end of the conversation? If her father buy a new computer, she will give the old computer to her father.
2. Compare answers with a partner. and teach him to use.

Stress

4 **Listening for Stressed Words.** Listen to the conversation again.

1. Some of the stressed words are missing. During each pause, repeat the phrase or sentence. Then fill in the blanks with words from the list.

another	faster	meeting	out	take	typed
computer	get (2 times)	new (3 times)	research	teach	worry
electronic	I	notebook	schoolwork	thinking	years
e-mail	laptop	old (2 times)	so	tricks	you
	library	online	software		

Ming: Dad, my ___computer___ broke down again. I think I need a ___new___ one.

Dad: A new one? You've only had this one for three ___years___.

Ming: Yeah, I know. But it's _____out_____ of date already. I need a _____faster_____ one with more memory.

Dad: You and your _____electronic_____ toys . . .

Ming: It's not a toy, Dad. I need a computer for my_____schoolwork_____. I use it every day for _____research_____, for writing, for . . .

Dad: . . . for _____meeting_____ guys online . . .

Ming: Nooo, I don't do that, don't_____worry_____. Anyway, I was _____thinking_____ . . . how about a_____laptop_____? For Christmas, maybe?

Dad: Why a laptop?

Ming: Because I can _____take_____ it to class to take notes, take it to the _____library_____ . . . A lot of students have them. Believe me, it would make my life _____so_____ much easier.

Dad: I don't _____get_____ it. When _____I_____ was in college, I did just fine with a _____notebook_____ and a pen.

Ming: I know, I know. And you _____type_____ your papers on a typewriter.

Dad: That's right. No _____software_____, no hardware, nothing to plug in.

Ming: Okay, then here's _____another_____ reason you should _____get_____ me a computer. If you get me a _____new_____ one, you can take my _____old_____ one. Then I'll _____teach_____ you and mom how to use_____e-mail_____. And then we can talk _____online_____ every day.

Dad: Hmm. You think you can teach an _____old_____ dog new _____tricks_____?

Ming: Sure I can. Even _____you_____!

2. Now read the conversation with a partner. Practice stressing words correctly.

After You Listen

5   **Vocabulary Review.**   Walk around the class. Ask your classmates about the information given here. Find someone who says "yes" to each question and write his or her name on the line. Use each name only once.

Find Someone Who . . .

_____Isabel_____ owns a laptop computer.

_____Joyce_____ has never used a typewriter.

Aura	has some computer hardware for sale.
Anna	has bought some computer software recently.
Luis	has a passport that is out of date.
Kate	has bought something online recently.
Maria	plugs headphones into a CD player at home.

Pronunciation

> ### The American /t/
>
> In some words, speakers of American English pronounce /t/ between two vowels as a quick /d/ sound. You can hear this sound frequently when we say "it" after /t/:
>
>   _Get it._   _Take it off._   _Fill it in._   _Put it out right away._
>
> This pronunciation change does not happen in British English.
>
> For example: American English: "better"   /beder/
>   British English: "better"   /beter/

6   **Listening for the American /t/.**   Listen and repeat the following examples from the conversation.

1. But it's out of date already.
2. How about a laptop?
3. A lot of students have laptops.
4. I don't get it.
5. I need a computer for my studies.

7   **Pronouncing the American /t/.**   Work in pairs. Each student looks at a different box and follows the instructions in the box.

> ### Student A
>
> Ask the questions below. Your partner will answer with a word containing the American /t/.
>
> 1. What day comes after Friday?
> 2. What's the capital of Mexico?
> 3. What's the opposite of "ugly"?
> 4. My jacket is too warm! What should I do?
> 5. I called my friend, but she isn't home. What should I do?
>
> Now change roles. Listen and answer your partner's questions with one of the words below.
>
>   British English   better   Eat it   Fill it out   I go to work (or school)

Student B

Listen to and answer your partner's questions with a word containing the American /t/. Choose from the list below.

P<u>r</u>e<u>tt</u>y   Call her la<u>te</u>   Take i<u>t</u> off   Mexico Ci<u>t</u>y   Sa<u>t</u>urday

Now change roles. Ask your partner the questions below.

1. Where do you go every morning?
2. What should I do with this new application?.
3. What the opposite of "worse"?
4. What kind of English do people speak in England?
5. This apple looks delicious, and I'm really hungry. What should I do?

Talk It Over

Discussing Technology in the Home

1. Work in small groups. Together make a list of electronic items in your homes.

desktop	motion detector	washer machine
laptop	oven	answering machine
T.V. ✱	dishwasher	telephone
DVD player	toaster	dryer
microwave	vacum	blender
rice cooker		lawn mower

2. Which of these items did not exist when your grandparents were your age?

3. What would your life be like without these things? Describe your life without them.

   Example:

   > If I didn't have a VCR, I couldn't tape my favorite programs on TV.
   > I also couldn't rent movies from the video store.

4. Name three electronic items that you don't own, but would like to have. Explain why you want to have them.

   Example:

   > I would really like to have a personal digital assistant, like the Palm Pilot. It could help me organize my appointments and phone numbers and keep important Websites and other information. It's very small, so I could keep it in my pocket or bag all the time.

PART 2	# Recalling Main Ideas

Before You Listen

1   **Prelistening Questions.**   Before you listen, talk about electric cars with a partner.

1. Do you know anyone who has an electric car? Have you ever driven one?
2. What are some differences between traditional (gas-powered) and electric cars? Guess if you're not sure.

2   **Vocabulary Preview.**   You will hear the following underlined words in the speech. Before you listen, write the letter of the correct definition beside each sentence.

	Sentences	Definitions
G 1.	Smoke from factories and cars <u>pollutes</u> the air.	a. dirt and dangerous chemicals
A 2.	This city is not clean or healthy: it has too much air <u>pollution</u>, water pollution, and noise pollution.	b. a box that keeps electricity
F 3.	Before going on a long trip, I need to buy <u>gasoline</u> for my car.	c. come to an end; have no more
B 4.	My cell phone doesn't have a very good <u>battery</u>; it dies after five days.	d. put energy back into something
C 5.	Be careful. Your car has almost no gasoline. It's going to <u>run out</u> in 10 minutes.	e. share a car (with other riders)
D 6.	When my cell phone is dead, I have to plug it in and <u>recharge</u> it for a few hours.	f. liquid made from petroleum
E 7.	My son <u>carpools</u> to school with four other children every morning.	g. make dirty

Listen

3   **Taking Notes on Main Ideas.**

Listen to the speech. Take notes in the space provided. Focus on the good points, the bad points, and the future of electric cars.

_____

_____

_____

_____

4   **Reviewing Notes.**

Hints for Remembering

It is easier to remember information if you organize your notes into an *outline*. An outline has numbers and letters to separate main ideas from details in a clear way. An outline has key words and phrases—not complete sentences.

Look at your notes in Activity 3. Separate the main ideas from the details and write them in the outline below.

I.   Advantages

  A. _____

  B. _____

  C. _____

II.   Disadvantages

  A. _____

  B. _____

  C. _____

III. Future Developments

  A. _____

  B. _____

  C. _____

5   **Listening for Specific Information.**   Look at the outline while you listen again. Make changes or fill in missing information.

After You Listen

6   **Summarizing Main Ideas.**   Compare notes with a partner. Summarize the story by acting out the role of David and a friend.

Example:

  Dave: Tell your friend that you bought an electric car.

  Friend: You think Dave is crazy for buying an electric car. Tell him about all the negative points.

  Dave: Tell your friend about all the positive points.

7 **Vocabulary Review.**   Discuss the following questions with a partner. Use the underlined vocabulary in your answers.

1. What do you do when your money <u>runs out</u> while you are on vacation?
2. What machines or electronic items in your house work with <u>batteries</u>?
3. Have you ever used a <u>carpool</u> to go to work or school? What are the advantages and disadvantages of carpools?
4. Is there a lot of <u>pollution</u> where you live? What kind of pollution? What is your government doing to reduce it?
5. Look at this sentence and discuss its meaning: "I was so tired that I went to Hawaii for week *to recharge my batteries*." Where would you like to go to "<u>recharge</u> your batteries"?

PART 3   # Reading

Before You Read

1 Discuss the pictures in small groups.

1. What area of science and technology might each picture or symbol represent— for example, atomic energy, chemistry, mechanics, and so on?
2. If you are an expert in one of these subject areas, tell the class a few facts about it.

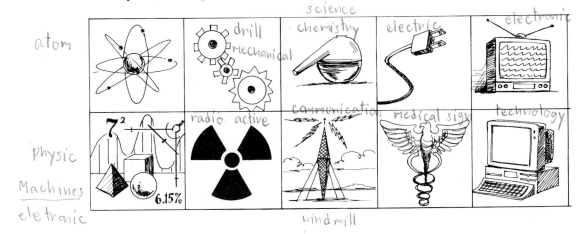

2 Think about the answers to these questions. The reading selection answers them.

1. What are some controversial issues in science and technology today?
2. How can using a computer improve someone's social life and ability to communicate?
3. What are some examples of computer technology in the home?
4. What are some examples of advances in medical technology?

3 **Vocabulary Preview.** Here are some vocabulary items from the reading selection. You can learn them now or come back to them later.

Nouns
- issues
- radiation
- samples
- criminals
- an aspect
- terminals
- connections
- the wish
- the body
- X-rays
- scans
- surgeons
- surgery
- treatments
- a schedule
- an ambulance
- the hospital
- a patient
- a victim

Verbs
- create
- dial
- collect
- distribute
- turn on
- turn off
- record
- program
- advance

Adjectives
- controversial
- convicted
- separate
- warmed-up
- electrical
- interactive
- high-tech

Adverbs
- automatically
- photographically

Phrases
- e.g. (for example)
- a microwave oven
- the medical sciences
- emergency medical technicians
- in the meantime
- radioactive tracers
- organ transplants

Read

4 Read the following material quickly. Then read the explanations and do the exercises after the reading.

Everyday Uses of Technology

A We often hear and read about controversial issues in science and technology. For example, will radiation from electronic equipment negatively change or destroy the environment? Should the DNA samples of convicted criminals be put into a computer data base so investigators can compare it to the DNA of blood at murder scenes? Should medical scientists change gene structures to prevent genetic disease or to create "more perfect" human beings? While people are arguing about these and other controversial subjects, technology continues to influence every aspect of everyday life—the home, health and education, entertainment and communication, etc.

B Some people carry on active social lives with computers—their own or the ones available at terminals in public places like cafés, social centers, libraries, etc. Communicating with others on electronic bulletin boards or in chat rooms, computer users can get to know people they might never meet in traditional ways. Some look for potential dates or mates by computer: they might place personal ads with photos on the screen or even produce digitized video segments for their Websites. With live online video connections, two people with cameras in their computers can see and talk to each other from separate places.

C With modern telephone technology, most people stopped writing letters—especially personal letters and notes. But now, writing to communicate has returned in electronic form, or e-mail, which is a way of sending messages from one computer to another. When a computer is ready to "mail a letter," it dials a server—i.e., a central computer that collects and distributes electronic information. Delivery time from the sender to the receiver is no more than a few seconds, even from one country to another. For some computer users, the wish to communicate intelligently or creatively with others makes them want to write better.

D   Computer technology has also made it possible to run a house electronically. From turning lights on and off on a regular schedule to starting the coffee and cooking the hot cereal, computers are taking care of people at home. Many modern machines (e.g., kitchen appliances) contain computer chips that allow their owners to program them. For instance, you can "instruct" a microwave oven how to cook a certain dish. You can program your electric or gas range, dishwasher, washing machine and dryer, etc., to "do the housework" on their own. Most entertainment equipment operates with computer technology too: some examples are radios, television sets, VCRs (i.e., video-cassette recorders), which can be set up electronically to go on and off, go to certain channels or stations, record specific programs at certain times, and so on. Computers can even start cars automatically so that on cold winter mornings you can get into a warmed-up vehicle and drive off. And of course, the typical U.S. family has a microcomputer (a computer that fits on a table or desk) in their home, which they use for everything from keeping household records and writing letters to playing computer games.

E   Largely because of the computer, technology continues to advance in the medical sciences. One example is the use of computer information in an ambulance before a patient even gets to the hospital. Emergency medical technicians can attach small sensors (i.e., devices with cables) to the patient (e.g., a heart-attack victim) to get information about electrical activity in the heart and the brain. By radio and computer, they can send the information to the hospital so that medical specialists can get ready for the patient's arrival. In the meantime, technicians can get advice on how to keep the patient alive. Later, doctors can look into the patient's body in new ways—not only with X-rays but with CAT (computerized axial tomography) scans and DSA (dynamic spatial reconstruction) scans that photographically "slice through" an organ from any or many different angles. Other methods of collecting medical information are based on sound (sonography), temperature (thermography), radio waves, radioactive tracers, tiny cameras that patients swallow, and so on. Technology extends to new surgical procedures as well: for instance, with cameras and lasers (devices that produce very narrow beams of light), surgeons can do heart surgery through tiny holes in the chest; they can do surgery on babies even before they are born.

F   Although much of the technology in our everyday lives has positive effects, there are some uses that raise controversial issues and questions. For example, are interactive media (i.e., a combination of television, telephone, and computer) going to control minds, destroy privacy, and cause people to forget about family life and personal relationships? What effects will the genetic engineering of foods (e.g., changing the gene structure of fruits and vegetables) have on people's health? High-tech medical treatments (organ transplants, changing the gene structure, etc.) can increase the longevity of individuals, but can they improve the health and happiness of human beings in general? Only time will tell, but, in the meantime, science and technology will continue to move forward.

After You Read

5   **Review of Outline Organization.**   For an informational reading selection with a lot of facts and details, an outline will probably give the clearest picture of the organization of the material. It will have at least three levels of detail: numbers like I, II, III, and IV for the major divisions; capital letters (A, B, C, etc.) for the main topics in each division; and numbers (1, 2, 3, 4, etc.) for the details of each topic. Even smaller details can follow small letters like a, b, c, d.

Here is one way to organize the information in the reading selection. To complete the outline, write words and phrases for the major divisions of the material, topics, and important details in the blanks. Look back at the reading if necessary. (The letter in parentheses refers to the paragraph that contains the information.)

Everyday Uses of Technology

I. Social lives through electronic bulletin boards (B)

  A. Locations of computers

    1. ___Own places___

    2. Public places

  B. Advantages

    1. Can meet people you might never meet in traditional ways

    2. ___Look for a potential dates or mates___

      a. ___Photos___

      b. Action videos on Websites

      c. ___Online video connection___

II. Communication through e-mail (C)

  A. How it works

    1. ___Dial sever___

    2. ___Send electronic info.___

  B. Advantage: ___Delivery time from the sender to the receiver is no more than a few seconds.___

III. Computerized equipment in homes (D)

  A. Running a house electronically

    1. Kitchen appliances

      a. ___Microwave oven___

      b. Gas or electric range

      c. ___Dishwasher___

      d. ___Washing machine and dryer___

    2. Entertainment equipment

      a. Radios

      b. ___Television sets.___

      c. ___VCR. [video, cassette recorders]___

    3. Cars and other vehicles

    4. ___Microcomputer___

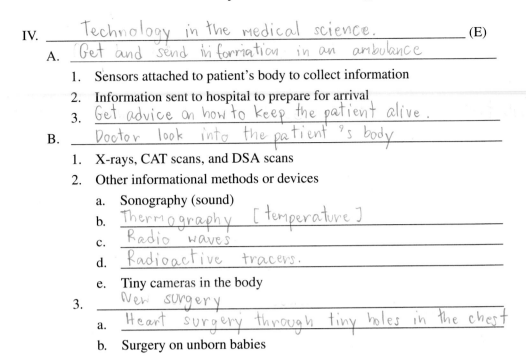

IV. <u>Technology in the medical science.</u> (E)
   A. <u>Get and send information in an ambulance</u>
      1. Sensors attached to patient's body to collect information
      2. Information sent to hospital to prepare for arrival
      3. <u>Get advice on how to keep the patient alive.</u>
   B. <u>Doctor look into the patient's body</u>
      1. X-rays, CAT scans, and DSA scans
      2. Other informational methods or devices
         a. Sonography (sound)
         b. <u>Thermography [temperature]</u>
         c. <u>Radio waves</u>
         d. <u>Radioactive tracers.</u>
         e. Tiny cameras in the body
      3. <u>New surgery</u>
         a. <u>Heart surgery through tiny holes in the chest</u>
         b. Surgery on unborn babies

Circle the number of the main idea of the reading.

(1.) Although there are controversial issues, modern science and technology continue to influence every area of life.

2. Radiation offers both benefits and disadvantages to human beings and the environment.

3. To have a good social life, everyone can make new friends with the help of electronic bulletin boards.

4. Computer technology such as e-mail improves people's communication skills.

6   Understanding the Main Idea. In addition to stating information clearly and directly, the writer of a reading selection may imply or suggest certain facts or personal views. Readers infer, or figure out, what the writer wants to communicate on the basis of what they already know, the information in the text, and context clues in the material.

For which of the following statements does the reading "Everyday Uses of Technology" give or suggest information or views? On the lines before those items, write an *X*. Put an *O* before those items not suggested. In the reading, underline the sentences or parts of sentences that lead you to your answers. Give your own opinions about all the statements, but make it clear that they are your views, not the views of the writer.

_____O_____ 1. Because electronic machines are destroying the environment, science and technology cannot advance.

_____X_____ 2. Computer technology can help people to meet others, make friends, and get married.

_____X_____ 3. Instead of always using the telephone to communicate, some people are sending e-mail messages or looking at and talking to each other on the computer screen.

_____ *0*_____   4.   Kitchen appliances of the future will be much more colorful.

_____ *X*_____   5.   Modern medical technology can prevent disease, and it can also help save or extend lives.

_____ *0*_____   6.   The worst problem caused by modern technology is computer crime.

7   **Special Uses of Punctuation.**   If a word or phrase has a new or special meaning in a specific context, it may be in quotation marks (" ") or italics (a special kind of slanting type).

Example:

> When a computer is ready to "mail a letter," it dials a *server*.
>
> (What does "mail a letter" mean? The quotation marks show that in this special context, the phrase means that the computer is going to send a message electronically. A server is a computer that serves a special function.)

Sometimes common, everyday words take on new or special meanings. In a small or old dictionary, you may not find the exact definition you need, but you can often figure out the meaning from the modern context.

Example:

> Are there *computer terminals* at the *bus terminal*?
>
> (A *bus* terminal is a starting and ending point for buses. A *computer* terminal, then, must be a starting and ending point for electronic information.)

From the definition of the everyday words or phrases in italics, try to figure out the meaning of the items in quotation marks in their new or special contexts. Then answer the questions. To find the item in context, you can look back at the reading selection; the capital letters in parentheses indicate the paragraphs. You can also check your dictionary to see if it contains the specific definition you need.

1.   (A) *Data* is collected information. What might crime investigators do with a "database" of DNA samples?

   compare the DNA of a crime suspect with it

   Perfect means "with no faults or defects." How might medical science change gene structure to create "more perfect" human beings?

   modify the gene structure to prevent disease

2.   (B) A *bulletin board* is a board on the wall on which people put messages. What is an "electronic bulletin board"?

   Computer

   To *chat* is to talk in a friendly, casual manner. What is a computer "chat room"?

   Communicating with others on electronic bulletin boards.

What can computer users do on electronic bulletin boards and in chat rooms?

Computer users can get to know people they might meet in the traditional ways.

3. (B) The *personals* are ads that people place in newspapers or other print media, usually with the purpose of finding potential dates or mates. What are the "personals" on Websites?

computer user

Digitized means "put into electronic instead of physical form." *Video* is "motion pictures." What are "digitized video segments"?

Live means "broadcast at the present time; not pre-recorded," and *online* means "controlled by computers." What are "live online video connections"?

To *meet* means to "come together by chance or arrangement." How might computer users "meet" in nontraditional ways?

4. (C) *Mail* is the postal system of sending and receiving letters. What is "e-mail"?

A *server* is a person or thing that collects and gives out food. Some computers are "servers" too. What do they do?

How do computers "deliver" information from senders to receivers?

5. (D) *Chips* are small pieces of material. What are "computer chips"?

Small pieces of material in computer

A *program* is a plan of what someone intends to do. When people "program" a computer, an appliance, or another piece of equipment, what do they do to it?

How might a household that is "programmed" with "computer chips" operate?

6. (E) To *sense* means to "get a feeling about." Medical technicians can attach "sensors" to a patient's body. What do these devices do?

_____

To *slice through* means to "cut into flat pieces." How does photographic equipment such as CAT and DSA "slice through" body organs?

_____

A *procedure* is a way of doing something. What is a "surgical procedure"?

_____

In medical investigation and health care, how is science advancing?

_____

_____

7. People *interact* when they have an effect on one another. What do television, telephones, and computers do in "interactive media"?

_____

Engineering is "using scientific principles to design and build structures." What is "genetic engineering"?

_____

The word *tech* is a short form of "technical." What is "high-tech" equipment?

_____

What are some of the controversial issues and questions raised by "interactive media," "genetic engineering," and "high-tech" medical treatments?

_____ more couch potatoes _____

_____

Discussing the Reading

8   In small groups, talk about your answers to the following questions.

1. Do you use or have you ever used an electronic bulletin board, a chat room, or e-mail? If so, explain how they work. Give your reactions to your experiences.

2. What electronic or computerized equipment or appliances do you have in your home? How do you use them?

3. Have you ever been in an ambulance or a hospital during an emergency? If so, what do you remember or know about modern medical technology?

4. Do you think that computers and interactive media benefit or hurt family life and personal relationships?

5. What is the effect of high-tech medical treatments on the health and happiness of people in general?

6. Should medical scientists change gene structures to create "more perfect" human beings?

PART 4

Writing

Before You Write

Exploring Ideas

1   **Discussing Computer Networks and Newsgroups.**   Read the following article. Then discuss the five questions near the end of the article.

The Information Superhighway

In recent years, there has been a revolution in communication that has connected people all over the world. You can now sit at your desk, make a telephone call from your computer, and connect to a network which will allow you to explore information in computers from Acapulco to Zhenjiang.

You can find out soccer scores for your hometown team, shop for the latest computer equipment, have an electronic "chat" with other people about your favorite movie star, read and post articles on the latest international crisis, or play chess with a team of international players. You can use search engines to look for information stored in computers all over the world. In thousands of computer discussion groups you can read and send messages on almost any subject—some of which you wouldn't want your children to see. You can even play your favorite music and send photographs to your friends and family.

The network with the most information is the Internet (or "Net"). The Net started as a way for scientists and computer experts to communicate and share information. Universities, research groups, and governments paid for it, and only people with advanced computer knowledge could use it. Now almost anyone can access the Internet, and they can send or receive almost any kind of information. This freedom of access can be good or bad, and there are many unanswered questions about it, such as:

■   Should governments, or any other group, try to control the Internet?

■   What role should advertising play on the net?

■   Should the Internet carry *any* kind of communication? What about censoring criminal activity, racist messages, or sex discussions or pictures?

■   Should people be allowed to "flame" (verbally attack) *anyone* or *any* subject?

■   Should people be able to control the amount of "spam"(electronic junk mail) sent to their e-mail address?

These questions of freedom versus control will never be answered to everyone's satisfaction, and they will probably be the subject of interesting discussions for a long time.

2   **Building Vocabulary.**   This chart has examples of terms commonly used in computer networking. Add other words you used in your discussion to the list. Then choose the correct terms from the list to complete sentences 1 to 6 that follow the chart.

Nouns	Verbs	Other
network	network	_____
chat room	censor	_____
e-mail	download	_____
censorship	upload	_____
spam	flame	_____
electronic	access	_____
search engine	e-mail	_____
_____	_____	_____
_____	_____	_____
_____	_____	_____

1.   When you want to send a message you have already written to a discussion group, you can _____ it to the group in only a few seconds.

2.   An electronic _____ is a group of computers connected together to communicate and share information.

3.   By using a _____ , you can search for information on any subject on the Web.

4.   When you connect to the Internet, you have _____ to computers around the world.

5.   You can _____ a message from a newsgroup to save it on your computer.

6.   People on the Internet do not agree on how to _____ illegal activity.

Organizing Ideas

You are going to write a message to a computer discussion group on the topic of censorship. In your message, you will give your opinion about one of the four questions in the article you just read.

Messages to discussion groups are generally organized like other writing, with a few minor differences. Here are a few special rules for organizing e-mail messages. Many of these "rules" have developed informally and are referred to as "netiquette." (*Netiquette* is a combination of the words *network* and *etiquette*; the word *etiquette* means "*a set of rules for good behavior.*")

Internet Netiquette

- Because so many messages are sent to computer newsgroups, keep your message short.

- Keep to the topic of the discussion group. You may be flamed if you don't!

- Keep your message simple and informal. Discussion groups are for ordinary people.

- If you are responding to another message, quote a few lines from the message so people who didn't read it know what you are talking about.

- Give your main idea in a few sentences so people can quote a few lines from your message when they reply to it.

- People on the Internet express their opinions strongly, and you can find some very strong personal attacks on the Net. Express your opinion strongly, but don't call people names or attack them personally when you disagree with them.

- Don't only criticize other messages—offer positive suggestions.

- Don't type in all capital letters. On computer networks, this means you are angry and are SHOUTING.

3   Read the following two messages from the newsgroup on censorship. Each one contains information that is not on the subject of computer network censorship. Find that information and cross it out.

Topic: Ban Advertising on the Internet
Written 10:10 am Jan 5 by lmbewe@dlu.edu
***Advertising ruins our cities, our highways, our magazines, and our TV. Every night I have to throw away dozens of pieces of junk mail I receive that advertise products I don't want. The U.S. mail system has gotten so bad that I don't receive mail I need, only stupid advertisements. Now the same thing is happening to the Internet! Everyday I receive e-mail advertisements from companies I have never heard of. Can't there be at least one place where human beings can communicate without some people trying to make money off us?
Lionel Mbewe
lmbewe@dlu.edu

The second message is a response to Lionel. Note that when some Net users sign their name, they may also include their regular address and/or one of their favorite quotations.

Written 8:32pm Jan 7 by freebie@freepr.mrfs.qu.ca
>Can't there be at least one place where human beings can communicate without some people trying to make money off us?

It would be nice, but let's be real: it would be impossible to keep advertising out of the Internet. In fact, it is already here, in special discussion groups that share information about different products. One of the freedoms that we have is the freedom to make money, as long as the making of money does not break some other law. We have to make realistic rules to control advertising on the Net, not to ban it completely. Why don't all the people involved in this question—companies who want to advertise, ordinary people against advertising, the groups that provide access to the Net, and experienced users—get together on-line and seriously work toward setting controls on advertising? Right now it's just talk, talk, and more talk!

So many people who send messages to the Internet are scientists and university researchers who live far away from the real lives of most of us who need to make money. They don't need to advertise on the Internet—they have good safe jobs. University professors should be required to spend time outside in the real world before they go into the classroom and try to tell us ordinary people the way it is. Cindy McPherson, People's Free Press, 7592 rue Berri, Montreal, Quebec, H2J 2R6, Canada freebie@freepr.mrfs.on.ca
''None can love freedom heartily, but good men—the rest love not freedom, but license.'' John Milton

4   In groups, discuss what you crossed out in Activity 3 and why it doesn't belong.

5   Cindy quoted the lines she thought gave the main idea of Lionel's message. What lines would you quote as the main idea of Cindy's message? What positive suggestion did Cindy give?

6   Choose one of the five questions in the article on page 271. Write two or three sentences that give your opinion about the question. Offer positive suggestions if possible and make sure you are writing only about that topic. If you want to respond to one of the messages on pages 273-274, mark the sentences that you will quote to give the main idea of the message you are responding to.

Supporting Your Opinion

While your e-mail message should be short, it should include support for your opinion. That is, you need to give examples or reasons that illustrate your point of view or prove your argument.

7   In her reply to Lionel, Cindy wrote that it would be impossible to keep advertising out of the Internet. She gave one supporting example and one supporting reason. What are they?

Supporting example: _____

_____

Supporting reason: _____

_____

8   Look at the sentences you wrote in Activity 6 giving your opinion. Write each sentence again. Under each sentence, give reasons and examples supporting your opinion.

Writing e-mail Topic Lines

E-mail messages don't include titles. Instead, the topic is written after the word *Topic* or *Subject*, which appears on the computer screen. This topic is just like a title: It should give the main idea of your message and make people want to read it. The topic is included in the index of messages, which people use to decide which messages to read, so it is important. When writing your topic, follow the same rules of capitalization as you do for titles.

9   Write a topic for the message you are going to write.

Topic: _____

Write

Developing Cohesion and Style

Unifying Your Writing with Synonyms and Pronouns

One way of unifying your writing is to refer to the same word or topic several times. However, a paragraph doesn't flow smoothly if you often repeat the same word in phrases that are near each other. To refer to a word or topic in a nearby phrase, you should use:

■ pronouns such as *it, they, this* and *these*, or
■ synonyms (words with the same or similar meaning), often used with *this* or *these*

If you haven't used a word in a few sentences, then you can repeat it.

---

10   Look at this list of words with similar meanings. Insert the appropriate words in the sentences that follow.

computer (used as adj.) — electronic   access (v) — connect to
censor — control (v)1   criminal (used as adj.) — illegal

The Internet is a huge computer network. People connected to the Net can participate

in _____ discussions called bulletin boards. Because so many
                  1

people can now _____ these bulletin boards, the question of
                                    2

who should control information on the Internet is an important topic for discussion.

For example, should the government try to _____ the Internet for
                                                                3

racist messages or _____ activity?
                                  4

Language for Giving Opinions and Suggestions

There are phrases you can use to give polite opinions; there are also suggestions and phrases you should avoid if you want to be polite. Use *should, need to, it would be better if*, or *why don't / doesn't* instead of *must.*

Examples:

■ The Internet *should* censor messages for racist language.
■ *Why doesn't* the Internet censor messages for racist language?
■ The Internet *needs to* censor messages for racist language.
■ *It would be better if* the Internet censored messages for racist language.

11 Find the language Cindy and Lionel used on pages 273-274 to give opinions and suggest ways they can make their messages more polite. Look at the opinions and suggestions you wrote in Activity 6. Have you expressed them politely?

Writing the First Draft

12 Using the opinions and supporting reasons and examples you have written, write your e-mail message. Make sure you state your main idea in your message and support your opinion with reasons and / or examples. First write a topic line, your message (quoting another message if you like), and then your name and electronic address. If you don't have an electronic address, write your first initial and last name, the "@" symbol, the initials of your school, a period, and then "edu," as in the following example:

blelieu@und.edu

Edit and Revise

Editing Practice

Spelling and Grammar in Computer Messages

One of the netiquette rules is not to flame people for grammar or spelling mistakes. Of course, you should use correct grammar and spelling so your message is clear and easy to read. If you are writing on a computer, use a computer spell-check program.

---

13 Edit this reply to Mike Janovic, who wanted censorship in the Internet. First omit any personal attacks or lines that aren't on the topic. Then add support to the opinion expressed and/or give a positive suggestion. Finally, use pronouns and/or synonyms in place of the word "Internet" and correct spelling and grammar.

(Note that since you can't underline on the Internet, writers use asterisks ** instead.)

>I don't understand how anybody can argue for total freedom from censorship on the Internet . . . There are controls on sex and violence in other media: why not on the Internet?
>That's just the point: the Internet is *not* like all other media. It is selfish peabrains like Mr. Janovic who one day ruin the Internet. The Internet not for childs, the Internet for adults. If peple want a Sesame Street Internet, they should make there own Internet and not ruining our Internet. Childs must to be controled. Parents let them run wild in the street. They taking drugs and killing peple.

Editing Your Writing

14   **Editing Using a Checklist.**   Edit your message using the following checklist.

Editing Checklist

1. Content
   a. Does the message express your opinion strongly without personal attacks?
   b. Have you given reasons and examples to support your opinions?
2. Organization
   a. Are all your sentences on the topic of the discussion group?
   b. Does your message contain a sentence or two that gives the main idea of your message?
   c. Does your topic line give the main idea of your message and make people want to read it?
3. Cohesion and Style
   a. Does your message use pronouns and synonyms to unify your writing?
   b. Have you used polite phrases to give opinions and suggestions?
4. Grammar
   a. Are your verbs correct?
   b. Have you used correct grammatical forms to give opinions and suggestions?
5. Form
   a. Have you avoided writing in all capitals?
   b. Have you capitalized the important words in your topic line correctly?
   c. Have you put front brackets before lines quoting other messages?
   d. Have you written a signature under your message with your name and electronic address?

15   **Peer Editing.**   Give your message to another student to check.

Writing the Second Draft

16   Rewrite your message using correct form. Then give it to your teacher for comments.

PART 5

Grammar

A. Introduction to the Passive Voice

Most verbs that take an object can be used in both the active voice and the passive voice. The passive and active forms have similar meanings, but different focuses. The active voice focuses on the person or thing that does the action. The passive voice focuses on the person or thing the action is done to. In the passive voice, the object of an active verb becomes the subject of the passive verb.

Examples		Notes
Active *subject* *verb* *object* Alexander Graham Bell invented the telephone.		focus of active sentence: Alexander Graham Bell
Passive The telephone was invented by Alexander Graham Bell. *subject* *verb* *agent*		focus of passive sentence: the telephone
Active *subject* *verb* *object* My brother sent the message.		focus of active sentence: my brother
Passive The message was sent by my brother. *subject* *verb* *agent*		focus of passive sentence: the message

Note: The agent can often be left out of a passive voice sentence, as in: *The message was sent.*

1 Write an *A* next to the sentences that are in the active voice, and a *P* next to the sentences that are in the passive voice.

1.   __A__   Technology is changing our lives.
        __P__   Our lives are being changed by technology.

2.   __A__   Many people own cellular phones.
        __P__   Cellular phones are owned by many people.

3.   __P__   Millions of documents are sent by fax machines every day.
        __A__   Fax machines send millions of documents every day.

4.   __P__   Phone messages are taken by answering machines.
        __A__   Answering machines take phone messages.

5.   __A__   The Internet connects people around the world.
        __P__   People around the world are connected by the Internet.

B. Passive Voice: Uses

Uses	Examples
When the doer of the action isn't known	New technology **is developed** every day. (Passive) *Instead of:* People **develop** new technology everyday. (Active)
When it isn't necessary to mention the doer because the doer is obvious	He **was arrested**. (Passive) *Instead of:* A policeman **arrested** him. (Active)
When we are more interested in the action than the doer	A computer room **was added** to the community center. (Passive) *Instead of:* The town council **added** a computer room to the community center. (Active)
When we want to avoid placing direct "blame" on a doer	Too many long-distance calls **were made** this month. (Passive) *Instead of:* You **made** too many long-distance calls this month. (Active)

write 10 sentences about passive

C. The Passive Voice with the Simple Present and Simple Past Tenses

	Examples	Notes
Simple present tense	Active: The repairman **checks** the phones every week. Passive: The phones **are checked** every week (by the repairman).	The passive voice of verbs in the simple present tense is formed with *am / is / are* + the past participle. The negative is formed by adding *not* after *am / is / are*.
Simple past tense	Active: The repairman **checked** the phones yesterday. Passive: The phones **were checked** (by the repairman) yesterday.	The passive voice of verbs in the simple past tense is formed with *was / were* + the past participle. The negative is formed by adding *not* after *was / were*.

2   Fill in the blanks with either the active or the passive form of the verbs in parentheses. Be sure to use the correct tense (simple present or simple past).

The history of modern communication technology began when the electric

telegraph ___was invented___ by the American Samuel Morse in the 1830s.
1 (invent)

The telegraph ___linked___ two places by electric wire. By switching
2 (link)

the electricity on and off, messages ___were sent___ down the wire by a code
3 (send)

Salsa is being danced by Jordan
The homework will be done by him.
Arepas have been eaten by me.

Mistakes were made
Frank built and fixed airplanes.
Airplanes was built and fixed by Frank.

In 1876, Alexander Graham Bell invented the telephone when he __discovered__ a way to send human speech down an electrical wire. Eventually,
4 (discover)

telephones became so common in many parts of the world, that they __were taken__
5 (take)

for granted by many people. Only international calls __remained__ expensive and
6 (remain)

difficult to make.

This began to change when the first communications satellite __was launched__
7 (launch)

into space in 1962. Satellites made it possible to bounce telephone signals around the

world quickly and easily. It quickly __became__ much easier and cheaper to
8 (become)

make international calls. (Today,) more than 150 communication satellites

__orbit__ the earth.
9 (orbit)

Another important step in communication technology was the invention of

the cellular phone. These phones __were developed__ in the early 1980s and quickly
10 (develop)

became became a very popular and common technology. This __was followed__
11 (follow)

by the most important invention of the 1990s: the Internet. The Internet

__linked__ computers around the world. It __is used__ to send
12 (link) 13 (use)

millions of messages (each day.)

Communication technology never stops developing. Improvements

__are made__ and new technologies __researched__ all of the time. What
14 (make) 15 (research)

new kinds of communication technology do you think we will have in the future?

Video Activities: Sight for the Blind

Before You Watch. Discuss the following questions with your class or in small groups.

1. How can technology help physically challenged people? Give examples.
2. As a child, did you ever try to "pretend" you were blind (unable to see)? How did it feel?

Watch.   Write answers to these questions.

1. Who is Jerry, and who is Craig? _____

2. How does the new technology help Jerry? _____

3. Jerry is _____ years old. He became blind _____ years ago.

4. Craig has been blind for _____ year(s).

Watch Again.   Circle the correct answers.

1. Craig became blind _____.
    a. at birth   b. in an accident   c. because of a disease

2. According to Craig, when people pretend to be blind, they always cheat.
    He means:
    a. They ask someone to help them.
    b. They never really close their eyes.
    c. They open their eyes just a little

3. The new device that helps Jerry to see uses a _____.
    a. camera   b. computer   c. transistor

4. Craig's biggest dream is to _____ again.
    a. work   b. drive   c. see

5. How does Craig feel about the future?
    a. sad   b. hopeful   c. worried

After You Watch.   Fill in the blanks with the active or passive form of the verb
in parentheses. Be careful to use the proper verb tense or modal.

Eyeglasses _____ (invent) in Italy around 1284 by the inventor

Salvino D'Armate. These early glasses _____ (can, use) only for

reading. Glasses for seeing far away _____ (invent) later. A portrait of

Pope Leo X, which _____ (paint) by Raphael in 1517, shows the

Pope wearing them.

In 1794, the American inventor Benjamin Franklin _____

(invent) bifocals. Such glasses _____ (divide) into two parts, one

part for seeing far and the other for seeing near. For hundreds of years,

eyeglasses _____ (make) of glass. In recent years, however,

plastic lenses _____ (become) more popular.

The first contact lenses _____ (develop) by Adolf Fick in

1887. These lenses _____ (make) of glass. They were uncomfortable

and _____ (could, not, wear) for long. Hard-plastic contact

lenses _____ (became) popular in the U.S. in the 1960s, and soft

contact lenses _____ (introduce) in the 1970s. Nowadays, soft

lenses _____ (wear) by millions of people all over the world.

Appendices

Appendix 1

New Year's Day

Date: January 1

Reason: To celebrate the arrival of a new year

Special customs: People stay home from work. Many people watch football games on television. Most shops and businesses are closed. There are big parties the night before and at midnight, people drink champagne to toast the New Year.

Valentine's Day

Date: February 14

Reason: To celebrate love

Special customs: People give their loved ones greeting cards shaped like hearts. They can also give each other candy, flowers, or jewelry.

Symbols: hearts; the color red

Foods: chocolate; candy

Easter

Date: a Sunday in March or April (It changes every year)

Reason: Christians believe that on this day, Jesus came back to life. It is also a celebration of the beginning of spring.

Special customs: Religious people go to church. Families color eggs and hide them; then the children hunt for them. Most families get together for a big dinner. Most shops and businesses are closed.

Symbols: baby animals, especially rabbits and chickens (to symbolize spring)

Foods: colored eggs; chocolate eggs and rabbits

Memorial Day

Date: May 30

Reason: To honor the men and women who have died in military service

Special customs: People visit the graves of their loved ones who have died in military service. Many towns have parades in their honor. It is also the unofficial beginning of summer, and people get together for picnics and barbecues.

The Fourth of July

Date: July 4th

Reason: To celebrate the independence of the United States in 1776

Customs: Cities have big fireworks events after dark; people get together for picnics. Many cities hold parades. Some people hang a U.S. flag outside their houses.

Foods: typical picnic or barbecue foods such as hot dogs and hamburgers; watermelon; corn

Halloween

Date: October 31

Reason: Originally for Christians to celebrate the night before All Saints' Day. On this night, people used to believe that the spirits of dead people came out. Therefore, Halloween is considered a scary (but fun) holiday. Nowadays most Americans observe Halloween as a nonreligious holiday.

Customs: Children dress up in costumes. After dark, they go from house to house and say "Trick or Treat." Then people give them candy. Popular costumes include scary characters like witches, ghosts, and monsters. Also on this holiday, people carve faces on pumpkins. They put a lit candle inside the pumpkin and place it on their front porch.

Foods: candy

Thanksgiving

Date: The fourth Thursday in November

Reason: Around 400 years ago, the first European settlers in North America ate a special meal with the Indians to give thanks for the food they grew together. Today we celebrate Thanksgiving to remember that occasion and to give thanks for our good luck.

Customs: Families get together for a big midday meal. People often travel long distances to be with their parents on this holiday. Nearly all shops and businesses are closed. Americans of all religions celebrate Thanksgiving.

Foods: turkey with cranberry sauce; corn; sweet potatoes; squash; pumpkin pie

Christmas

Date: December 25

Reason: For religious Christians, to celebrate the birth of Jesus Christ. Most Americans now also observe Christmas as a nonreligious holiday.

Customs: People put a cut pine tree in their homes and decorate it. They buy each other gifts and put them under the tree; then they open the gifts on Christmas morning. Small children are told that a man called Santa Claus comes down the chimney and leaves their gifts under the tree. On Christmas Day people get together for a large midday meal. All shops and businesses are closed.

Appendix 2   Irregular Verbs

Simple Form	Past Form	Past Participle	Simple Form	Past Form	Past Participle
be	was/were	been	leave	left	left
bear	bore	born	lend	lent	lent
become	became	become	lose	lost	lost
begin	began	begun	make	made	made
bite	bit	bitten	mean	meant	meant
blow	blew	blown	meet	met	met
break	broke	broken	pay	paid	paid
bring	brought	brought	put	put	put
build	built	built	read	read	read
buy	bought	bought	ride	rode	ridden
catch	caught	caught	ring	rang	rung
choose	chose	chosen	run	ran	run
come	came	come	say	said	said
cost	cost	cost	see	saw	seen
do	did	done	sell	sold	sold
draw	drew	drawn	send	sent	sent
drink	drank	drunk	shake	shook	shaken
drive	drove	driven	shoot	shot	shot
eat	ate	eaten	shut	shut	shut
fall	fell	fallen	sing	sang	sung
feed	fed	fed	sit	sat	sat
feel	felt	felt	sleep	slept	slept
fight	fought	fought	speak	spoke	spoken
find	found	found	spend	spent	spent
fly	flew	flown	stand	stood	stood
forget	forgot	forgotten	steal	stole	stolen
freeze	froze	frozen	sweep	swept	swept
get	got	gotten	swim	swam	swum
give	gave	given	take	took	taken
go	went	gone	teach	taught	taught
grow	grew	grown	tear	tore	torn
hang	hung	hung	tell	told	told
have	had	had	think	thought	thought
hear	heard	heard	throw	threw	thrown
hit	hit	hit	understand	understood	understood
hold	held	held	win	won	won
hurt	hurt	hurt	write	wrote	written
keep	kept	kept			
know	knew	known			

Appendix 3

Spelling Rules for *-s*, *-ed*, *-er*, *-est*, and *-ing* Endings

Rule	Word	-s	-ed	-er	-est	-ing
For most words, add –s, -ed, -er, -est, or –ing without making any other changes.	clean cool	cleans cools	cleaned cools	cleaner cooler	cleanest coolest	cleaning cooling
For words ending in a consonant + *y*, change the y to *i* before adding –s, -ed, -er, or -est. Do **not** change or drop the *y* before adding –*ing*.	carry happy lonely study worry	carries studies worries	carried studied worried	carrier happier lonelier	happiest loneliest	carrying studying worrying
For most words ending in *e*, drop the *e* before adding –ed, -er, -est, or –ing. Exceptions:	dance late write agree canoe		danced	dancer later writer	latest	dancing writing agreeing canoeing
For many words ending in one vowel and one consonant, double the final consonant before adding –es, –ed, -er, -est, or –ing. These include one-syllable words and words with stress on the **final syllable.**	hot plan shop run quiz begin admit occur refer	quizzes	planned shopped quizzed admitted occurred referred	hotter planner shopper runner quizzer beginner	hottest	planning shopping running quizzing beginning admitting occurring referring

287

Rule	Word	-s	-ed	-er	-est	-ing
In words ending in one vowel and one consonant, do **not** double the final consonant if the last syllable is not stressed. This includes words ending in *w, x,* or *y.*	enter happen open travel bus fix play sew	buses	entered happened opened traveled bused fixed played sewed	opener traveler fixer player sewer		entering happening opening traveling busing fixing playing sewing
For most words ending in *f* or *lf,* change the *f* to *v* and add –*es.* Exceptions:	half loaf belief proof safe	halves loaves beliefs proofs safes	halved			halving
For words ending in *ch, sh, s, x, z,* and sometimes *o,* add –*es.* Exceptions:	church wash class fix tomato dynamo monarch piano radio studio	churches washes classes fixes tomatoes dynamos monarchs pianos radios studios				

Appendix 4 Punctuation Rules

Period

1. Use a period after a statement or command.
   We are studying English.   Open your books to Chapter 3.
2. Use a period after most abbreviations.
   Mr.   Ms.   Dr.   Ave.   etc.   U.S.
   Exceptions: UN   NATO   IBM   AIDS
3. Use a period after initials.
   H. G. Wells   Dr. D. R. Hammond

Question Mark

1. Use a question mark after (not before) questions.
   Where are you going?   Is he here yet?
2. In a direct quotation, the question mark goes before the quotation marks.
   He asked, "What's your name?"

Exclamation Point

Use an exclamation point after exclamatory sentences or phrases.
   I won the lottery!   Be quiet!   Wow!

Comma

1. Use a comma before a conjunction (*and, or, so, but*) that separates two independent clauses.
   She wanted to go to work, so she decided to take an English course.
   He wasn't happy in that apartment, but he didn't have the money to move.
2. Don't use a comma before a conjunction that separates two phrases that aren't complete sentences.
   She worked in the library and studied at night. Do you want to go to a movie or stay home?
3. Use a comma before an introductory clause or phrase (generally if it is five or more words).
   After a beautiful wedding ceremony, they had a reception in her mother's home.
   If you want to write well, you should practice writing almost every night.
4. Use a comma to separate interrupting expressions from the rest of a sentence.
   Do you know, by the way, what time dinner is?
   Many of the students, I found out, stayed on campus during the summer.
5. Use a comma after transitional expressions.
   In addition, he stole all her jewelry.   However, he left the TV.
6. Use a comma to separate names of people in direct address from the rest of a sentence.
   Jane, have you seen Paul?   We aren't sure, Mrs. Shapiro, where he is.
7. Use a comma after *yes* and *no* in answers.
   Yes, he was here a minute ago.   No, I haven't.
8. Use a comma to separate items in a series.
   We have coffee, tea, and milk.
   He looked in the refrigerator, on the shelves, and in the cupboard.

9. Use a comma to separate an appositive from the rest of a sentence.
   Mrs. Sampson, his English teacher, gave him a good recommendation.
   Would you like to try a taco, a delicious Mexican food?

10. If a date or address has two or more parts, use a comma after each part.
    I was born on June 5, 1968.
    The house at 230 Seventh Street, Miami, Florida, is for sale.

11. Use a comma to separate contrasting information from the rest of the sentence.
    It wasn't Maria, but Parvin, who was absent.
    Bring your writing book, not your reading book.

12. Use a comma to separate quotations from the rest of a sentence.
    He asked, "What are we going to do?"   "I'm working downtown," he said.

13. Use a comma to separate two or more adjectives that each modify the noun alone.
    She was an intelligent, beautiful actress. (intelligent and beautiful actress)
    Eat those delicious green beans. (*delicious* modifies *green beans*)

14. Use a comma to separate nonrestrictive clauses from the rest of a sentence. A nonrestrictive clause gives more information about the noun it describes, but it isn't needed to identify the noun. Clauses after proper names are nonrestrictive and require commas.
    It's a Wonderful Life, which is often on television at Christmastime, is my favorite movie.
    James Stewart, who plays a man thinking of killing himself, is the star of *It's a Wonderful Life*.

Quotation Marks

1. Use quotation marks at the beginning and end of exact quotations. Other punctuation marks go before the end quotation marks.
   He said, "I'm going to Montreal."
   "How are you?" he asked.

2. Use quotation marks before and after titles of stories, articles, songs, and television programs. Periods and commas go before the final quotation marks, while question marks and exclamation points normally go after them.
   Do you like to watch "Friends" on television?
   My favorite song is "Let It Be."
   Do you like the story "The Gift of the Magi"?

Apostrophes

1. Use apostrophes in contractions.
   don't   it's   we've   they're

2. Use an apostrophe to make possessive nouns.
   Singular: Jerry's   my boss's
   Plural: the children's   the computers'

Underlining

Underline the titles of books, magazines, newspapers, plays, and movies.
   I am reading <u>One Hundred Years of Solitude</u>.
   Did you like the movie <u>The Wizard of Oz</u>?

Tapescript

Chapter 1 — School Life Around the World

PART 1 — Listening to Conversations

3   Listening for Main Ideas. Page 3.

Jack:	Hi. How're you doing?
Peter:	Hi. You're . . . Jack, right?
Jack:	Yeah. And, sorry, you're . . .?
Peter:	Peter. Peter Riley.
Jack:	Oh, yeah, we met on campus last week. Peter, this is my friend, Ming Lee. She's just moved into the building.
Peter:	Hi, Ming Lee.
Ming:	Nice to meet you. You can just call me Ming. Lee's my last name.
Peter:	Oh. "Ming." That sounds . . .?
Ming:	Chinese. My parents came over from Hong Kong before I was born.
Peter:	Really? I was thinking of taking Chinese this term. Maybe you could help me.
Ming:	Well, my Chinese really isn't very good . . .
Jack:	Listen, Peter. We're really hungry. Do you want to get something to eat with us?
Peter:	Sorry, I can't. I have to go meet my new roommate.
Jack:	Oh, okay. Well, stop by sometime. I'm up in 212.
Peter:	Hey, I'm on the same floor. I'm in 220.
Jack:	No kidding . . .
Peter:	Well, nice meeting you, Ming. I'm sure I'll see you guys soon.
Ming and Jack:	See you later.

4   Listening for Stressed Words. Page 4. See student text.

5   Comparing Long and Reduced Forms. Page 5. See student text.

6   Listening for Reductions. Page 5.

1. How're ya feeling?
2. See ya in an hour.
3. Jack, d'ya wanna eat at the cafeteria?
4. When d'ya hafta meet your roommate?

8   Distinguishing between –s Endings. Page 6.

1. plays	3. hopes	5. drives	7. washes	9. mothers
2. misses	4. stops	6. phones	8. summarizes	10. puts

Recalling Main Ideas

3 Listening for Main Ideas. Page 9.

Hello everybody. Welcome to the American Language Center! I'm Gina Richards, your academic advisor. You can all just call me Gina. I know today is your first day at our school, so you're probably a little nervous and maybe a little shy, too. So, I want to tell you right at the beginning: if you don't understand something, please ask questions. Okay? And listen very carefully because we're going to give you a lot of important information —information that will make your experience here enjoyable and useful. Okay, here we go.

Let me tell you about the plan for today. There are three things on your schedule. First, you will take a placement test. This test will measure your English level. You'll take a reading, grammar, and composition test. Oh, and also listening. A listening test. The whole test takes three hours.

Next, you will meet in small groups, with a teacher, for an orientation. This orientation meeting will be about important things you need to know, like where to buy your books, what type of classes you'll have, how to find a roommate, things like that. This is where you can ask a lot of questions.

Then, finally, this afternoon, you will take a campus tour. We'll show you the main buildings where your classrooms are; you'll see some of the sports facilities, you know, the tennis courts, the swimming pool, places like that; and you'll also visit the library and the computer lab. I think you'll be surprised how large and how beautiful our campus is. All right. Are there any questions before we begin?

5 Listening for Specific Information. Page 9. Listen again. See text for Activity 3.

Chapter 2 Experiencing Nature

Listening to Conversations

3 Listening for Main Ideas. Page 33.

Peter: Hey, look outside. It's raining cats and dogs — again! I hate this weather. When does winter break start?

Jack: Winter break? It's only October.

Peter: I know, but I'm sick of studying. I want to go someplace warm and lie on the beach for a week. Someplace where it's sunny and dry. Florida or Hawaii, maybe?

Jack: Yeah. We can go swimming and snorkeling and get a great tan. Now that's my idea of a perfect vacation.

Ming: Not mine. I can't swim very well, and I don't like lying in the sun. I prefer the mountains, especially in winter. I'm crazy about skiing and snowboarding. In fact I'm planning to go to Bear Mountain with some friends in December. Do you want to come?

Jack: No thanks. I went there last year. I was freezing the whole time. Anyway, I don't know how to ski very well. I fell about a hundred times.

Ming: How about you, Peter?

Peter: Sorry, I agree with Jack. I don't want to go anyplace where it's below 70 degrees.

Jack: By the way, what's the weather forecast for tomorrow?

Ming: The same as today. Cloudy, cold, and a 90% chance of rain.

Jack: Oh, no! How am I going to go to the library?

Ming: Take an umbrella!

4 Listening for Stressed Words. Page 34. See student text.

5 Comparing Long and Reduced Forms. Page 35. See student text.

6 Listening for Reductions. Page 35.

Jack: Hi Ming. Hi Peter.

Ming and Jack: Hey Jack.

Ming: What's happening?

Jack: I'm going to the campus recreation center. Do you want to come?

Ming: What are you going to do there?

Jack: Well, it's a nice day. We can swim and lie in the sun.

Ming: Thanks, but I don't want to go. I'm too tired.

Jack: How about you, Peter?

Peter: I can't. I've got to stay home and study. Maybe tomorrow.

8 Distinguishing between *Can* and *Can't*. Page 36.

1. She can't swim very well.
2. Mike can drive.
3. The boys can cook.
4. I can't find his phone number.
5. Kenji can't speak Spanish.
6. He can speak Japanese.
7. I can't understand him.
8. Pete can come with us.
9. She can't take photographs in the rain.
10. Herb can play tennis very well.

| PART 2 | **Recalling Main Ideas** |

---

3 Listening for Main Ideas. Page 38.

Manager: You're all wet and muddy. What happened to you?

Woman: You're not going to believe this! It's the most incredible thing! It all started when we decided to go hiking this morning.

Man: Yeah, the weather was sunny and clear when we got up. So we put on shorts and t-shirts and started up the mountain. Half an hour later it started raining cats and dogs!

Woman: So we hiked back to our tent as fast as we could. We couldn't wait to change into dry clothes.

Man:	Right. But when we went into our tent, we couldn't find our clothes! So we went back outside to look around. And then we saw the craziest thing. Two great big brown bears came out of the woods, and guess what? They were wearing our clothes!
Manager:	Aw, come on. That's impossible! What do you mean, the bears were wearing your clothes?
Man:	Well, one bear had my t-shirt around his neck. And the other one had Mary's pants over his head. We still don't know where the rest of our clothes are!
Woman:	I know it sounds funny, but we were so scared! Those bears were big! And now we have a big problem.
Ranger:	What's that?
Woman and man:	We don't have any dry clothes to wear!

4 Taking Notes on Specific Information. Page 38. Listen again. See text for Activity 3.

Chapter 3 Living to Eat or Eating to Live?

PART 1 Listening to Conversations

3 Listening for Main Ideas. Page 59.

Mr. N:	Well, dear, I got a few things that aren't on the grocery list.
Mrs. N:	I can see that! You're not shopping for an army, you know.
Mr. N:	You know I always do this when I'm hungry.
Mrs. N:	Well, let's see what you have here.
Mr. N:	Some nice, fresh strawberries for only a dollar nineteen a pound.
Mrs. N:	Well, that's fine. They always have nice produce here. But why do you have all these cookies?
Mr. N:	I don't know; don't you like them?
Mrs. N:	Oh, I suppose. I hope you have a box of soap here.
Mr. N:	Oops, I forgot. Where's the soap in this market?
Mrs. N:	Aisle 3.
Mr. N:	I'll go get it.
Mrs. N:	Wait – This steak you got looks really expensive!
Mr. N:	Well, it isn't. It's on sale for just $3.99 a pound.
Mrs. N:	And what's this? More ice cream? We already have a gallon at home. Go put it back. Meanwhile, I'll get in line.
Cashier:	I'm sorry, ma'am; this is the express line. You have too many groceries, and we don't take checks here.

4 Listening for Stressed Words. Page 60. See student text.

5   Comparing Long and Reduced Forms. Page 61.   See student text.

6   Listening for Reductions. Page 61.

Customer:	Waiter?
Waiter:	Yes sir. Do you know whatcha want?
Customer:	D'ya have the spaghetti with mushroom sauce tonight?
Waiter:	Yes, we do.
Customer:	Well, are the mushrooms fresh or canned?
Waiter:	We get lotsa fresh mushrooms from the produce market every day.
Customer:	Great, I'll have that.
Waiter:	What kind of wine d'ya want with that?
Customer:	I dunno. Why doncha recommend something?
Waiter:	Our California wines are excellent.

8   Distinguishing between Teens and Tens. Page 63.

1. We waited in line for 30 minutes.
2. My sister is 14 years old.
3. We've lived in this city for 15 years.
4. Sixty people came to the party.
5. The groceries cost seventy dollars.
6. There are 18 students in the class.
7. I live 90 miles from my parents.

9   Listening for Teens and Tens. Page 63.

1. This turkey weighs 14 pounds.
2. The market is open until 10:30.
3. We spent $40 on groceries yesterday.
4. This milk is good until November 13th.
5. Those peaches cost $1.90 a pound.
6. Everything in this store is about 15 percent cheaper today.
7. My daughter is getting married. I need 30 bottles of champagne.
8. Please hurry up. The store will close in 15 minutes.
9. By using this coupon, you can save 70 cents on this ice cream.
10. Canned vegetables are on aisle 19.

PART 2   Recalling Main Ideas

3   Listening for the Main Idea. Page 66.

Do you think you're overweight? Are you thinking of going on a diet? Here are some things you should and shouldn't do if you want to lose weight. First, the best way to lose weight safely is to lose it slowly. This means about 2 pounds, or one kilogram, a week, no more. If you lose weight too quickly, you'll probably gain it back anyway. So how do you lose weight slowly?

First, eat right. Stay away from fast food and prepackaged foods—you know, canned and frozen foods. They may save you time, but they're bad for your health because they're high in fat and salt.

In addition to changing your eating habits, you should also exercise regularly. To lose 1 pound, you must burn about 3,500 calories. You can do this by exercising just one hour, three times a week.

Finally, to lose weight safely, don't take diet pills and don't go on crash diets. Diet pills can be very dangerous. They can hurt your muscles, bones, and heart. They can even cause death. Crash diets promise quick results in a very short time.

For example, they say you can lose five pounds in two days if you just eat grapefruit. But crash diets are bad because the weight you lose always comes back. Don't try them. Remember, the best way to lose weight is to eat right, exercise, and be patient.

4 **Taking Notes on Specific Information. Page 66.** Listen again. See text for Activity 3.

Chapter 4 In the Community

Listening to Conversations

3 Listening for Main Ideas. Page 89.

Kenji: Peter, are you going downtown today?

Peter: Uh-huh. Why?

Kenji: Can you give me a ride? I have to run some errands.

Peter: Where do you need to go?

Kenji: Uh, a lot of places. First, I've got to go to the bank. Could you drop me off at the corner of King Boulevard and Second Avenue?

Peter: King and Second? Oh, sure. I know where that is. But why are you going to the bank? Why don't you use the ATM on campus?

Kenji: 'Cause I need to cash a check my dad sent me. And the cleaner's is next door to the bank. I have to pick up some clothes there anyway.

Peter: There's a laundry room right here on the first floor. You can do your laundry there much cheaper.

Kenji: I'm not picking up laundry. It's dry cleaning. By the way, is there a photo shop near there? I need to drop off some film to develop.

Peter: A photo shop? Oh, yeah. There's probably one in the drugstore, across the street from the bank.

Kenji: Oh, that's convenient. So what are you gonna do downtown?

Peter: I'm going to the courthouse. I've got to pay a traffic ticket.

Kenji: No kidding! I'm going there, too. I also got a ticket.

Peter: But, Kenji, you don't drive!

Kenji: I know. I got a ticket for jaywalking!

Peter: Really?!

Kenji: Yeah. *Man*, sometimes I miss living in Japan. I could cross the street and not worry about stupid rules like jaywalking!

4 Listening for Stressed Words. Page 90. See student text.

5 Comparing Long and Reduced Forms. Page 91. See student text.

6 Listening for Reductions. Page 91.

      Male: D'ya know where the Central Library is?

   Female: Sure. You hafta take Bus #9.

      Male: Couldja walk with me to the bus stop?

   Female: I'm sorry. I don't have time 'cause I've gotta do a lotta things.

      Male: Oh. Then kinya jus' gimme directions to the bus stop?

   Female: Arya kidding? It's right there across the street.

PART 2   # Recalling Main Ideas

---

3 Listening for Main Ideas. Page 94.

   Peter: Phew. . . I'm glad I don't live in the city. The traffic is terrible. I have a headache from the noise and all the smog.

   Ming: You think cities here are bad? Ask Kenji about Tokyo.

   Kenji: Yeah, Tokyo is noisier and much more crowded than the cities here.

   Ming: Yeah, and I hear the smog's worse, too.

   Kenji: That's right.

   Peter: So, I guess you don't miss *that,* huh?

   Kenji: Well, I don't miss *those* things. But a big city like Tokyo can be very exciting.

   Peter: Yes, I'm sure that's true. But I prefer the peace and quiet of a small town like ours.

   Kenji: Well, I like it here, too. The people are friendlier and things are cheaper.

   Ming: Well, you know, I come from a small town, and it can be so conservative and boring. When I graduate, I want to live in a big city like New York or Chicago. You can make more money there, too.

   Peter: Yeah, but it's more dangerous there.

   Ming: Yeah, that's a disadvantage. But there are also lots of advantages.

   Peter: Yeah? Like what? The long lines at the bank or in the stores?

   Ming: Waiting in line doesn't bother me. I really love shopping in the city. You can find anything.

   Kenji: Great! The next time we need something downtown, we'll send *you.*

4 Taking Notes on Specific Information. Page 94. Listen again. See text for Activity 3.

Chapter 5 Home

Listening to Conversations

3 Listening for Main Ideas. Page 117.

Jennifer: I'm so stressed out. My landlord just raised my rent. I think I'll have to move.

Ming: Really? My building has some vacancies. It's a pretty nice place and it's just ten minutes from campus.

Jennifer: Oh? How much is the rent for a studio?

Ming: There're no studio apartments in our building. My neighbor just moved out of a one-bedroom. He paid $850 a month, I think.

Jennifer: That's not bad. Tell me more.

Ming: Well, one-bedrooms come with a bathroom, a kitchen, a fireplace in the living room, pretty big closets and uh. . . Are you looking for a furnished or unfurnished place?

Jennifer: Unfurnished. I have all my own stuff. What about parking and laundry?

Ming: There's no garage. You have to park on the street. But there is a laundry room downstairs.

Jennifer: Hmm. I think I'm interested. Could you give me the address?

Ming: Sure. It's 1213 Rose Avenue. The manager's name is Jerry Kohl. Call him up or stop by and talk to him.

Jennifer: Thanks, Ming. I'm gonna do that tomorrow for sure.

4 Listening for Stressed Words. Page 118. See student text.

5 Comparing Long and Reduced Forms. Page 119. See student text.

6 Listening for Reductions. Page 119.

A: Mr. Kohl, I have to talk to you. I have another problem.

B: Could you call me later? I'm busy now.

A: No, I need the plumber again. Could you call him right now?

B: I have a lot of things to do. I'll call him tomorrow morning, okay?

A: No, I need him right now!

B: Are you having trouble with the toilet again?

A: Yes. Look, just give me the plumber's phone number. I'll call him.

B: All right, all right. Just give me a minute and I'll do it.

8 Distinguishing between *–ed* Endings. Page 120.

1. turned
2. rented
3. mixed
4. asked
5. recommended

6 walked
7. tested
8. followed
9. moved
10. changed

Recalling Main Ideas

3   **Listening for Main Ideas. Page 122.**

Manager:	So, here's the living room. Oh, and please don't touch the walls; we just painted them. I hope you like green.
Jennifer:	Well, green is not my favorite color . . .
Manager:	As you can see, there's lots of light in here. And here's the fireplace. It's great in the winter.
Jennifer:	Whew, it's warm in here, isn't it? Is there any air conditioning?
Manager:	No, there isn't. Just keep this window open. Oh, it's almost never this noisy.
Jennifer:	I'm sorry, what did you say?
Manager:	Come this way. Here's your kitchen, all electric, a dishwasher. . . This big refrigerator is included; and there's room for a breakfast table here. . .
Jennifer:	That's nice. Could I see the bedroom?
Manager:	Sure, it's over here. We just put in new carpeting, so . . . uh. . . we raised the rent $25.
Jennifer:	Oh, really? Hmm . . . the bedroom looks a little small.
Manager:	But look at all the closet space! And here is the bathroom, with a shower and bathtub.
Jennifer:	Oh, what about that leak?
Manager:	Hmm. I can't believe it. The plumber just fixed it last week.
Jennifer:	Uh, if I decide to take this apartment, when can I move in?
Manager:	It's available on the first of the month. That's actually the day after tomorrow.
Jennifer:	I see. And, uh, do I have to sign . . . I mean, is there a lease?
Manager:	It's up to you. You can sign a 1-year lease or you can pay month-to-month. So, uh, are you interested?
Jennifer:	Possibly. I need to think about it a little more. And I have a few more questions.
Manager:	No problem. Let's go to my office and talk.

4   **Taking Notes on Specific Information. Page 123.** Listen again. See text for Activity 3.

Chapter 6   Cultures of the World

Listening to Conversations

3   **Listening for Main Ideas. Page 147.**

Kenji:	Is this your first trip to the U.S., Simone?
Simone:	Yes, it is.
Kenji:	What's your impression so far?

Simone:	Well, the streets are very clean, and the people are so friendly. But the food is not so good.
Kenji:	That's what I thought too, when I first got here. But I'm used to it now. I really love hamburgers and french fries.
Simone:	French fries? What is that?
Jennifer:	You know, fried potatoes. I think you call them "pommes frites" in France. But we call them french fries, for some reason. And a lot of people eat them with ketchup.
Simone:	Ketchup! That is very bizarre. We eat our pomme frites with salt, or maybe mustard.
Jennifer:	Last night I took Simone to a Mexican restaurant. I wanted her to try something exotic.
Kenji:	Did you like it?
Simone:	The food was delicious, but it was too much. I couldn't finish it all.
Jennifer:	Simone was amazed when I said she could take the leftovers home in a doggie bag.
Kenji:	Yes, that's funny, isn't it? They call it a doggie bag but it's for people. Was there anything else that surprised you?
Simone:	Yes. The restaurant was so cold! We don't use air conditioning so much in France. And the water had ice in it too. I had to put on my sweater!
Waiter:	Excuse me miss, but there's no smoking here.
Simone:	Oof, I forgot, you can't smoke in restaurants here. That is the strangest thing of all for me. In France you can smoke almost everywhere, and almost everybody smokes. It's normal for us.
Kenji:	It's not normal here. Most Americans don't smoke, and it's illegal to smoke in most public places. If you want to smoke in someone's home, you'd better ask for permission first.
Simone:	I know. Last night Jennifer made me smoke outside.
Jennifer:	I'm sorry Simone.
Simone:	It's OK. When in Rome, do as the Romans do.

4 **Listening for Stressed Words. Page 147.** See student text.

5 **Comparing Long and Reduced Forms. Page 148.** See student text.

6 **Listening for Reductions. Page 149.**

Anita:	Well, it's time to get back to the office. I'll see you soon, Brenda.
Brenda:	OK, see you. . . Wait, Anita, is this your cell phone?
Anita:	Oh my goodness, yes, thanks. By the way, I almost forgot: My parents are coming for a visit next week.
Brenda:	Really? I'd love to meet them.
Anita:	Well, do you want to have lunch with us on Saturday?
Brenda:	Saturday? Hmm . . . I told my roommate I'd go shopping with her that day. Could we get together for a drink later in the afternoon?
Anita:	I don't know, they might be busy. I'll ask them and let you know.

Recalling Main Ideas

3   **Listening for Main Ideas. Page 151.**

At what age does a child become an adult? The answer depends on your culture or religion. Here are a few examples.

First, in some North American Indian cultures, a boy became a man around the age of 13. At that time, he would go into the woods alone, without food or water, for several days. When he returned safely, he became an adult man. Girls became adult women as soon as they were old enough to have babies, also around the age of 12 or 13.

To give another example, in the Jewish religion, children spend years studying their history and religion. Then, at age 13 for boys and 12 for girls, they go through an important religious ceremony called a *bar mitzvah* for boys and *bat mitzvah* for girls. From that day, they are adults, and they become responsible for their own religious development.

In Japan today, young people become legal adults at age 20. Each year on January 15, they celebrate "Coming-of-Age Day," when all the twenty-year-olds in a town are invited to attend a special ceremony. They wear traditional clothes, listen to speeches, and visit with old friends.

Finally, in the United States, the passage into adulthood takes several years. American teenagers look forward to their 16th birthday, because in most states that is the age when can get a driver's license. The <u>legal</u> age of adulthood is 18, when Americans can vote, get married, and work full-time. However, they must wait until age 21 to buy alcohol. Many people celebrate their 21st birthday by having a drink with friends in a bar.

4   **Taking Notes on Specific Information. Page 151.** Listen again. See text for Activity 3.

Chapter 7 ## Entertainment and the Media

Listening to Conversations

3   **Listening for Main Ideas. Page 175.**

Ming: Hey, listen to this. The average American family watches six hours of TV a day.

Jack: A day? You're joking.

Ming: No, it says so right here in this magazine. Hmm, I guess <u>you're</u> an average American, Jack. When I come over to your place, you always have your TV on.

Jack: Come on. Are you saying I'm a couch potato?

Ming: Yeah. I really think watching TV is a waste of time.

Jack: Well, I disagree. Some programs are bad, like those soap operas. But what about sports or the news? You watch those sometimes, don't you?

Ming: Well, actually, for the news, I prefer the newspaper. Or the Internet.

Jack: Why?

Ming: First, because they give you a lot more information. And I can read them any time I want. Plus, I hate all the TV commercials.

Jack: I know what you mean. That's why, when the commercials come on, I just turn down the volume or change channels.

Ming: Yeah, I noticed that. Channel surfing drives me crazy.

Jack: Well, then, next time you come over I'll let you have the remote control.

Ming: That's so sweet. But I have a better idea. Next time I come over, let's just turn the TV off.

4 Listening for Stressed Words. Page 176. See student text.

5 Comparing Long and Reduced Forms. Page 177. See student text.

6 Listening for Reductions. Page 177.

B: Are ya calling the movie theater?

A: Uh-huh. Why, what's wrong? Don'tcha wanna go to the movies tonight?

B: To tell you the truth, I'm pretty tired. But we can go to an early show. D'ya know whatcha wanna see?

A: Not really. I'll letcha choose. Terminator III is playing at 8:00 and James Bond is at 10:00.

B: Let's see Terminator. I'm tired now and by 10 o'clock I'm gonna be dead.

PART 2   # Recalling Main Ideas

3 Listening for Main Ideas. Page 180.

Radio Announcer: Good evening. Our top story tonight: About an hour ago, a small airplane carrying six people landed safely in traffic on Highway 1. Two of the passengers received back injuries and one of the passengers suffered a broken leg. Here's reporter Larry Jones at the scene of the crash.

Reporter: Good evening, Mark. I'm standing here on Highway 1 with two drivers who almost hit the plane as it landed. Could you tell me what you thought as you watched the plane coming down?

Witness 1: Well, at first I wasn't scared. But then I saw it was flying very low. So I drove to the side of the road in a hurry.

Reporter: And you, sir?

Witness 2: I almost didn't see the plane at all. It happened so fast. When I finally heard the plane's motor, I knew something was wrong. And then I hit my brakes. Phew . . . it was real close. I'm still shaking.

Reporter: Fortunately, no one on the ground was hurt, but the plane blocked traffic for over an hour. Officer John McNamara of the local highway police thinks the plane ran out of gasoline. A complete investigation will begin tomorrow. Back to you, Mark.

4 Taking Notes on Specific Information. Page 181. Listen again. See text for Activity 3.

Chapter 8 | Social Life

PART 1 | ## Listening to Conversations

3 Listening for Main Ideas. Page 203.

Karen:	Yolanda, look! I can't believe it! It's Peter Riley. Hey Peter! How are you?
Peter:	Karen? Yolanda? Wow! I haven't seen you guys since graduation night!
Yolanda:	I know. You look great!
Peter:	Thanks. So do You.
Yolanda:	So what have you been up to?
Peter:	Well, I go to Faber College.
Karen:	Really? Do you like it?
Peter:	Yeah, so far. But I've been studying really hard.
Yolanda:	Sure you have . . .
Karen:	What's your major — body building?
Peter:	No, actually it's computer science.
Yolanda:	Ah-h-h. That makes sense. You always *were* good at math and science.
Peter:	Thanks. Anyway, what have you guys been up to?
Yolanda:	Well, I'm a sales rep for a publishing company.
Peter:	No kidding! How do you like that?
Yolanda:	Oh, I love it! I'm on the road a lot, but I get to meet some interesting people.
Peter:	That's terrific. And how about you, Karen?
Karen:	I'm a nurse in a hospital.
Peter:	You always were good at science too. Well, it was great seeing you both. We should be sure to keep in touch from now on.

4 Listening for Stressed Words. Page 204. See student text.

6 Pronouncing Exclamations. Page 205. See student text.

7 Matching Statements and Responses. Page 206.

1. My sister just had triplets.
2. Guess what? I'm getting married next month.
3. Would you like a job for a dollar an hour?
4. I've been exercising a lot, and I've lost 30 pounds.
5. Someone hit my car yesterday. It's going to cost $1,000 to repair.
6. I met the President of the United States yesterday.
7. My sister likes to eat peanut butter and banana sandwiches.
8. I locked the keys in the car.

Recalling Main Ideas

2 Listening for Main Ideas. Page 207.

Karen:	Listen, a friend of mine is coming to town next week. I think you might like him.
Beverly:	Well, I really don't like blind dates. But tell me about him anyway.
Karen:	Well, he's very good-looking.
Beverly:	Oh, yeah? Tell me more.
Karen:	He's got dark hair and green eyes and a wonderful smile. He had a beard the last time I saw him. And he has his own business.
Beverly:	That's nice. What kind of business?
Karen:	Import/export. And he loves to travel.
Beverly:	About how old is he?
Karen:	He's almost thirty.
Beverly:	Does he like dancing or music?
Karen:	He loves jazz, and he's played the piano for years. I'm sure he likes dancing too.
Beverly:	Wow, he sounds great! Maybe he could come with me to the football game next weekend.
Karen:	Oh, I don't know if Franco would like that.
Beverly:	Why is that?
Karen:	Well, they don't play American football in Italy. They play soccer.
Beverly:	Italy? You mean he's Italian?
Karen:	Yes. So there is one small problem, I guess.
Beverly:	Don't tell me . . .
Karen:	Right. He doesn't speak English.

3 Taking Notes on Specific Information. Page 207. Listen again. See text for Activity 2.

Chapter 9   Customs, Celebrations, and Holidays

Listening to Conversations

3 Listening for Main Ideas. Page 231.

Clerk:	Hello. Can I help you with anything?
Kenji:	I'm looking for a Valentine's Day gift for my girlfriend. Well, actually, she's not my girlfriend yet, so I really don't know what to get her.
Clerk:	How about some chocolate?
Kenji:	Well, I think she's on a diet.
Clerk:	Hmm, then how about some jewelry?

Kenji:	Like what?
Clerk:	Well, look at this bracelet. It's simple but very elegant, don't you think?
Kenji:	It's pretty, but I really can't spend that much money.
Clerk:	OK. Let's see . . . What else? . . . Well, here's a nice bottle of cologne. I'm sure she'll like that.
Kenji:	Actually she once told me that she doesn't like any kind of perfume. And anyway, I really wanted to give her something . . . unusual.
Clerk:	I'm afraid something unusual might be expensive. Look, I have an idea. Why don't you get her a nice card and give it to her with one perfect red rose. Most women love to get flowers. Doesn't that sound romantic?
Kenji:	Yeah, I guess so. OK, that's what I'll do.
Clerk:	Don't worry. I'm sure she'll like whatever you give her.
Kenji:	Oh, I hope so. Thanks for your help!

4   **Listening for Stressed Words. Page 232.** See student text.

5   **Comparing Long and Reduced Forms. Page 233.** See student text.

6   **Listening for Reductions. Page 234.**

Jane:	Hi Helen. Are you going out?
Helen:	Yeah, I'm going downtown. It's my brother's birthday tomorrow, and I wanna buy 'im a gift. Do you wanna come with me?
Jane:	I really can't . . . I hafta study for a big test. But can ya do me a favor?
Helen:	OK.
Jane:	Could you buy me some film? My sister just had a baby boy . . .
Helen:	Really? Congratulations! What's 'is name?
Jane:	Jeremy. He's so cute, but my poor sister is so tired. I'm gonna visit 'er this weekend and give 'er a hand. 'n' while I'm there, I'm gonna take some pictures of the baby.
Helen:	OK, no problem.
Jane:	Thanks. See ya later.

PART 2   # Recalling Main Ideas

---

3   Listening for Main Ideas. Page 237.

Kenji:	Everything is delicious, Mrs. Riley. It really was nice of you to invite me.
Mrs. R:	Well, nobody should have dinner alone today. Thanksgiving is a time for families and friends to be together. Is this your first Thanksgiving in the United States, Kenji?
Kenji:	Yes. In fact, I don't really know much about it.
Peter:	Well ask Robbie. He'll tell you all about it.
Robbie:	Ah, come on. What's this, a history lesson?
Kenji:	No, I'm really interested. Come on, tell me.
Robbie:	Well, see, these guys came over from Europe like maybe a thousand years ago . . .